D1570832

Augsburg Sermons

SERMONS ON GOSPEL TEXTS FROM THE NEW LECTIONARY AND CALENDAR

AUGSBURG SERMONS

GOSPELS

SERIES A

AUGSBURG PUBLISHING HOUSE
MINNEAPOLIS, MINNESOTA

AUGSBURG SERMONS — GOSPELS — SERIES A

Library of Congress Catalog Card No. 74-77679

International Standard Book No. 0-8066-1430-7

Manufactured in the United States of America

Contents

Introduction

The Calendar and Lectionary introduced by the Inter-Lutheran Commission on Worship (ILCW) in Advent 1973, has become one of the most popular liturgical tools for contemporary worship and preaching. It is the answer to many requests in Lutheran churches for a revision of the church year and a new lectionary.

The church year calendar has been modified and modernized. The lectionary has been extensively overhauled by drawing on parallel efforts by the Protestant Episcopal, Presbyterian, and Roman Catholic churches.

This new lectionary has proved to be just what preachers have been asking for.

The New Church Year Calendar

This new calendar is similar to all previous calendars in that Easter is still the heart of it, and the Gospel still tells the story of Jesus Christ throughout the year.

The revisions in the new calendar are these:

- The *gesima* Sundays, sometimes known as pre-Lent, are now listed as Sundays after Epiphany. The season of Epiphany is therefore lengthened, which makes possible a fuller development of Epiphany themes.
- The Sundays between Easter and Pentecost will be known as the Sundays *of* Easter, rather than *after* Easter.
- The Latin titles for the Sundays of Lent and Easter have been deleted.
- Passion Sunday has been moved from the Fifth Sunday in Lent to the Sixth Sunday (Palm Sunday).
- The Sundays in the Pentecost-Trinity season have been numbered *after Pentecost* instead of *after Trinity.*
- In color terminology, *purple* replaces *violet,* and *red* is suggested for use during Holy Week.

The New Lectionary

The new lectionary presents a three-year cycle of lessons for the church year. The texts designated for a specific year will be chosen alternatively from Series A, Series B, or Series C of this lectionary.

This lectionary follows the traditional pattern of appointing an Old Testament lesson, an Epistle, and a Gospel for each Sunday. During the Easter season, however, a reading from the Acts of the Apostles replaces the Old Testament lesson.

Perhaps the outstanding feature of the lectionary is its use of a *Gospel of the Year.* In each series, one of the Synoptic Gospels is featured, providing continuity to the reading and telling of the Gospel story throughout the entire church year. The reading of the *Gospel of the Year* is interrupted annually by the insertion of the Gospel of John from Easter Sunday through Pentecost. Certain festivals for which only one Gospel is appropriate (the Epiphany for example), also are outside the domain of the *Gospel of the Year.*

Series A in 1974

The Lutheran churches in America will receive their first exposure to Series A of the new *Calendar and Lectionary* beginning in Advent 1974. Matthew is the *Gospel of the Year* in this series and thus will be the primary source for most of the sermons preached in 1974-75.

The *Gospel of the Year* approach enables the pastor to study the Gospel of Matthew in depth and to share his insights with his congregation through his sermons. This will help make visible the uniqueness of each of the New Testament Gospels. The same kind of organized in-depth study and proclamation of the Gospels is continued in Series B which features Mark and Series C which is based on Luke.

The first volume of *Augsburg Sermons,* based on the Gospel texts of Series C, was published in the summer of 1973. The enthusiastic response to those sermons, plus the wide acceptance of the new *Calendar and Lectionary,* provided the encouragement to issue the present volume based on the Gospel texts of Series A. This book, like its predecessor, is offered in the hope that the sermons, the calendar, and the lectionary will contribute to the renewal of preaching.

THE SECRET INGREDIENT

First Sunday in Advent
Matthew 24:37-44

Sometimes magazine cartoons show a barefoot man in a long tattered robe carrying a sign, "The End Is Near." We smile at the fanatic.

Once in a while we see a home-made sign on a fence post warning us, "Prepare to Meet Thy God." Some nut put that up.

In the new three-year schedule of Scriptures, the First Sunday in Advent focuses on the Second Advent of Christ. This same Gospel is being heard by millions of Christians—reminding us on this Sunday that the end is near and that we should prepare to meet our God. Are we all crazy?

Or are we just going through the motions? After all, the Second Advent is part of the Bible and it has to come up some time. Let the preacher sound off; it's part of his job. Meanwhile time marches on as it always has. We'll go home and eat dinner and then lie on the floor and watch football according to plans we made yesterday. Or maybe not even by plan. Just a pattern we followed last week and the week before that and the week before that. Like "Ol' Man River," life "jus' keeps rollin' along," and what's to prevent it?

So who cares about this unworldly teaching that Jesus is coming again? Wouldn't it be more profitable to dwell on what would help us in the present moment?

The Secret Ingredient Makes the Difference

I propose that this difficult doctrine does indeed do something for us right now, that it adds a *secret ingredient* to our daily round, changing us from flat, tasteless creatures who're just existing into human beings for whom life may throb with increasing excitement.

Am I promising too much? Let's look again at what Jesus says:

> As were the days of Noah, so will be the coming of the Son of man. For as in those days before the flood they were eating and drinking, marrying and giving in marriage, until the day when Noah entered the ark, and they did not know until the flood came and swept them all away, so will be the coming of the Son of man.
>
> Matthew 24:37-39

But isn't that a pretty good life? "Eating and drinking, marrying and giving in marriage"—what's wrong with enjoying these things? Not a thing. Then what's the complaint? Jesus says the fault lay in this: *"They did not know* until the flood came and swept them all away." What didn't they know? *What* was happening and *why.* That is, they didn't know God. They took no account of him as they ate and drank and got married. They were what we call "secularists," people living without the up-and-down dimension, cut off from their source and pretending no accountability to a judge.

Jesus further illustrates:

> Then two men will be in the field; one is taken and one is left. Two women will be grinding at the mill; one is taken and one is left. Watch, therefore, for you do not know on what day your Lord is coming.
>
> Matthew 24:40-42

This is where I get the idea it's a secret ingredient. To all appearances the two men in the field were alike. No difference apparent from the outside. The same with the two women grinding at the mill. The way they worked and the results they produced were identical; in fact, one couldn't do it without the other. They put their grain between two heavy stones: the lower one stationary, the upper one movable by means of a handle long enough for two women to tug upon, for it took the strength of two. Both were needed. Yet—as with the men also—"one is taken and one is left." One is ready, the other not. One has the secret ingredient, the other doesn't. One eats and drinks and gives in marriage and knows the Lord. The other simply eats and drinks and knows nothing more. One is alert for the coming of Christ, the other isn't. Yet from the outside, both look exactly alike.

The Secret Ingredient Affects Our Outlook

Yet although others may not detect this secret ingredient within us, *it still affects our whole outlook on life.*

Like oatmeal without salt or bread without yeast, it can affect us by its absence. Can we imagine the terror when the flood came in the days of Noah, when the windows of heaven and the waterspouts of the deep opened up and gushed forth forty days and forty nights? Hear the unprepared scream. Watch them scramble up the trees. Look at them perched on the topmost branches. Turn your face away as the water keeps rising.

Nor was it pleasant for the people in Jesus' day (far poorer than any of us by comparison) to have come home to find that a thief had dug his way through their clay walls and emptied their house of what few keepsakes they had. In the same way, the day of the Lord will surprise the secularists and steal all their guilt projections and pretenses and leave them standing there, bare and defenseless—no masks or alibis to cover them—naked in the lightning of God's Law, shuddering at the sight of their deformities and warts. Dogs and hogs eat and drink and (in a sense) marry and are given in marriage, and they can live without reference to their maker because they weren't formed in his image. But when human beings attempt to live on no higher level than the animals and when human beings cut themselves off from their source and clench their eyelids shut against their judge, they may suppress reality for a time but not forever.

Truly, the secret ingredient (being tuned in to Christ and alert to his coming) does affect us negatively by its absence. It also affects us positively by its presence. That is, it enriches our lives. For we live in the consciousness that God is aiming all history at our redemption. We walk in the awareness, "This Is My Father's World." We breathe the air of confidence that this universe was made for us. For we're not meant to be bought like animals to be butchered. Nor shall we be sold like motors or ladders to be used. Oh yes, we've been purchased, but for an entirely different purpose—to be the companions and colleagues of the living God!

The View of Eternity

So we live in the view of eternity. This is the secret ingredient. You can't weigh it on the scales. You can't dissect it with a scalpel. You can't photograph it on an x-ray film. The one man chopping weeds with his hoe—he'll have it; the other man sweating just as much and perhaps doing just as good a job—he may not have it.

And what it does—this secret ingredient—for our sense of humor! We grow in our capacity to laugh at ourselves, because we don't need to pretend anymore we're something we're not. We don't have to get even or score points or make rebuttals. We're gradually losing the compulsion to justify ourselves as we become more and more aware that Christ has already justified us. So when we get caught doing something silly, we don't wither and pout if others chuckle. And we're being set free to join them in their amusement.

This is why I claim this secret ingredient affects our whole outlook on life: it brings us to live in view of eternity and makes us aware that all history is aimed at our redemption; it even sets us free to laugh at our own foolishness as we realize that Christ's atonement makes it unnecessary to be defensive.

Put it this way. There's not much practical difference between being ready for the Messiah and being ready for our own death. Someone has said, "Practice for death is practice for Christ's coming." Now suppose one morning you feel a lump on your body. You go to the physician. Yes, it's malignant. You're told, "This is it. At most, you have six months." Won't that affect how you look at a landscape? The way you savor your food? Your tone of voice with the family?

Six months, six decades or six minutes—who knows how long we shall live? In plain truth, by the grace of God this is the only day I have. Then how small of me—on my last day—to gossip and cheat. How disgraceful—on my last day—to be sour and surly. How dangerous—on my last day—to be found ~~in a den of iniquity.~~ in all the wrong places.

On the other hand, what a privilege—on my last day—to be living in the presence of God. What a breath of fresh air—on my last day—to be honest and open with my family, forgiving and being forgiven, loving and being loved. What a pleasure—on my last day—to give honor to every neighbor, to respect the image of God in every color, to reverence the blood of Christ shed for each Jew and Gentile, each male and female, each slave or free person. This is the only day I have. I live it in view of eternity, without being frightened by my Judge, without needing to ease my inner tension by making light of the Lord. I dare to live in his presence because he has clothed my nakedness with the righteousness of his Son.

So the hope of the Second Advent of Christ (which many poke fun at) is not so pointless after all. It does indeed do something for us in the present moment, affecting our view of ourselves and our attitude towards others. It rescues us from merely existing, like dogs or hogs which eat and drink and know nothing more. It's the secret ingredient, giving taste and zest to our lives.

Keep us alert, Lord. Help us watch and be ready.

ALVIN C. RUETER
Bethlehem Lutheran Church
St. Paul, Minnesota

PREPARE THE WAY OF THE LORD!

Second Sunday in Advent
Matthew 3:1-12

Who can forget the vivid opening of the rock musical "Godspell"—based primarily on the Gospel of Matthew? A cluster of characters all wearing gray sweatshirts are seated on the stage with their backs to the audience. One by one they arise and stand in the spotlight revealing the name imprinted on the front of their shirt; and they sing persuasively of their own ideology: Socrates, Plato, St. Thomas Aquinas, Martin Luther, Karl Marx, Nietzsche, Sartre, Martin Luther King. Then in a chorus called "The Tower of Babel" each sings his song simultaneously with the others.

As this concludes, suddenly down the aisle of the theater appears a modern-day John the Baptist. First he blows a ram's horn, and then he begins to sing to them over and over again in a moving and hauntingly beautiful melody his one sentence message: "Prepare ye the way of the Lord!" And John soon joins them on the stage and they all begin singing this song and dancing around in the excitement that sentence evokes. John is carrying a pail of water and a big sponge, and as a symbol of his baptism of repentance he washes each participant. And then these eight representatives go dancing down the aisle and out the back as the song, "Prepare ye the way of the Lord," fades away. And when they come back on the stage after John the Baptist and Jesus have encountered each other, they are no longer wearing their identifying sweatshirts; instead they are wearing joyous colorful clown-like attire and their faces are brightly painted.

Not only does "Godspell" begin with John the Baptist; all four gospels begin with the message of John the Baptist. And his first word is "Repent!" (Matthew 3:2), just as the first word of Jesus' message in Matthew is "Repent!" (Matthew 4:17).

The Speaker

John the Baptist, the great Advent figure, is a colorful man. He dresses like an Old Testament prophet (2 Kings 1:8; Zech. 13:4). His coat is made of coarse camel's hair—a symbol of penitence. Around his waist is a leather belt—a symbol of poverty. His food is insect food: grasshoppers and wild honey—very simple and immediately at hand, requiring no planting or cultivation or harvesting or manufacture or shipping. His drink is Adam's ale. His hair and his beard are long and uncut; he has taken the life-long Nazirite vow (Luke 1:15) never to go near a barber shop, as well as never to touch alcohol or any dead or unclean thing. The idea behind this vow is entire dedication to

God no matter what the cost. He lives in the desert where his body is bronzed from the hot sun. When he is pictured in art, he carries a long staff in the form of a cross on which in Byzantine art is a scroll with the words: "Repent for the kingdom of heaven is at hand"; and on which in Latin art is a scroll with the message: "Behold the Lamb of God!", with a lamb at his side and with his index finger pointing—obviously to Christ who is the Lamb of God.

The Setting

The wilderness of Judea where John preaches—he empties the cities and fills the wilderness—is chalky dust with some small rocks. It gets 110 degrees there in June, July, August, and the first part of September. There is not a sign of any living vegetation. The blue sky overhead is cloudless; on yonder horizon the gaunt gray hills of Moab shimmer in the heat. Time seems to stand still—temporal things seem unimportant. Judgment—and eternity—seem to hover very near.

The Sermon

John the Baptist is a man sent from God (John 1:6) on a mighty mission: to get people ready for the coming of Christ (Luke 1:16, 17 and 76-79). His great Advent cry, from Isaiah 40 and applied to him by Matthew, Mark and Luke—and which he applies to himself in John, rings across the centuries to us today: "I am the voice of one crying in the wilderness: 'Prepare the way of the Lord!' "

Let Us Prepare Our Homeland for Christmas

There has been a growing awareness on the part of Christians in our day that we are involved in the sins of our social and political order, that we do not repent in a vacuum. We share in the sins of our nation. John the Baptist in his short ministry which could have lasted no more than a year and a half before he was imprisoned for a year and then had his head cut off at Herod's birthday party, dealt directly with every one of the problems that beset us in our land today. He rebukes for instance our gluttony and our drunkenness and our drug abuse by his simple diet and his disciplined life. He rebukes our materialism and our greed and the waste of our resources and our befouling of the environment with his simple apparel, his home in a cave, and his transportation which was always by means of his two sturdy legs. He rebukes our corruption, our payola, when he tells the taxgatherers, the hated minions of Rome, to cut out the graft (Luke 3:12-13). He rebukes our economic injustice in a world half stuffed and half starved in which the two most common questions in our land are: "How can I lose weight?" and "Where can I park my car?" when he tells the multitudes: "If you've got two shirts, share one; if you have extra food, share" (Luke 3:10-11).

He rebukes our smug complacency—and this is the great sin of our land, "We are special people, we are God's pets, somehow we'll get by." This was the same attitude that the Jewish multitudes had. They figured that they might get as close to the fires of hell as to be singed a little bit but then they were sons of Abraham, so Abraham would wisk them away. And John rebukes them with withering words, which must have been like great hammer blows right in the teeth. He says as he points to the rocks out there in the wilderness at his feet there amidst the dust: "God out of these rocks can raise up children of Abraham" (Luke 3:8). In other words, he excommunicates the whole nation.

And he rebukes the sins of militarism when he cries out to the soldiers to cut out the three sins of soldiers in all ages; namely, the violence, the extortion and the griping. Yes, cut out the bullying, the blackmail and the grabbing (Luke 3:14). And he rebukes our nation's immorality and impurity when he points to King Herod and then to his consort Herodias, the woman whom King Herod had stolen from his half brother Philip when he had been to Rome, and says, "What you are doing is against the eternal laws of God." And he rebukes the religious leaders—vipers, he calls them, crawling on their belly in a false humility and stinging with a poisoned tongue: "You bunch of snakes, how are you going to flee from the wrath to come?"

And so there's not a probem that besets us, not an ulcer, not a running sore in our nation—and we surely have them—that John doesn't confront in his short and violent ministry. His illustrations, all from nature, all laced with the fire of judgment.

1. The scorpion flees from the approach of the burning stubble.

2. The woodsman, finding an unproductive tree on which he must pay tax, rests his axe against the trunk while he doffs his cloak—then the blows ring out, then into the fire.

3. The harvester, having had the grain on the big flat threshing rock trodden by oxen or pounded by a flail, waits until the evening breeze, then takes his winnowing shovel and tosses the grain into the air. The heavy kernels fall back to the

ground, the light chaff is blown in a pile to the side and then burned.

John says the choice before our land is Pentecost or holocaust. And we come back to the words of the Second Book of Chronicles (7:14), "If my people who are called by my name will humble themselves and pray and seek my face and turn from their wicked ways, then I will hear from heaven and I will forgive their sins and I will lay my healing hand upon their land."

Let Us Prepare Our Homes for Christmas

Advent is a new broom. It is spiritual housecleaning time for our homes too. In a "Charlie Brown Christmas" Charlie says to Linus: "Everything I do turns into a disaster." And Linus says to Charlie: "You're the only person in the world that can take a wonderful thing like Christmas and turn it into a problem." Would that Charlie were the only one; but I fear he has a lot of company. The budget begins to take a beating, the datebook gets jammed, the scale begins to ascend, the bottle of Tums disappears and we get that hurried and harried look and lose our perspective so that Christmas, the message of the great Burden-bearer begins to become a burden. You recall that Linus tells Charlie the real meaning of Christmas by reciting Luke 2. "That's what Christmas is all about," says Linus. And Charlie Brown concludes: "Nobody is going to commercialize my Christmas for me."

The Grinch is right when he says on Christmas morning: "Christmas came to Who-ville without ribbons or tags; without boxes or bags. Maybe Christmas doesn't come from a store. Maybe Christmas means a little bit more."

Let Us Prepare Our Hearts for Christmas

The human heart—that is the real battleground. John quotes a stirring passage from the 40th chapter of Isaiah as he tells the people in effect: "My message is the message of the Road-Builder" (Isa. 40:3-5; Luke 3:4-6).

The roads would get powdery dusty in the dry season. Then heavy winter rains would dig ravines and gullies, loosen boulders, deposit all sorts of scrap. The people would go scrambling over all this debris.

Suddenly a herald would come riding on horseback into the village, blow the trumpet and announce in a loud voice: "The king is coming this way! Prepare the way! Get ready!" Then the people would scurry out to make a straight and smooth highway for their king.

In like manner, says John the Baptist, we are to build in our hearts a superhighway for our God.

Let God bulldoze off the mountains of pride. "I" is the middle letter of pride and of sin; we are by nature ego-maniacs, "I" specialists.

Let God lower the great craggy hills of prejudice.

Let God fill up the swampy valleys of low living with thoughts that are clean and pure.

Let God fill up the great barren lowlands of neglect with deeds of love and thoughtfulness.

Let God fill up the dark bogs of ignorance with a study of his living Word.

Let God fill up the deep murky caverns of depression and despair with his sure promises.

Let God disc out the ruts of bad habits.

Let God straighten out our crooked thoughts and plans, the twistings and turnings of a deceitful heart.

Let God smooth out our rough ways with one another—our irritability, our impatience, our crankiness, our low boiling point (not least these December days).

Repent! What does that mean?

It means to be sorry for the wrong things we've thought and said and done.

It means to say: "I'm sorry!" Those seven letters are the hardest in the English language to pronounce without any "ifs," "ands," or "buts." Repentance doesn't come easy to respectable people. Many today deny the reality of sin; their greatest peril is a lack of awareness of the human predicament. Others look on the Ten Commandments as only ten suggestions. Others pick say three out of the Ten and forget about the others. Others are busy confessing other people's sins.

It means being sorry enough to want to quit doing the bad things—not just being spared from the embarrassment of getting caught or from the consequences of the wrong deeds.

It means putting things right with people we've wronged, as much as possible. John the Baptist told the multitudes and the taxgatherers and the soldiers to bring forth the fruit of repentance. Zaccheus the publican had likely been under the influence of John's preaching.

It means to turn from evil and to turn to God.

The Hebrew word for repentance, *Macham,* means to have compassion; the Greek word for repentance *metanoia* means to change your attitude. Doesn't that sound like what our hearts need? Christian youth especially are raising their voices against the unhuman, uncaring, unbending qualities they see in life about them. The moment we turn around we fall into the arms of pursuing Divine Love.

Christmas is a personal thing. It came not to the masses but only to a few: the watching Wise Men and to the waiting shepherds. Christ is born when?—not in the blazing sun of noon day but at night, in the nighttime of sorrow over sin. And where? —not in proud Jerusalem but in humble Bethlehem. And not in a great palace or temple but in a stable cave.

Over the place of the manger crib in Bethlehem there is now a church called The Church of the Nativity. The most memorable thing about that church is the door. It is very low; you have to stoop down and bend and kneel in order to get into the church. This is because in the persecution days the Mohammedans would drive donkeys into the church and beat them to disrupt the service—and would ride in on their horses. I think there is a parable there. The proud and the smug and the complacent and the self-satisfied, they never get to Christmas, because they don't know how to bend. Only the humble and reverent get to Christmas.

Advent with its four Sundays is a great season which has as its purpose to bring each of us—and our families—to Christmas on our knees in penitence, in expectation, in awe, in wonder, in gratitude that the God of a million million birthdays has laid his Son on the doorstep of the world to be our Savior ("He shall save his people not in their sins but from their sins" Matt. 1:21) and our Companion ("Emmanuel—God with us" Matt. 1:23) and our Guide ("Wonderful Counselor" Isa. 9:6) and our Peace ("Prince of Peace" Isa. 9:6).

Wilton E. Bergstrand
Holy Trinity Lutheran Church
Jamestown, New York

WALK BESIDE ME!

Third Sunday in Advent
Matthew 11:2-11

One of the most dramatic, and in some ways, overbearing figures in the New Testament is John the Baptist. What a character he must have been! He was an impetuous, emotional man, with piercing eyes, heavy beard, a voice that would shake you right down to your bones, dressed in animal skins often whipped by the desert wind.

You could do many things with John, and people did, but one thing they could not do was to ignore him. Scholars believe that he belonged to a monastic group called the Essenes who spent their time in seclusion waiting for the coming of the Messiah. When we first hear of John on the pages of the New Testament, we hear him announce: "I am the voice of one crying in the wilderness, make straight the way of the Lord." With the assurance often found in a man conscious of his own personal calling, he was now sure that he had found the Jewish deliverer in his own cousin, Jesus of Nazareth.

However, when Jesus came to be baptized by John in the Jordan, it was John who would have turned him aside: "I need to be baptized by you, and do you come to me?" But baptize Jesus he did. And later on, Jesus says of this most unusual man: "Truly I say to you, among those born of women, there has not risen one greater than John the Baptist."

When we encounter this same man a year later in the filth and boredom of an oriental prison, we see that this ordeal has eroded his confidence. His physical strength has waned; his spiritual stamina seems to have been drained. Calling two of his disciples to the prison window, he asks them to go and ask Jesus one question: "Are you he who is to come, or shall we look for another?"

Life with Meaning

In these two contrasting pictures of John, we see first of all a man driven by a purpose. A man who has a deep sense of meaning in his life. And then in the second instance, a man who is not sure of himself, a man whose life has suddenly been drained of meaning.

Many of you have found yourselves in similar situations. For a young person it may have been some critical study in college; for others it may have been an illness, or a personal disappointment.

So much meaninglessness is evident in our day. The writer of Ecclesiastes might well have been our spokesman: "What has a man from all the toil and strain with which he toils beneath the sun? For all his days are full of pain, and his work is a vexation; even in the night his mind does not rest."

The issue of meaningless living is not basically that of drudgery—but motion without purpose, activity without a goal. Don

Heiges in his book, *The Christian Calling,* tells of a gang of laborers who blasted through asphalt and concrete streets with air hammers to a depth of five feet. After they had finished, the boss would inspect the hole and then say to them, "Okay, fill 'er up." This seemingly pointless routine went on all morning long. At noon, the men came to the foreman: "We quit. Pay us off." The astonished foreman asked whether the work was too hard or the pay too low. One of the workers blurted out the truth: "We quit because no one is going to make fools of us—digging holes and filling them up!" With the explanation that because records had been lost, they were trying to relocate the water mains, the men went back to work. They could now see some meaning in their mindless drudgery.

There must be a sense of meaning to work, or we live under a "sense of being damned." Kagawa, the famous Japanese Christian, put it well:

> I read
> In a book
> That a man called
> Christ
> Went about doing good.
> It is very disconcerting to me
> That I am so easily
> Satisfied
> With just
> Going about.

If our young people were given three choices on some sort of mystical Aladdin's lamp, what do you think their choices would be?

For some it might be the hope that the handsome athlete or lovely cheerleader would respond to them in love. For others, it might be that we would get an athletic contract with the Milwaukee Bucks, or another of the pro teams. For others, it might be some sense of absolute security, or a job that would take them to the four corners of the world. I once asked this question of a group of South Dakota University students. One young man, speaking for many of them in the group, replied, "I would want a life with meaning."

John felt himself on the verge of losing just that. And so he sent his disciples to Jesus and said, "Are you he who is to come, or shall we look for another?"

It is this sense of significance that modern man has lost.

So many of our poets, novelists, dramatists, philosophers, even our theologians have been preoccupied for more than a century with the anatomy of meaninglessness. Whether you have read a Christian like T. S. Elliot, or a Jew like Franz Kafka, or an atheist like Jean-Paul Sartre, you get a bleak prospect of life without essential meaning.

Theodore Hacker, German philosopher and translator of Kirkegaard, made this observation: "The function of literature for almost one hundred years has been understood to consist of describing as exactly as possible how the world looks without God." How does it look without God? Without meaning? The novelist Koestler has one of his characters say this: "The place of God has become vacant . . . and the wind is blowing through it as an empty flat before the new tenants move in."

Our society is filled with decent, self-respecting people whose lives, once moored to great religious certainties, are now dangerously drifting on the high seas of uncertainty and indifference.

Most of them never deliberately turned their backs on faith or repudiated their religious convictions. Their falling away, their loss of meaning in life, was much more subtle than that. Some, like G. K. Chesterton's memories as a youth, put their religious beliefs in a drawer. Chesterton adds, "When I went to look for them again as a man, I found the drawer empty."

Leonard Griffith of Canada, tells of attending a conference of intellectuals (as an observer, Griffith wants us to remember) who were discussing the topic, "The Predicament of Modern Man." A distinguished professor of psychiatry argued strongly that man will never resolve his human predicaments until he breaks loose from the inhibitions and superstitions of religion. To quote the psychiatrist: "It is time to recognize that within ourselves is the power to create a better life." The reply to these remarks at the conference was given by a Christian layman, also an intellectual and a scientist (and here Griffith expresses our mutual surprise at the popular illusion that to be an "egghead" is to be, by definition, an agnostic): "We cling to the Christian belief, as men have always done, not because we seek something outside ourselves, but because something outside ourselves has sought us and laid hold upon us. It is not we, but God who has taken the initiative."

Dare we believe this? Hundreds, I dare say thousands, in the academic community accept the good news that "God in Christ has taken the initiative." I think, therefore, it is appropriate that we make a few brief observations on the nature of this struggle.

Admit Need for God

Please note, John immediately admitted that he had a faith problem. He didn't beat around the bush. There was no subtle evasion. No ego-saving. No failure to face the fact that even an Essene could have doubts. The worst thing anybody can do is stay away from a doctor when he detects some physical symptoms not normal in his body. And certainly the worst thing that a religious man can do is to "make believe" when he doesn't really believe at all.

Who doesn't have doubts? I'm often amazed how people live year after year with burdens they do not have to carry—born out of fear, half-heartedness, or perhaps indifference—I don't know. But what a joy it is to come clean, to come directly to the point. "Lord, I believe, help my unbelief. I need help, O God, I need help!" For as with the Alcoholics Anonymous program, no man can find God's help until he admits that he *needs* God's help.

However, perhaps lack of faith is not a matter of mere emptiness. Isn't it true that tragedy isn't always something that *happens* to us; often, it is something wonderful that *should* happen to us, but doesn't. It's like the young person who says to you, "Im going somewhere," and five years later you see that he didn't go anywhere at all but down.

When in all seriousness we do admit our need to God, he will lay his finger on the one factor in our lives that we have never completely committed to him—the one thing that is blocking the advent of God into our lives. Until we have faced it, my friend, and put it right, it is going to spoil everything for us. Down with the barriers. Away with the reservations. Be done with the misery of a divided life.

The Answer—in the Life of Jesus

The wonder of the encounter with Christ for modern man, as it was for John the Baptist, is that he will give us a real answer in terms of empirical evidence. The answer of the Christian faith will not be in theories, philosophies, or explanations. The claim of the Gospel on our lives has always been presented in terms of historical facts—the life of Jesus. It isn't that Jesus had a magnificent theory about life and death, but that in him we find a magnificent life! And his terrible death and his resurrection from the dead give us a catalyst for living.

Our response will not be a matter of being convinced by argument or emotionally moved to "follow in his steps." For as with John, so too, with us. When John's disciples asked of Christ the agonizing question, "Are you the one, or shall we look for someone else?" the answer of our Lord is still with us today: "Go and tell John what you hear and see: the blind receive their sight and the lame walk, lepers are cleansed and the deaf hear, and the dead are raised up, and the poor have good news preached to them." No. Not theories, facts! Facts! It happened, things are changing!

The proof of the Christian faith is always a matter of changed lives—lives that suddenly find purpose and meaning. Permit me to share with you two examples, one far away and one as close as I stand before you.

Louis Evans, noted Presbyterian leader, tells of visiting a mission field in Korea, and spending time with a missionary doctor, who had relinquished a very lucrative practice in the States. One day Evans watched the doctor perform an operation. It took seven hours. Several times, Evans found the intense heat and the fumes so overbearing that he had to leave the room to refresh himself. When it was all over, he asked the surgeon, "Is every day like this?" The fatigued surgeon only replied with a wry smile at first. One of the men in Evans' party questioned, "What would this operation have cost in the United States?" The doctor said, "About a thousand dollars." When someone asked how much this poor Korean woman could pay, the doctor looked at her and said, "For this I will get her gratitude and my Master's smile, that's all. But that's worth more than all the praise and money that the world can give."

The second example is much closer to home—a Christmas card I received from a young man. As a graduate student, he came to see me last January with a very difficult personal problem. He came in hesitantly because he hadn't been to church for ten years. But he had been in Bethel the previous Sunday out of sheer desperation. He came back a week later. He heard, he felt, he sensed . . . and he came into my office the next day.

In the months that followed, we talked, shared, and agonized together about his problem. I found a mind and spirit rich in everything that makes for a fine human being—except he didn't feel that he had hold of anything spiritually helpful.

God was actually not far beneath the surface of this young man's thoughts and slowly faith and meaning began to assert themselves. This week, I received a Christmas card, the most meaningful card I've received this year. After expressing his gratitude for our talks, he wrote, "Pastor Bob, I thought you might be interested in the following:

Don't walk in front of me—I may not follow;
Don't walk behind me—I may not lead;
Walk beside me—and just be my friend.
—A. Camus

With sincere thanks for being 'my friend' and fond hopes for a sincere holiday." The card had one word printed on the front: "Joy."

He is coming, and when he comes, he will come as a friend. And he is the one who is willing to walk beside us and share our frustration, our loneliness, and our empty hearts. And to share in such a way that ultimately, we too, in spite of what life does to us, can put on a Christmas card the word "joy," and mean it!

R. G. BORGWARDT
Bethel Lutheran Church
Madison, Wisconsin

INCREDIBLE, BUT TRUE

Fourth Sunday in Advent
Matthew 1:18-25

Some time ago a young girl sat in our church library and revealed to me the bitterness of a hardened attitude toward the things of God. She was travelling through the area with a team of youth sponsored by a large midwestern congregation. As we sat there on the carpet, with several of her friends around, she openly shared her rejection of God's "Good News" of acceptance through Jesus Christ's atonement. "I deserve to be condemned," she said bitterly. "I have sinned, and I know it. I should have to pay the price for what I have rightfully earned and that is exactly what I intend to do!"

Religion vs. Christianity

That which makes the message of Christmas so complicated for so very, very many people is its utter simplicity. Perhaps that sounds like double talk. Nevertheless, it is true. Someone has characterized the difference between "religion" and "Christianity" in these terms: "Religion" is man's best attempt through some effort on his own part to re-establish what he acknowledges as a broken relationship with God, the Source of life. "Christianity" is unique among world religions in that it acknowledges that because man's relationship with God is broken, there is absolutely nothing he can do on his own to re-establish that broken, but vital relationship. God, instead, has done it for him. The message of Christmas is simply this, "What you and I cannot do for ourselves, God has done for us."

An Ego Problem

For people who are accustomed to understanding Christianity as just another religion, (a system of establishing justice through one's own efforts, or ultimate salvation through one's own merits), the message that God has done it for them is just too incredible to accept. In fact it is downright insulting to any responsible ego. Most of us have been taught all our lives that "no one ever gets anything for nothing." We've claimed the philosophy, "God helps those who help themselves," as the best policy for getting ahead. So subtly has that "Do-It-Yourself-Religion" preoccupied the truth of the gospel that many Christians have attributed that trite phrase to the Word of God. I hope every one of you knows that the phrase, "God helps those who help themselves," never came from the Bible! In fact, that phrase is *Anti-gospel!* It is completely the opposite of the message God has shared with us from the beginning of the Bible right down through its very last word.

The other day some friends were sharing their burden for an outstanding young man they knew personally. Their friend had been raised and nurtured within the influence of Christian community and yet, for some reason or another, he had strayed from any kind of regular involvement. Time and again, as the subject of "church" would come up, he expressed his hope that someday he would be back, involved in Christian fellowship. But today wasn't the day for he knew that first he owed it to God to demonstrate a "reasonable show" on his own part that he had brought his life back together and could prove to God by his actions that he was sincere, . . . then and then only would God be interested in receiving him back.

The message of Christmas is simply this, "You and I can't Get Our Own House in Order by Ourselves." In fact, the longer and harder we work at it, the more we realize, (if we are honest), what an impossible futility that kind of religion is. The message of Christmas is, "Be of Good Cheer, God Has Done It for Us." *Incredible, but true!"*

History Has a Goal

The simplicity of the gospel message involves a very complicated plan according to human logic. So foreign to human experience is the plan that God chose to bring salvation to you and me that it has often been referred to as "the scandal of the gospel." At the fall God who had been rebelled against, God whose perfect authority had been challenged by the very subjects he had created, . . . this same God should be the one to initiate a plan by which the offenders could be reconciled to himself; the offended one, . . . the initiator of the offenders' redemption; the innocent party paying the price owed him. How foreign to human logic! God, who could have by his word created instant salvation by saying, "Be clean! . . . Be gone, sin!" should nevertheless choose an intricate plan of self-sacrifice, through acts in human history, through the use of fallen human-beings as his mouth-piece and his hands, through the commonness of human experience

The Scandal of the Gospel

The Gospel text for the Fourth Sunday in Advent, Matthew 1:18-25, supremely illustrates the scandal of God's plan. It carries a very simple, yet profound message for each one of us. It's a message that is scandalous in its illogic. Here in this text God presents us with a microcosm of the process that occurs in every human life as God seeks to bring the message of Christmas into a living, vital human experience. The fact exists that unless Christmas becomes living, and vital, and personal to us, its reality has no personal relevance for our lives.

God Has a Plan

Have you ever wondered if God really does have a plan for your life personally? Have you ever asked yourself if it isn't all left up to the powers of fate? Considering the few verses that precede our text for this Sunday we are immediately confronted with the testimony that God is a God who has a plan. That plan so bursts the logic of the human mind it is almost staggering to see and consider. God began that plan way back in the Garden of Eden when, after man's initial rebellion, he promised to send a Savior through the seed of the woman, and that plan of God would conquer sin and death once for all. You see, God is a God who acts, and in our text from Matthew we see that complete unfolding as the author, before announcing the birth of Jesus, traces the long list of ancestry from Abraham to Joseph. It's interesting to notice that Luke's account of the plan traces the lineage clear back to "Adam, the Son of God."

Even more interesting, as one considers the text, is the stature of divine relationship over and against human genealogy. How foreign to human logic! It was through Eve's seed the child was to be born, a process that would move biologically through Abraham, and King David, culminating in Joseph. And yet when the time was fulfilled for Jesus' birth, it was not through Joseph's biological seed but instead through a divine intervention of God, . . . a conception by the power of God's Holy Spirit within the woman engaged to be Joseph's wife. This child was to be God's Son, . . . the second Adam, consecrated, not through the biological seed of Joseph but through his wife Mary by virtue of her engagement. God had a plan. It began back in the garden and was unfolded through the prophets of old, even as Isaiah, 800 years before Christ, foretold the news, "A virgin shall conceive and bear a son, and his name shall be called Emmanuel," which means "God with us." Here at the beginning of our text we see this intricate plan of God coming to its supreme fulfillment as Joseph is visited by an angel.

God has a plan for your life today, just as certain as he has a plan for mine. It is an intricate plan. It may be so foreign to your logic and mine that we have difficulty identifying it as even being of God. But God has that plan and we must individually discover it through Jesus Christ, in a personal relationship with "Emmanuel," God with us.

God, No Liar

How many times have you bemoaned the fact that God's way seems so difficult for you to follow? You always seem to be "blowing it." Time and again you end up a defeated Christian. "If only I had more faith," you say, "then things would be better." Let me ask you a question. How much faith does it take to be a Christian? Only enough to believe that God would not lie. If that is your problem, it was Joseph's problem too, for Joseph was an earth-bound human being as well. As I read about this man Joseph, I thought, "Wow, here must be a supreme evidence of trust." Joseph was engaged to this woman he no doubt considered the perfect one for him. He was making these plans for marriage only to discover that Mary, the one he was engaged to, was already pregnant, and of course he knew the pregnancy wasn't his seed. Joseph had every reason in the world to become disillusioned and skeptical. By human standards anyone would have had a right to be bitter about it all. The one he loved had been unfaithful to the degree of total intimacy.

Now openness, in honest integrity, is an avenue to God's truth, and Joseph must have been open in that way for our text says that Joseph, being a just and righteous man considered not to humiliate the girl he loved but instead to quietly put her away. Obviously he had never for a moment closed his mind to the possibility that God had a plan in all of this seeming confusion. The text says he lay down in his state of confusion to rest when suddenly he was confronted with a dream. In this dream an angel of God came to him and said, "Joseph, do not be afraid to take Mary as your wife for the child that has been conceived inside of her is the very Son of God and has been conceived by the Holy Spirit." For this is the fulfillment of the age-old prophecy that a virgin shall conceive and bear a son and shall call his name, Jesus, Emmanuel, which means, God with us."

I tried to think how I would have reacted had I been Joseph. Sad to say, the incident might well have been a terrible blunder! You know what I mean, God comes to us as Christians many times a day, challenging us to trust his Word, even though things seem to be falling to pieces. He asks us in our family life, when relationships appear to be totally hopeless, to place our trust in him and believe that his plan from ages old is going to be fulfilled in our life if we will only give it all up to his control. Whatever your life-shattering dilemma might be, God challenges you as he does me, each day, to be willing to trust him though chaos itself seems to have broken loose—and that is exactly what Joseph did. He trusted God. How much faith does it take to be a victorious Christian? Only enough to believe God would not lie.

Ultimate Risk

A well-known theologian once defined faith as *ultimate risk*. That's being willing to follow the one you acknowledge as God anywhere he leads, even though you don't perceive in advance where you are being led. The Bible says, "And without faith it is impossible to please him (God), for he who comes to God must believe that he is, and that he is a rewarder of those who seek him." Down through the pages of biblical history we see the pattern, over and again, of men of God, called to trust God with no present evidence of the future. A Noah, called to build an ark in preparation for a flood, ridiculed and mocked for his apparent folly; an Abraham, called to leave the grandeur of Ur of the Chaldees and a position of respect among fellow citizens to become a wandering nomad; a Moses, called to challenge Pharaoh's authority and power on behalf of a trembling, grumbling Israel; a David, no more than a child with a sling-shot, called to fight the mighty Philistine, Goliath. And the list goes on and on. "For by grace you have been saved through faith."

In the Christian life, the blessing of God becomes a reality after we have demonstrated, before God, our faith and willingness to trust him. You see, God wants to know if our faith is in him or if it is in human logic and physical evidences. And as long as we are basing our decisions on those physical things that lead us to decide through human logic alone, there is no way we can ever claim the decision by faith, that is purely trust in the Lord. God wanted to bless the people of Israel. From ages old he had promised to send the Messiah, the Christ, and now because Joseph is willing, in the face of utter confusion, to trust God anyway, the promised Messiah is born, flesh and blood, into the world. The promise is fulfilled, after the exercising of faith. He shall be called "Emmanuel" which means that God has actually visited us in flesh and blood so that we don't have to wonder anymore what he is like. We can see for ourselves as we look at Jesus and experience in him exactly what God's love is like. Fantastic, But True!

Just as fantastic is the fact that God wants to bless every one of us here today! But God needs to know first . . . *Who are we trusting?* In what have we placed our ultimate confidence? Is it in material evidence given us ahead of time? Is it in seeing the gigantic problems in our life resolved before we come to worship? Or is it stepping-out in faith and saying to God, "I believe you! . . . Even though I can't see where you're taking me, . . . I praise your name anyway! I continue to worship you, God, for you are the only one worthy of my trust." And at that moment God unfolds his blessing. He unfolded that blessing to Joseph. He gave him a marvelous dream in which the angel, in a sense, said, "Do not fear, Joseph, for you have been appointed by God to receive a blessing that will in turn be a blessing to all peoples."

Have you ever wondered where we'd be today if Joseph had not trusted God? The Mosaic Law commanded death as the punishment for those committing adultery. That means that according to Israelite justice, Mary could have literally been put to death as her pregnancy was discovered. And through that death, the child conceived would never have been born. Where would we be if Joseph had not trusted God? And where will other people be if you and I refuse to trust God? Where will our children be, . . . where will our husbands and wives be, . . . where will all the people who have never heard the name of Jesus be if you and I, because of human logic, reject the simple message that God has done it all for us, by becoming one of us through a "virgin-birth?"

Trust

If there is one word here to remember it is the simple word *trust*. Trust the Lord. Here is where it's at! Here's where God breaks into our lives and makes Christmas the vital, living experience he intended it to be when Jesus was born in flesh and blood almost two thousand years ago. Trust, trust him, . . . trust him by placing everything you are and have into his hands, knowing that he is the only one who is trustworthy. What is that really to give up, anyway? Trust him with the little things. Trust him with the big things. Trust him now for the plan he has for your on-going life, for he has a plan. In any critical moment the danger is that you and I will by human logic, in the flesh, impose our plan upon God instead of trusting him and allowing him to act in his faithfulness. Turn to God in prayer. Be available to him and let him do it, and I can assure you that your steps will lead to blessings. In that walk you will be a witness to the truth that Jesus Christ is the meaning of Christmas; that Jesus Christ is the Son of God and the Savior of those who call upon his name; that Jesus is the answer. I leave you with that short word, . . . that simple word, . . . *trust*. In many respects the entire Christian walk can be summed up in that word. Trust the Lord! He has done it for us! *Incredible, yes, but true!*

Richard G. Matson
La Jolla Evangelical Lutheran Church
La Jolla, California

THE SIMPLE WONDER IN SIMPLE WORDS

The Nativity of Our Lord — Christmas Day
Luke 2:1-20

The angel who announced the birth of Jesus to the shepherds on the fields of Bethlehem was a messenger of few words. "Be not afraid; for behold, I bring you good news of a great joy which will come to all the people; for to you is born this day in the city of David a Savior, who is Christ the Lord. And this will be a sign for you: you will find a babe wrapped in swaddling cloths and lying in a manger."

This first Christmas sermon was a marvel of simplicity. In these simple words everything that needed to be said was said.

In the years that have followed since the night our Lord was born, this simple sentence sermon of the angel has grown to endless volumes of comment from the lips and pens of men. The glory of the heavens that flooded the Judean skies that holy night has become a festival of Christmas light that encircles the entire globe. The simple worship of the shepherds in the presence of the ox and ass within the lowly grotto has become a glorious ritual in elaborate cathedrals. The swaddling cloths and manger dark have blossomed into priestly robes and marble altars. And the sweet simplicity of Christmas and the Christmas Gospel has been lost along the way.

Listen closely to the angel! "This will be a sign for you: you will find a babe wrapped in swaddling cloths and lying in a manger." That's where you will find him. Not within the royal splendor of Jerusalem, but in the lowly squalor of a Bethlehem. Not in the palace of the king, but in a small Judean cattle cave. Not in the incense perfumed presence of the high priest, but in the company of smelly shepherds and in the dense aroma of a cow barn.

Simply Wonderful

Christmas is a simple wonder, and its message comes in simple words. That's what makes it wonder-filled because it is so simply wonderful. It is simple in its message, simple in its circumstance, simple in its characters, and simple in its faith. It is *simply* wonderful. And I submit that when we lose the wonder of this holy season, we lose it because we look in wrong directions. We seek its wonders in the beauty of our Christmas lights and in the thrill of Christmas pageantry, in anything to complicate the celebration. We forget the simple manger and the simple swaddling cloths. But if we want a Christmas that is simply wonderful, that's where we have to look. These are the tokens we must mark, and when we find the Christ child there, then our lights will glow much brighter and the Christmas music will have a beauty we have never heard before.

The Glory

We dare not, of course, forget the glory of this holy night, for Christmas is simply wonderful in glory. When the evangelist, St. Luke, recorded the event, he scarcely said a word that would identify the deity in Jesus Christ to mark him as the God of God and Light of Light and very God of very God. He simply told the story of a humble birth in humble circumstance to humble peasant parents. A decree of Caesar for a tax increase brought Joseph and his young bride, Mary, down to Bethlehem, the ancient city of a famous ancestor named David. The town was crowded at the time, the inn was filled, and everywhere they went, no vacancy. And so it was that while they were there the days were accomplished that she should be delivered. And she brought forth her first-born son and wrapped him in swaddling cloths and laid him in a manger. That's how it happened—just that simple. A child was born. A miracle of life had taken place just as it happens now 11,000 times a day across our country. Pregnant mothers do not choose convenient circumstances for delivery.

But this was different. Suddenly a halo formed around the humble setting. Shepherds tending flocks in midnight darkness suddenly were bathed in terrifying light. The voice of heaven's angel spoke his simple sentence sermon and the heavens echoed with the carol of the cherubim and seraphim. In a distant eastern sky a star appeared, and a company of eastern sages started on their pilgrimage to Bethlehem to seek the new-born king.

This child is Christ, our God and Lord. The infant as a helpless suckling at his mother's breast is Wonderful, Counsellor, the Mighty God, the everlasting Father, the Prince of Peace. The fulness of the time had come. God had sent forth his Son, made of a woman. The Word has become flesh to dwell among us. God who in times past spoke to our fathers by the prophets now speaks to us in the most glorious revelation of them all—through his Son. This is the simple wonder of the Christmas glory that the infant, virgin-born of Mary, is our God! And Christmas is simply wonderful!

No Ordinary Child — No Ordinary God!

But the point of emphasis is this today that Christmas is simply wonderful. If the Christmas Gospel tells us that the child of Bethlehem is not an ordinary child, it is much more concerned with telling us that the God of heaven is not an ordinary god. That the infant is our God and Lord is one side of the coin, and it may terrify us. But the other side is this, that God has become an infant, that he has appeared in human flesh and blood, that he has taken to himself the form of a servant and is made in the likeness of men. The majestic Lord of heaven, the Creator of the earth, terrible and terrifying in his holiness and in his glory, is born an infant small. Where in all the record of the deities that humans have created can you find a god like this God who created humans and who himself became a human. He doesn't hide himself behind the veil of his majestic glory. He does not remain beyond the earshot and the heart-beat of our human need and tears. He doesn't come to speak a word of vengeance and to wield the sceptre of his righteousness and execute his judgment. He assumes our human flesh and blood to take the burden of our guilt upon himself and save us from our sins and from our death. He appears in simple form to declare the love of God for us and Christmas is simply wonderful.

This does not explain the lowly circumstances in which the Christ was born, but certainly it helps to understand. The mighty God appeared in swaddling cloths and in a manger—why not in robes of royal purple and in the palace of a king? He was born of Mary, a simple peasant maiden from a village in the hinterland of Galilee—why not to a woman from the ranks of royalty? His birthplace was a little town of Bethlehem, the least of all of Judah's thousands—why not Jerusalem, the ancient capital of Israel, site of the holy temple, the home of Israel's important people? The message first was caroled to the shepherds on the fields of Bethlehem—why not to Pharisees and Sadducees and to the company of priests and Levites?

The Message Must Get Through

This message must get through—this man receives sinners! This message must get through—he has come to be the Savior of the world and not the private property of some select and segregated few who are conscious of their class distinctions and the color of their skin and their clean and wholesome living standard. This message must get through—in Christ we have a Savior sent from God who is our brother, who can be touched with the grief of our infirmities. And this is how God gets the message through, not just by saying so, but doing so. This is the way he invites us to himself—he becomes as one of us, as small as us, the pledge and promise of God's love for us. There is no greater consolation God has given us than this that he became a man, a child, a baby—to bear our sins and save us. This is the simple wonder, that God has come from the other side of majesty and glory so that we can see him on our side in swaddling cloths and in a manger.

But does the message get through? In one of his comments on the Christmas Gospel Martin Luther once said, "The Christian faith is foolishness." And if we apply our measurements and standards, we agree. The way God did things is not the way we would have done things. The God who spoke the majestic "let there be light," who pinned the sun and moon and stars into the skies, who fixed the orbit of the planets, surely God could have found a more dignified way to save. Why did he have to go to such preposterous lengths as these?

The Foolish for the Wise

God has chosen the foolish things of the world to confound the wise. He has chosen the weak things of the world to confound the things which are mighty. No flesh shall glory in his presence. This is what it took—not a dignified way, but the way of the manger and the cross. This is the Christ we need—not a mighty Conqueror of nations, but a Servant suffering for sinners. This is the Christ we look for—the Christ who makes our Christmas simply wonderful—not for analysis in science laboratories, but for acceptance with a childlike faith.

"This will be a sign for you: you will find a babe wrapped in swaddling cloths and lying in a manger." It's the last place we might expect to find him, but, thank God, this is the place we find him. And we add that if we want a simply wonderful Christmas, this is where we still find him. We find him among the lowly, the poor in spirit, the humble, the oppressed, the sorrowing. He comes to us along our pathways where we least expect. He confronts us in the presence of the hungry and the thirsty, the rejected and the homeless, the lonely and the ill, the burdened and the bored. And you will hear it from his lips, "As you did it to one of the least of these my brethren, you did it to me." The joy of Christmas is not determined by the extravaganza we can stage. It does not depend upon our state of health or state of wealth. Christmas is a simple wonder in a simple way—by the simple sharing of the love we see in him who first loved us.

A Personal Confession

I believe that on the night of Jesus' birth there were shepherds in the fields of Bethlehem, tending flocks. I do not ask to see the proof for this in the records of the county clerk at Bethlehem. I believe that in the dark Judean sky the glory of the Lord appeared and an angel sent from heaven told the shepherds of the Savior's birth. I do not ask a psychological analysis of this phenomenon. I believe that in the eastern skies a special star appeared to guide the Wise Men to the new-born king. I do not have to ask the astronomers for explanations. I believe that Mary was a virgin and that the holy child is God's own Son, and that the science of obstetrics wouldn't know about such things. These are miracles—some folks call them fables. For St. Luke and for me they are facts.

But in the simplest, yet the greatest, wonder of them all, I believe that in the fulness of time, God fulfilled his promise and God came to earth and God became an infant human being to bear my guilt of sin and die my death for me and rise again to bring his life to me. He became a man and he identified himself with me so that through all eternity I can be identified with him.

Nor dare I forget this wonder—the wonder that I believe it!

Because I do believe it—because I believe him—Christmas is simply wonderful, and I am wonder-filled!

ALTON F. WEDEL
Mt. Olive Lutheran Church
Minneapolis, Minnesota

LESSONS OF GOD'S PRESENCE

First Sunday after Christmas
Matthew 2:13-15, 19-23

One of the earliest memories I have is of a particular picture that hung in one of our bedrooms at home. It was not a great art and it was only a print, but I remember it. It portrayed two little children on a rickety bridge across a deep canyon amidst steep mountains. An angel with outstretched wings appeared to be leading them safely through this treacherous scene. The message was clear: God's guardian angel is with you during the dangerous periods of your life.

The story of the Flight to Egypt depicts a similar situation, as Joseph, Mary and the infant Jesus make their way across the Negeb under the protection of the angel's instructions. In this Matthean birth story, we can find many lessons for our lives.

The Lesson of Intervention

First of all, there is *the Lesson of Intervention.* Verses 13 and 19 are saying the same thing (And, by the way, it's amazing how similarly these two parts of the story are constructed): "... an angel of the Lord appeared to Joseph in a dream and said, ..." This is what you call intervention. In a situation of imminent danger someone is sent to bring the warning. In this instance, it was an angel . . . in a dream.

But this raises a number of difficulties: Who believes in angels these days, anyhow? And this bit about a dream is a bit "spooky." More than that, only too often church people get bitter and upset when they feel that God deserted them during a serious crisis in their lives. "Where was God then?" they ask. "If God really was loving and good, he just wouldn't have allowed that to happen." Well, this is a misunderstanding of the way God works. You have to make a distinction between what is possible and what is actual. It is possible for God to intervene in each situation of crisis, but it isn't very probable. He doesn't work that way—like Superman coming to the rescue. He rather depends on us to be his angels. He works through our sensitivity to and our compassion for others. This is the actual. The meaning of the word "angel" is "messenger"; an angel is someone who is sent to speak some helpful word or take some specific action. You and I are God's angels—God's messengers; and we are the instruments by which he intervenes in situations of crisis. The old gospel hymn says, "God has no hands but our hands, . . . no feet but our feet, . . . no tongue but our tongue. . . ." This is the first lesson of God's presence: God intervenes in situations of human crises. He does so through you and me who are his ministering angels to others. As we see human need and as we are moved to respond to it, we become messengers to others. And so other people are his ministering angels to us. But if we do not, or they do not—then God does not, and the need goes unmet.

The Lesson of Protection

Secondly, there is *the Lesson of Protection.* The reason why God intervened was to protect the "Holy Family," as we call it. The angel said, "Rise, take the child and his mother, and flee to Egypt, and remain there till I tell you; for Herod is about to search for the child, to destroy him." The second time the angel spoke, it was like a ringing of the bell at the end of a fire-drill at school; the students and teachers are standing in a line on the sidewalk or in the playground when the signal comes that the fire drill is over. The tension relaxes and the lines move back into the building. In both instances, it is protection from danger. In the case of Mary and Joseph, it was the danger of King Herod who was jealous of a possible rival to the throne. He wanted to make sure that no one would take his place. So, Matthew tells what happened between the "before" and "after" which our two texts describe; it's what is known as the "slaughter of the innocents." Pieter Breugel, the Dutch artist, has portrayed that scene in the version of the 16th century world in which he lived. It's an ugly scene of blood on the snow, screaming mothers and mounted soldiers hacking away at defenseless babies with their swords. This was that from which the angel was sent to protect Jesus.

And God protects us from danger, too! On Wednesday night of this week I have a funeral for a middle-aged man who died of cancer after spending one-hundred fourteen days in the hospital. Imagine that! One hundred fourteen days in the hospital dying of cancer! It doesn't sound like much protection, does it? But the protection was of a different kind. It wasn't from death—we all have to face that—but it was from despair. As I called on this charter member of the church over these weeks, I felt so badly for him, apparently not being able to die; just suspended there between life and death with no hope of getting better. But he was strong; he was patient; he lived in hope of life beyond death. We talked about that. We prayed together. We shared God's Word. We shook hands firmly. We reflected faith and courage into each other's faces. And he kept the faith. He did not become cynical or bitter. He fought the fight. He was able to stand! This, because God protected his spirit by the Holy Spirit in the giving of faith. This is the Lesson of Protection.

The Lesson of Guidance

Thirdly, there is *the Lesson of Guidance.* The guidance which God gave to Joseph and Mary through the angel involved time and place. In the initial warning, the instruction was, ". . . flee to Egypt, and remain there till I tell you." On the return journey, the instruction came after the death of Herod, "Rise, take the child and his mother, and go to the land of Israel, for those who sought the child's life are dead." Further guidance is given to Joseph that they should neither stay in nor pass through the territory of Judea but go north to the province of Galilee.

A number of years ago my wife and I took our family west to

Glacier National Park for two weeks in the summer. We had a camping trailer which we put up at St. Mary's Lake and enjoyed the time visiting friends who were there, going fishing, watching campfires and hiking the trails in the mountains. One day, particularly, one of my sons and I went over to Many Glacier lodge and took a hike up to see Grinnel glacier. This was a trail of about five miles each way and it took most of the day. A group of twenty vacationers of different ages and sizes made up the party which was under the direction of a forest ranger who served as a guide. A trip up the mountainside led around the shores of a few lakes on the way, after which we began to climb up the mountainside. When we came up to the timber line, the ranger stopped the group and gave us a warning about bears. He said that we may encounter a grizzly on the path, and if we did, we should not panic, but halt in our tracks remaining absolutely silent. The bears, he said, only attacked when they were startled, and because they are near-sighted, a sudden movement or noise could arouse them to anger. Needless to say, our eyes were big and watchful as we turned every corner of the trail. But, fortunately, we saw no bears and had a most enjoyable time climbing over the glacial moraine to the ice of the glacier itself. The view from there was breath-taking. But we wouldn't have started out without the experience and presence of a guide.

In the same way, we have a guide. Ultimately, it is Jesus himself who is our guide, even as he said, "I am the way, the truth and the life; no one comes to the Father but by me" (John 14:6). But the way he guides us, is through his Word. There is a Latin saying which declares, *nulla dies sine verba;* it means, "no day without a word." This is the way the Spirit of God guides us along the way we should follow in everyday life. That's why reading the Scripture every day is important. That's why prayer should accompany Scripture-reading, and Scripture-reading our prayers. The two go together as two parties in conversation. It is this way that we are guided in our decisions and goals of life, assured of the fact that, if we are open to this word of guidance, we will follow along the path which leads to life.

The Lesson of Promises Fulfilled

Finally, we have *the Lesson of Promises Fulfilled.* It is significant to note that, at the conclusion of both sections of our text (Matt. 2:15, 23) there is a specific statement that the action described was a fulfillment of a promise which had been made by God through one of the Old Testament prophets. The movement to Egypt was a fulfillment of Hosea 11:1 ("Out of Egypt have I called my son"), and the return from Egypt to Nazareth in Galilee was a fulfillment of a more obscure statement of Isaiah 11:1 ("There shall come forth a shoot—*Nezer*—from the stump of Jesse . . ." = "He shall be called a Nazarene"). Matthew, writing chiefly to the Jewish community of his day, made this a characteristic of his style, that he saw the episodes in the life of Jesus as fulfillment of Old Testament prophecy. Nevertheless, it suggests that promises of God were fulfilled, both in the immediate safety of the Holy Family, as well as in the larger view of God entering history in the form of human flesh.

It's impossible to live in a human relationship when promises which have been made are broken. One day a man called asking if he and his wife could have an appointment with me. He seemed in distress. This was arranged and I was in my office waiting for them. When they arrived, both of their faces looked unhappy and strained. They sat down; I closed the door and, taking my own chair, asked, "Did you want to talk to me about a problem? As she looked down stony-faced and angry, he blurted out, "I have committed adultery!" They did have a problem. The crisis of broken promises threatened to destroy their marriage. It had been a long road of frustration and misunderstanding that had brought them to this position, and it would be a long road back in the re-building of a relationship of openness and trust. For, in order to live together, there must be a relationship of mutual trust.

God, we know, is as good as his Word. He kept his promises tc Mary and Joseph about their safety. And he keeps his promises to us which he makes through Jesus Christ our Lord. These promises are of forgiveness and life as the fulfillment of his will for us and for all his people. They are contained in what is called a covenant relationship which he has initiated with us. And he is as good as his Word. We can depend on that. We can trust his promises to us. We can bet our life upon them, knowing that they grow out of his loving concern for us and our needs. He wants to be our God; he wants us to be his people.

On the back cover of an art catalog that came to our house in the mail was a print of a drawing by Albrecht Dürer, the artist who was a contemporary of Luther. It showed Joseph leading the donkey, on which sat Mary holding the infant Jesus, through the woods. A cluster of angel cherubs floated in the upper, right-hand corner. The trees and underbrush were thick and dark. This was Dürer's version of the "Flight to Egypt." The hovering angels symbolized the presence of God and this presence was giving to them and to us the Lessons of his Presence: the Lesson of Intervention, the Lesson of Protection, the Lesson of Guidance and the Lesson of Promises Fulfilled. Remember these for today and tomorrow!

INGOLF B. KINDEM
Mt. Zion (English Ev.) Lutheran Church
Wauwatosa, Wisconsin

WHAT'S IN A NAME?

The Name of Jesus
Luke 2:21

Several years ago a California teacher wrote a purely secular play under the title "A Cat Called Jesus." As a result, she created a furor that stirred up the wrath of hundreds of citizens and almost cost her her job and her credentials.

If the incident revealed little else, it pointed up how scores of people, even those with little genuine faith in God and little commitment to Christianity, are very touchy or sentimental about the way its treasured titles are used or abused. The reaction reveals, as well, how superficial religion can become.

Names are obviously rather important to the human creatures of God, even the names or initials that precede the surname. We are in danger of giving away much in our depersonalized society; but, lest we lose all sense of individual identity, we insist on retaining and treasuring our names.

In the case of Jewish boys, name-giving took place at the rite of circumcision. Whereas we recognize Jesus to be someone very special, and his mother at the time of her annunciation and Joseph through a dream had already been told what our Lord's name was to be, it was made official during the rite of circumcision. Thus on the eighth day he was named "Jesus," a name that was probably given to many Jewish boys but in this case signified all that this Bethlehem-born child was destined to fulfill. "She will bear a son, and you shall call his name Jesus, for he will save his people from their sins."

This circumcision and name-giving event was only partially understood by those who participated in this ceremony around the baby Jesus. We, from this side of the Easter event, can see how it may have identified and interpreted Christ's future career and saving work. The rite of circumcision signified our Lord's willingness to obligate himself to obey the whole law of God in order to "redeem those who were under the law, so that we might receive adoption as sons." It was the beginning of his active obedience in behalf of all men. Some also see in this act of circumcision his passive obedience, his suffering, for here is paid the first drop of blood as the price for our souls—the full payment to be completed at the end of his earthly journey—on the cross.

We may not fully comprehend it, but we accept its mystery—this circumcision of our Lord and the name of Jesus which will forever identify him. What may be far more difficult to accept is the significance of another name-giving ceremony and sacrament which took place with each one of us when we were brought to the baptismal font eight days or eight months following our births. There is a very real relationship between the name of Jesus and the name which each of us acquired on that very important day in our lives. I am not referring to the names that were inscribed on our baptismal certificates, but to that name or title that was branded upon our lives by the grace of God and which unites every one of us to the family of God as his sons and daughters forever.

Our name is Christian. We have no argument with the name given to our Lord, but I am afraid that many of us tend to shy away from the implications and the consequences of the name or title he gave to each one of us: the name "Christian"—a follower of Christ. This is neither presumption nor some recent revelation. It is the life and power and responsibilities that each of us has inherited as a disciple of Jesus Christ.

Our name is Christian. As Christ was the Son of God, so we who follow him have through his reconciling and redeeming act become the very sons and daughters of God. "Truly," said Jesus, "he who believes in me will also do the works that I do; and greater works than these will he do, because I go to the Father." And Paul, the apostle, writes: "When we cry, 'Abba, Father!' it is the Spirit himself bearing witness with our spirit that we are the children of God, and if children, their heirs, heirs of God and fellow heirs with Christ, provided we suffer with him in order that we may also be glorified with him. . . . For as many of you as were baptized into Christ have put on Christ. . . . I have been crucified with Christ; it is no longer I who live, but Christ who lives in me. . . . God chose to make known how great among the Gentiles are the riches of the glory of this mystery, which is Christ in you, the hope of glory."

Thus, *our name is Christian.* When Jesus walked with his disciples he was Christ, the Son of God—God revealing himself to those following few through the man Jesus. Completing his earthly sojourn, he died on the cross, rose from the dead, and ascended into heaven. A few days later the Spirit of God, who was so perfectly manifested in Christ, returned to indwell and empower the lives of Christ's followers. From that hour of Pentecost to this hour in which we meet together the Holy Spirit of God and of Christ dwells in the lives of every one who commits himself to God as revealed in Christ. With the fulfilling of the Spirit is granted everything that God is or promises. Do we understand what this means? It means, and this by Christ's repeated commands, that we are assigned to carry on the same task that Jesus began. We are not to redeem the world as did Christ; this was done once and for all by God through Christ. But we are to be "little Christs," authentic sons and daughters of God who are responsible for communicating and relating the power and the healing of this redemption to the creatures of this world.

Our name is Christian. It is a humbling truth—to think that we, sinful and self-centered, fallible and failure-fraught, are appointed and empowered to be "Christs" in this distorted, sin-ridden world. I am the very greatest of sinners, the least apt to deserve anything from God. I have nothing within myself worthy of his love and esteem. And yet I am one of those whom he has chosen to carry out his purposes, to continue that which Jesus began, to actually be a son of God amongst the children of this world, to represent and reflect Christ to the milling multitudes.

Our name is Christian. It is an awesome, even terrifying truth. Not only does our great God accept us and forgive us—in spite of faults and errors, our sin-permeated natures—but he reinstates us in his kingdom, reunites us to his divine family, and commissions us to manifest and demonstrate his power and purposes in his created world amongst his beloved creatures.

Our name is Christian. It is a very disturbing truth. What Jesus began in the three years of his visible presence he has appointed us to continue. He set the example, got the ball rolling; he reached out in self-sacrificing love to touch people in their need and to communicate to humanity the power of divinity. Now he gives us direct access to his source of power and commands us to go out and perform even greater works than he did in the short time he was upon this earth.

Our name is Christian. It is an upsetting, shattering truth. It means that we are not here to blow our horns, to perpetuate our personal ambitions. We are God's personal representatives, his envoys, his servants, his priests, with the express assignment of dedicating our very lives as well as the gifts he has made available to us to the carrying out of his purposes, the advancement of his kingdom, to channel his divine love and power into this fractured humanity about us. It means that we are no longer our own, that we really are not free to go about satiating our own lusts, but are free only to yield up our freedom to hold him and to others for his sake. And it means that until we do this, we are disjointed, disorbited beings without essential meaning or purpose for our lives.

Our name is Christian. It is an incomprehensible truth. We don't know why or how, but we have been created in the very image of God. This image was destroyed in our selfishness only to be restored through the redemption of Jesus Christ. Now, while we are still basically self-centered, we are nonetheless ordained for eternal purposes—the very objectives and purposes of God. And in spite of the crass imperfections of our beings, he does carry out his purposes through us in the measure that we surrender all that we are and have to his control.

Our name is Christian. It is a very expensive truth. It costs us everything that we have. We must "sell out" in order to relate to it. We must deliberately choose to lose our lives, deny selves, renounce all that we have, and take up our cross to follow in the path of Jesus Christ. And we do not do this just once, but every day of our lives. This is the conflict that we must perpetually engage in, a daily putting to death of self-interests and concerns in order that Christ's love and concern for others may be imparted through us.

Our name is Christian. It is a strange and solemn truth. With Christ no longer visibly present, we are, empowered by his Spirit, the only means God has of relating to those in our path. They may never realize God or his claim upon them except through us. We must be "Christ" to these people—as Jesus Christ would be to them were he visibly present. This means that we must love—even to the point of loving God through them—recognizing that as we sacrifice to meet their needs, we are thereby sacrificing to God himself.

Our name is Christian. It is an agonizing truth. It underlines the depression and pain of failure and sends us daily to the Father's throne to claim anew his acceptance and forgiveness. It identifies us with the pain and hurts, the emptiness and loneliness, the struggles and defeats, the poverty and deprivation of others. When God's creatures suffer, God himself suffers. As members of the body of Christ we also must endure suffering, to share in the sufferings and sorrows of others, to help bear their heavy burdens, for our name is Christian.

It is a beautiful and joyous truth far greater in value and worth than any human can possibly conceive. To be sons and daughters of God—claimed by his love, redeemed through his grace, empowered by his divinity, and guaranteed his eternal and abundant riches—all this is beyond one's wildest imaginations, and all this is ours, for our name is Christian.

It is not presumption; it's the Gospel truth. Our name is Christian. Let us begin each morning of the week with this realization and we will discover the real meaning and purpose of our lives. We will be compelled to draw on the power made available to accomplish that purpose; we will be driven to our knees again and again in abandonment and surrender; we will repeatedly find it necessary to renew and reestablish our faith. But if we really and truly allow God to have his way with us—whatever the cost, we will be the means by which God touches the lives of others, for our name is Christian.

LESLIE F. BRANDT
Trinity Lutheran Church
Victorville, California

EXCITEMENT IN OUR LIVES

Second Sunday after Christmas
John 1:1-18

Only two weeks ago, we were all caught up in the great excitement of the season. After all the waiting, we knew Christmas was finally at hand. We had spent weeks in preparation; we had given days and days to our shopping and wrapping and addressing and mailing. In the last few hours before the day came we even experienced those times when we wondered if we had done everything, or if everything we had done was really worth the effort. But suddenly Christmas was upon us. We decided it was worth-while; it was that exciting.

But then we discovered just as suddenly that Christmas was gone, and with it, some of the thrill faded too. True, the church calendar tells us this is still the Christmas season, but the carols are not quite as exciting. True also, we still have our wreaths and our Christmas trees, but they're no longer quite as fresh. Some of the novelty is gone from the toys, some of the newness from the clothes, some of the excitement from life. It seems we are ready to settle in our routines once again, thankful for the excitement which interrupted them, but unable to escape the less exciting times which fill them.

That's precisely why we need a word such as the Gospel word for this Sunday. It declares a strong *no!* to boredom and empty routine and darkness, and it declares God's strong *yes!* to life filled with his presence. It's a word proclaiming an ongoing excitement for the people of God, counting their joy in Jesus, the Christ. In him is life, John insists; in him is the light of men. He has become flesh to dwell among us, to fill us with his grace and truth, and that's a word of excitement.

It's the same thrill we might have felt as we heard the Old Testament lesson this morning, when Isaiah told us:

> I will greatly rejoice in the Lord,
> my soul shall exult in my God;
> for he has clothed me with the
> garments of salvation. . . .

or the echo in the second lesson, when we heard Paul tell the Christians at Ephesus:

> . . . he chose us in him before the foundation of the world . . .

and

> He destined us in love to be his sons through Jesus Christ.

That's the excitement we would find for ourselves this morning, the thrill of the Word made flesh and dwelling among us. He *has* made us his sons through our Baptism. He touches us with his Gospel in Word and Eucharist. He reaches into the tiredness, the dullness, the anxiety and the darkness of our existence with his love. He ends the boredom of our living with the excitement of his presence. The Word has become flesh, and in him is life, and new meaning while we live it.

The Word has become flesh, we said, and you remember, that's exactly the way John speaks of Christ in our text. He does give us much more reason to be excited about it, though. He says:

> In the beginning was the Word, and the Word was with God, and the Word was God. He was in the beginning with God; all things were made through him, and without him was not anything made that was made. In him was life.

Perhaps we will better understand John's emphasis here, if we also understand a particular term he used. He said that in the beginning was the Word, and that's a name we have often applied to Jesus Christ. But it's much more than a name, and even though the church has used that name for Jesus for centuries, those same centuries may have dulled some of the added meaning this name had for the first hearers of some almost two thousand years ago. In the beginning was the Word, John said, the *logos*, for that's the Greek term translated as Word, and John is telling his readers that Jesus Christ is that *logos* made flesh, dwelling among his people. To us it is another name, but for them it was a very special name, a name which included all the reason and the power in the universe, even all the wisdom which exists in it, and as some have called it, the life force which gives meaning to it. John is telling us that all creation and all its meaning are somehow to be found only in Jesus Christ. So he can say that in him is life, and the life was the light of men, shining into the darkness of dulled lives, a darkness which cannot overcome him.

The darkness does exist, though, for as John tells us, not everyone sees this *logos* with all his meaning. He says:

> The true light that enlightens every man was coming into the world. He was in the world, and the world was made through him, yet the whole world knew him not. He came to his own home, and his own people received him not.

Remembering that this was written some years after Christ, we can only recognize the accuracy of its reflection on the reception accorded Christ. He came into the world unrecognized; he came to his own people unaccepted. Neither the world nor his people were willing to find light for their darkness in him. First century Greek society prided itself on its enlightened culture and beauty; Rome of the same period found its meaning in power and wealth. Christ's own people of the Jewish world had their desires focused upon a hope for a Messiah, but they could not receive Christ as the fulfillment of that hope. Instead their excitement lay in the possibility that one day David's kingdom would be restored to its political and economic greatness, and Judah would know glory once again. The tragedy is alike for all three. Rome, Athens, and Jerusalem insisted that each had its own light, but as history tells us, darkness overcame them all.

At this point this word intersects our lives in the present day, as the Word himself also does. Human nature has not changed since the day he became flesh and dwelt among men, nor have human ideas about the meaning of life. Nor is there change in the peculiar human weakness in insisting on its own ideas about that which gives light to live by. "Enlightened" nations are those which have carved leading roles for themselves in the military or political or economic affairs of the world. They are the successful ones, the meaningful ones. "Enlightened" individuals are those who cope with the problems of living in that world successfully, and success we define in terms of occupation, status, income, or power. These are not only the goals of life; they are its sources as well, for we are surrounded by a culture which finds its life in them, extracts its meaning from them, and even derives its validity through them. If our advertising is at all accurate in reflecting our life style, then it would seem that the newer automobile, the better balanced golf club, the drier gin, or perhaps the younger spouse possess the power to make life new and exciting, and nothing more radical than changing deodorants, popping a few pills, or moving to a new neighborhood is necessary to handle any other problems which occur.

That is not to say that national accomplishment or personal success, or for that matter, a new car or a better golf club or even a drier gin, are wrong in themselves. Far from it! They too are the products of God's creative activity in his world, and as John says, without him was not anything made that was made. They are his gift to life. That means though, they are not the source of it, nor can they provide meaning to it. So they become problems, when we invest them with meaning they do not have and with validity they cannot support. Then they are signs of the darkness, and carry the possibility of overcoming us.

Perhaps that explains why ours is the age of anxiety it has become. We are discovering that the gods we have been worshipping cannot sustain us. International turmoil threatens our security and our economy; national tensions disrupt our political integrity. A depression can threaten our financial stability. We thought we had life, and now it appears we do not.

Perhaps it also explains the increasing boredom so many feel in their jobs, their activities, even their marriages. After all, we are people with expectations, defeated when we discover their emptiness. We would suggest that some of the problems of our modern society arise from them, that the growing alcoholism, the increasing dependence on drugs, the climbing rate of emotional and mental illness, and even the skyrocketing rate of broken marriages reflect our defeat. That which we had hoped would provide meaning has not; that which we thought would be exciting is dull. The darkness overcomes.

As we said before, that's why we need this Word, and we need it for something more than just to combat a post-Christmas letdown. This is a word which builds excitement into all of life, through the Word, the *logos,* who became part of it, and gives his meaning to it. He is the Word who overcame darkness with his light, who would not even be defeated when the forces of darkness put him to death on a cross. He is resurrection and life, or as he also said on another occasion, I am the light of the world.

In him was life, John said, and he might well have said: In him alone is life, for in those words our whole sin-filled rebellion against God is revealed. We have tried to structure life for ourselves and to write its meanings by ourselves. But John would say that's the sign of darkness, and we are the children of light. Our life is to be found in the one who has made us sons of God, the one who would say to us:

> No wonder you find so much of life dull and routine; no wonder you find it insecure and threatening. You've tried to build it on your own. It's time to recognize that life isn't something you construct. Instead, it comes only as a gift, as my gift to you. You are free of the struggle to find meaning for yourself; I give it to you. You are free of the need to develop status; I confer it on you. You are free of the necessity to live for the sake of power; I pour a new power upon you, the power to be the sons of God, through my forgiveness to you. Life isn't something you earn; it's the new relationship with the Father I have earned for you; it's love I constantly share with you.

John says it this way: Life is that which happens to the children of God, who were born not of blood nor of the will of the flesh nor of the will of man, but of God.

For the people of God, that is the good news we find exciting today and every day. It's the good news of the Word who became flesh and dwelt among us. It was that becoming and that dwelling which made our Christmas celebration exciting. And it's the good news of the Word still becoming flesh and still dwelling among us which gives excitement and meaning now. It's the joy of experiencing the touch of our Christ as the Word, entering the reality of our lives in the bread and wine of the Eucharist. It's the good news of the glory of the only Son from the Father, as John called him, the glory worked out in his birth and his life, in his suffering and death and resurrection. It's the fulness of grace and truth we have in him, the fulness of love and forgiveness acted out by him. It's the new confidence, the new joy, the new excitement, the new meaning we find from him. He has overcome our darkness, to bring light to our dark corners, and excitement to our dull lives.

LAVERN FRANZEN
Our Redeemer Lutheran Church
Temple Terrace, Florida

THE QUENCHLESS QUEST

The Epiphany of Our Lord
Matthew 2:1-12

There is an ancient legend which tells of a sea king who longed for the fellowship of a human being. One day he heard a cry. He left his cavern under the sea and rose to the surface of the water to discover a lonely child in an abandoned boat. Just as he reached for the child a rescue party intervened and he missed the prize he wanted so much. But as the child's saviors left the spot of the rescue, the sea king threw a little salt wave on the head of the child. As he submerged, he said to himself, "That child is mine. When he grows to young manhood, the sea will call him and he will come home to me at last."

It is only a legend but it holds the suggestion of a larger truth: that "God has placed eternity in our heart." He has made us restless with a quest for something better, something eternal!

The story of the Wise Men is the account of man's quenchless quest for something more, something always just beyond, that makes him a pilgrim on the earth.

They Reached for Stars

The Wise Men's Quest. We should like to know something more about these men who had in common some stirrings of soul that made them searchers. We sense the electricity of their conversation and anticipation as they shared their hopes and confessed their dreams for some closer liaison with a world of mystery and wonder.

It was an assembly of adventuring spirits for whom life was a thrilling event. Before he died in 1916 as an American volunteer serving with the French Foreign Legion, Alan Seeger wrote a poem which has attracted attention from time to time in our periods of war. It bears the title, "I Have a Rendezvous with

Death." In it, one senses the longings of this man who wishes for a spring of apple blossoms rather than death.

But here was a rendezvous with life, this joining of hearts and hopes with a star to guide them; somewhat uncertainly, to be sure, but with titillating possibilities of promise in the end!

Of course, their science was rudimentary, laced with superstition. Still, it was accurate enough to become the avenue of discovery. "We have seen this star." What wonders God reveals, even through our limited knowledge and our imperfect insights and understandings.

It is obvious that these were men of position, "wise men," men of wealth. "They opened their treasures, they offered him gifts." With this understanding of their status in life, they still were not satisfied. They were aware of an emptiness within. So they set out on their quest for inner fulfillment.

Too many of us have no goal in life. We flip and flop from one empty pursuit to another. We are like rudderless ships which simply cannot drive straight for any shore of accomplishment or destiny.

But we may learn well from these Wise Men. For all that we have gains worth only in the measure that we relate it to life's highest good. So their quest now became involved in a person. "Where is he who is born king of the Jews?" Things are never enough. Our hope that one more gadget, one more toy, one more fling at life or one more million will provide the answer ends up with a futile expectation. With these seers we seem to need some one, a King who is able to fill the spaces of our hearts with meaning. We need the King to take these scattered strands, these wispy, undefined dreams and shape them into a pattern which alone can be fashioned into the dimensions of eternity.

God's quest. Our faith is more than a philosophy of life, a search for something—we're not quite sure what! Thank God, it's his search for us. From his question in the garden, "Where are you?" to his invitation of the Bible's last page, "The Spirit and the Bride say, 'Come' . . . and let him who is thirsty come," God seeks us.

Praise the Lord for that. For even as Adam ran, so do we. And our escapes can be defined as aptly today as they were by the Psalmist who wrote, "Whither shall I go from the spirit? or whither shall I flee from thy presence? If I ascend to heaven . . . make my bed in Sheol . . . take the wings of the morning and dwell in the uttermost parts of the sea, thy right hand shall hold me." The flights and escapes of this generation no less than in that far off day find the sound of steps following—the strong steps of a God who thirsts for us!

This is the kind of a world into which God entered. The sign of the star lured the Wise Men. Even the sophistication of this time which looks to science and technology for salvation cannot shut its mind to him or quench the mystery that draws us to the portents of possibility inherent in Christ's birth.

We still reach for stars. But thankfully, the one to whom the star pointed reaches for us. This is the central truth of our faith. He is the Good Shepherd who seeks the one lost sheep, but more, he is the father of prodigals who hope to find their answers in far countries and farther out transgressions. He is the father who will not violate our wills but patiently patterns his wait to our moment of response. He searches us through our frustration, seeks us through our tears, and haunts us in those scintillating moments of ephemeral happiness.

The incarnation says this. God could not stay at his distance. "He bowed the heavens and came down." He has never left us. His Spirit continues to haunt our unquiet spirits.

They reached—and he reached them!

They Reverenced

"They worshiped him." We do not know whether they were able to define the object of their search as they embarked on their quest. But we know that in the end they found God in Jesus Christ.

Could they have guessed that their long trek would end at the place of a manger cradle and a baby? Yet, there is no inkling that they were disappointed in their discovery. What reinforcement did they have that this was the end of their search? Well, Herod knew that a child had been born and asked that they search diligently for him. In God's plan, even those who seek to frustrate his purpose are used to glorify him.

Costly worship. Treasures and gifts were offered. How significant! We who fall down before our treasures fail our destiny. They who fell down before the child, achieved theirs.

True worship is always costly. There are no tinsel offerings that acknowledge him, no shoddiness of performance that honors him, no shallowness that revered him.

They Returned

"And being warned in a dream not to return to Herod, they departed to their own country by another way."

They went back by way of peace. God used a dream to warn the Wise Men that they were not to return to Herod. Being wise, they reasoned that he was a jealous man who brooked no challenges to his despotic rule, who wanted no child, born to be a king, to threaten his throne.

This Jesus, heralded by angels' song, "Peace, goodwill toward men," came to be the Prince of Peace. Ribbons of blood crisscrossed their world. War was the order of their day. But the Wise Men went back to their country with the gospel of peace.

When will we learn that there is "another way?" We have raped the world's resources of men and material to fill the voracious maw of the god of war!

They went back by way of a new concern. How can we do less than share a great experience? In their quest for truth, they had known many a thrill. But this was the most unusual of their revelations. They began by following a star. It was climaxed when "they fell down and worshiped him." Their initial question, "Where is he . . . " became an affirmation of faith in Christ.

They went back, new people. How could they help return anything but "new?" You cannot look into the face of God and remain the same.

Recently, I stood at the place of the birth of Jesus in the Church of the Nativity in Bethlehem. It was on the day of the Epiphany of our Lord. A group of modern day pilgrims from Germany had followed the star of their quest to this holy place. Led by their priest in worship, they stood in the place of humble shepherds and Wise Men and received the holy communion. I shall not forget their faces, as though transformed, lighted from within, made new, they worshiped their Lord in this sacred spot.

The quenchless quest? Yes, because in him there is always more for us ahead!

Paul H. A. Noren
Mt. Olivet Lutheran Church
Minneapolis, Minnesota

THIS IS MY BELOVED

The Baptism of Our Lord — First Sunday after the Epiphany
Matthew 3:13-17

The baptism of our Lord speaks powerfully in this day of much religious curiosity, novelty, and experimentation. From tracing the movement of the stars in the cosmic reaches through astrology to probing our inner recesses through transcendental meditation we are a people much concerned with religion and its trappings. While old forms of faith are being jettisoned—new forms of faith are springing fresh upon the scene. Even religious relics from antiquity are being hauled out—dusted off and refurbished for our perusal. In the midst of all of this preoccupation and busyness with religion we hear this little story of Jesus' baptism by John in the river Jordan. What does it mean and how do we take its measure?

Perhaps the best place to begin in our search for understanding is to examine the setting in which this brief episode appears—to view the text in light of its context. What does Matthew tell us of Jesus before his baptism and what does he recount about Jesus after he walks from the Jordan?

Jesus' Early Years

What we are told prior to Jesus' confrontation with John is extremely limited. He is born in Bethlehem to a maiden named Mary. Shortly following his natal day unknown and unnamed men from the East visit him and worship before his presence. Following this act of adoration those same men return to their homes and disappear in the shadows of history. There is a break in the action. The drama resumes. The parents are forewarned that a suspicious King Herod, fearful of his puppet throne, seeks the child's death. They pack hastily and plunge into exile in Egypt. The ensuing holocaust, instigated by Herod, bathes Bethlehem in blood but Jesus is spared. Herod dies. Joseph together with wife and child returns to his homeland and settles in the town of Nazareth. That is all we are told. The years that follow are shrouded in an impenetrable silence. The childhood days, the adolescent traumas, the maturing to manhood—nothing—we are told nothing at all. Imagination—guess work—all fumbling attempts to unravel the web of silence can only leave us the more impoverished with our jaundiced speculation. It is as if Matthew is telling us through the skeletal frame of his Gospel that this is not important—this is not ultimately the crucial issue.

There follows a brief interlude in the gospel as Matthew introduces us to John and his ministry of baptism. And then—suddenly—Jesus appears on the banks of the Jordan striding out of those years of silence from the cross roads of nowhere to be baptized by this same John. The Baptist hesitates—seemingly uncertain of his mission for the first time. "It must be so"—says Jesus. John consents. The baptism begins.

"And when Jesus was baptized, he went up immediately from the water, and behold the heavens were opened and he saw the Spirit of God descending *like* a dove, and alighted on him; and lo, a voice from heaven, saying, "This is my beloved Son, with whom I am well pleased."

The Meaning of Jesus' Baptism

Now follows a whole series of events that bracket Jesus' baptism. He plunges into the nearby wilderness to confront and do battle with man's most ancient foe. From that lonely solitude he returns to the teeming countryside and begins to preach in staccato phrases—"Repent, for the kingdom of heaven is at hand." Now the long years of silence are shattered and the quiet of Nazareth's pastoral scene is stirred in a cacophony of words and a scurry of action. Sermons are preached, commands are given, lepers are cleansed, the sick are healed, storms are stilled and demons driven from besieged men. The tempo does not subside—it increases. There is no end to the confrontations and challenges hurled at him. His authority is questioned—his motives made suspect. The religiously rich he chastises. The morally bankrupt he confronts. Blindness, deafness, paralysis and death itself stagger before his relentless onslaught. No need too small for his compassion. No piety too revered for his rebuke. Finally he is stilled and silenced in the agony and despair of the cross. His life, like that of all men was bounded by birth and death. But his ministry and mission hinged upon his baptism.

Jesus healed no one—taught nobody—snatched none from the clutch of death—cast out no demons until he had been baptized. In some inexplicable way his baptism serves as the line of demarcation between Jesus—son of Mary and the Christ—Son of God. His authenticity—his authority is inextricably tied to his baptism. At no time does Matthew make any claim or even hint that Jesus was some kind of spiritual athlete or religious savant or self-authenticated genius, a miracle worker or in the vernacular of the day—a Superstar. The very paucity of the gospel at this point would seem to indicate that both Jesus and his followers had divested themselves entirely of even the suggestion. We see him only as a child—the child of Mary—a man among men—a Jew among Jews—who was baptized, and in that baptism received the Spirit of the Most High. There is no other attempt to explain or understand his ministry apart from this. The very silence of Matthew and the other gospel writers at this point thunders its message at us. There is no power, there is no authority apart from God's Spirit which is given through the water and word of baptism. No man can lay claim to such—not even the Christ.

We Have Been Baptized

Today we are beleaguered by all manner of religious hucksters. Would-be world changers going about their self-appointed duties. Self-appointed prophets busy divining the future. We fever ourselves with much self-generated piety and trouble ourselves in endless quest for valid religious experiences. Self-proclaimed miracle workers and faith healers have come hard upon the scene to tickle us with the exotic. We question ourselves with much introspection and increasing intensity. But in all of this it seems we too often have failed at the crucial point. We have been baptized. We have received the Spirit and power of God through the water and the word. The word of promise. The word of power. We can be done with the new and the novel—the fads and the follies of this much religion. We are the sons and daughters of him who is the Ancient of Days. We are the brothers and sisters of him who died and rose again. We have been baptized into Christ. Everything hinges upon that.

If you don't "feel" religious—remember you have been baptized.

If you have not "experienced" God's presence—remember God has drawn near to you in the water of baptism.

If you doubt and despair—remember God has given you his promise in baptism.

If you traipse into the far country and swill in the pig sties of the earth—remember there is a Father who has named you and known you in your baptism.

If you renounce it all and give yourself over to meaninglessness and nothingness—remember in baptism God has not renounced you.

If you stumble in your sin and stammer in your confession—remember that in your baptism you who are guilty have received grace.

No ecstasy—no vision—no experience can make it more real. No doubt—no despair—no evil can take that from you.

For in your baptism, as with your Lord's, God has said—"This is my beloved—with whom I am well pleased."

KEITH KREBS
Emmanuel Lutheran Church
Walla Walla, Washington

NEW LIFE FOR THE NEW YEAR

Second Sunday after the Epiphany
John 1:29-41

Epiphany is more than a season of the church year. It is a way of life for Christians which gives meaning and purpose to living and the opportunity to change our world.
Lord, show us how to use the signs about us to point people to your grace in Jesus Christ. Having given us a purpose for living in the New Year make our life a doxology to your love. Amen.

Resolutions —Which Ones Work?

By now you have made your New Year's resolutions and are well on the way to accomplishing them or abandoning them. If you have already given up on your resolutions you may be wondering why it is that each year you go through the same futile motion. Perhaps you are like Charlie Brown who finds it difficult to resist running at the football when Lucy holds it for him at the beginning of the football season each year. Charlie Brown knows what the outcome will be but he must try anyhow. So he runs. Some of us approach our resolutions with the same morbid feeling of inevitability.

One of the reasons New Year's resolutions are hard to keep may be because they often deal with things which are on the periphery of our lives. I believe that when we get down to the things that really count we find the power to do them. That is why Satan carries on such an intensive campaign to make us think that our lives do not make any difference in the long run. The powers of evil win when we believe that we are not accountable to anyone in our living.

Yesterday I received a newsletter called the *Christian Leadership Letter*. It dealt with this very topic.

> The early church discovered the tremendous social value of confessing our sins to one another—being accountable. But the Roman Church came and said that we only had to confess our sins to the priest. When the Protestants came on the scene, they made it worse! They said we only had to confess our sins to God. Then Freud came along and blew the whole thing: he said we didn't have any sins to confess! (December 1973, p. 1.)

If we do not press that statement for historical and theological accuracy it can be useful in emphasizing that our life has accountability to God and to one another. Making a firm resolve to take God and his will seriously during the New Year can bring great purpose and satisfaction into our living.

The Agenda for the New Year

To guarantee that life will be rewarding in the new year we need to go beyond resolutions that have to do with losing weight or with curbing bad habits and creating new ones, to recommitting ourselves to pointing people to Jesus Christ during the next 350 days. In fact, I will be audacious enough to suggest that if we pursue that goal with vigor our lives can effect the course of human history in the years to come.

In order to change the world we need a plan. Our plan must be simple enough for everyone to understand and to become involved. The gospel for today contains the outline for such a plan. It clearly teaches that to change the course of history we need to start small. Begin where John the Baptist made his beginning—with himself. He took himself seriously. He prepared himself for what he understood God's will for his life to be. People like John the Baptist are the kind that change our world.

We received a beautiful Christmas card with the message: "As we are, so is our world." How true that is. Change yourself and you change the world. It is that simple and it is that possible.

God had a hand in John the Baptist's life even before his birth. John was aware of that. But that did not make it any easier for him to serve God. He sometimes seemed dissatisfied with the way God was doing things. Yet John was an important part of God's plan and God used the life of John the Baptist to bless his world.

God has had a hand in your life too. God put his mark on you in baptism. In your rebirth through faith you became a child of God. In the word of the Scriptures, in the action of the sacraments, and in the witness of those about you God is empowering you to serve him daily. This very day God is telling you that he loves you. And even if you think your life is quite insignificant in comparison to the life of Jesus Christ—nevertheless your life is crucial to the plan of God for the welfare of his world. God's purpose for your existence is the same as it was for the people of Israel. God always chooses people for an end greater than themselves. Thus he said to Israel through Isaiah: "I will give you as a light to the nations, that my salvation may reach to the end of the earth" (Isaiah 49:6).

John the Baptist was also chosen for a purpose greater than self-salvation. John said, "I myself did not know him; but for this I came baptizing with water, that he might be revealed to Israel" (John 1:31).

Our Means to God's End

In accomplishing his purpose that Israel would come to know Christ, John used a very simple means. John knew that saving Israel was God's business so he was satisfied to use his life to introduce people to God's salvation in the flesh. When John saw some people whom he knew he said to them, "Look, there is the Lamb of God who takes away the sin of the world." John used his life to point people to a Christ whom he had come to regard as Savior. And you can do the same thing!

John first pointed out Christ to his own disciples. He took a few who were close to himself and introduced them to the Lamb of God. I am not certain what that phrase meant to John's disciples. They might have thought from it that Jesus was the one who was to usher in the new age when all the forces of evil would be destroyed at the end of time. John often spoke like that. He was a hellfire and brimstone preacher who described Jesus in terms of God's judgment (John 3:1-17). Or, John's introduction might have reminded them of the Passover lamb whose blood prevailed in the sight of God to save the first-born of the Israelites from the angel of death when God was working out the freedom of his people in Egypt. We do know that at a later time Jesus was connected with the Passover lamb as Paul said, "Christ our Passover has been sacrificed" (1 Corinthians 5:7). On the other hand they might also have considered Jesus to be the suffering servant lamb of Isaiah 53 even though the disciples seemed not to understand that it was necessary for the Lamb of God to suffer and to die for the life of the world.

Whatever they understood the title to mean, it was enough that John introduced them to Jesus. Trusting their friend and leader they left his companionship long enough to discover for themselves what this person to whom John was pointing was all about. You can understand that John the Baptist made a significant sacrifice and took a great risk in sending his friends in pursuit of the Christ. But he loved his friends and understood his mission so the risk was worth it.

Then a marvelous thing happened. When Andrew was introduced to Jesus he went and got his brother Peter. When Philip was introduced to Christ he enlisted Nathaniel. And each of these in turn introduced many more to Jesus—all of whom became believers through their own encounter with the Christ. And thus the world was changed. It is a simple method but it is still the best I know. And the most marvelous thing about it is that in a plan such as that you too can be involved. Epiphany—revealing Christ to people and people to Christ is for you!

As we were shopping in the food store one evening I stood before the paper products counters with their empty shelf space and a big sign telling people that there is no paper shortage. The sign appealed to the common sense and the common decency of people saying that if we do not hoard them there will be no shortage of paper products. The thought struck me—what a great idea it would be to get a case of Kleenex, a carton of paper towels, or a big stack of toilet tissue and to stand on the corner of some busy street in Washington, D.C. giving it away to people. As I visualized myself doing that I saw myself urging people to look beyond the paper to the tree from which it came. I fantasized about telling people to look beyond the tree to the God from which it came. I thought I would ask people who took my gift to look beyond yesterday with its many problems to the God who loved us enough to send a Savior to live our life and to transform it so that it is now so much more than bread and paper and gasoline. I think I would plead with people to look beyond today to the God who loves us still and who provides for the greatest needs of life we can experience. Just think—one person could do that at a time such as this.

Our Epiphany Call

When Jesus was baptized, the Holy Spirit came upon him and it remained with him. It is the power and presence of that same Holy Spirit which Christ pours out upon us today urging us to join the Epiphany life. God is telling us to help people in our world discover him by our witnessing in word and in deed.

God has prepared the world for our witness. Not in a long time has the confidence of the American people in materialism and in the inherent goodness of mankind—even the inherent goodness of the so-called great men who can get themselves elected to high offices—been as low as it is right now. I have observed people listening to the patriotic editorial of Gordon Sinclair with almost religious attention. Sinclair is the Canadian radio and TV commentator who has written a commentary of how the United

States has helped other countries in their time of disaster and received little or nothing in return. The editorial has even been inserted into the *Congressional Record* and it has become the subject of many editorials in our own land. People are searching and grasping for something good in which to believe in the midst of a crumbling stock market, incredible scandals, and the unbelievable statistics which tell us that we have more oil and oil products available now than we had a year ago. God's grace can be most magnificently portrayed against the backdrop of our present historical circumstance.

I have read with keen interest the letters to editors which concern themselves with what families are doing on weekends since gasoline is unavailable. Thus far I have not discovered many letters from people saying that the shortages have given them more time and resources for worshiping the great God who loved us enough to travel from heaven to earth on our behalf. But the signs are hopeful as people are being moved closer to each other. There many may discover their need for God and give us opportunity to show by our own life of concern how much God yearns for them. And perhaps we too can come to appreciate that before all else, God would have us be about his work of sharing himself with those about us.

How exciting your life can be if you plan during this year to find just one person and say in your own way to that human being, "Look, here is Christ. He loves you. He gave his life for you because you needed that. He wants to count you as one of his followers. Christ will take over your life and open up a whole new way of living for you if you want him to do that. He will give you abundant life through the Holy Spirit with peace and power for living right now."

If you have caught the vision of what I am talking about then you are really in the Epiphany spirit and you know that you have gone far beyond the ordinary New Year's resolution which most of us make to serve ourselves. We have all been served by Jesus Christ. There is very little that you and I need for the new year besides each other. If we are firmly committed to each other we can go to the one who needs us—the one to whom God has been waiting to introduce us—that we might be ambassadors for Christ so that God can make his appeal through us.

If you have caught the vision of which I speak, you will not be bashful about yourself or about the person whom you introduce to Christ. Remember that God loves everyone—not just the people who are like us. Natural barriers must be crossed to do the work of God. For God wants to work through us to claim everyone for his own. And God will use you where he finds you to change his world. God put you where you are—for a purpose. There is someone who is near you to whom you can say, "Look, here is the Lamb of God." And when they find him, they will tell someone else. And our world will be different and it will be better because you lived in it.

GEORGE F. LOBIEN
The Lutheran Church of St. Andrew
Silver Springs, Maryland

HE'S BUILDING AN EMPIRE

Third Sunday after the Epiphany
Matthew 4:12-23

More often than not when the words, "He's building an empire," are spoken, they are meant to convey a negative criticism, denunciation and even censure. They are used to describe the activities and plans of leaders in every facet of society; they are spoken often in envy, sometimes in resentment and at other times with bitterness. They are uttered by competitors, defeated opponents and enemies. Many who speak them hope to tarnish the reputation, minimize the achievements and even destroy the one to whom they have reference.

But these words are also spoken with admiration and appreciation. As such, they come from the lips of colleagues and collaborators, supporters and stockholders. Today, I use these words in this approving and favorable sense, devoutly proclaiming them a description of our Lord and Savior. Before he came as the fulfillment of the promises of a coming Messiah, there were students of the Scriptures, who yearned for the day when the kingdom of God would be established on earth. Their interpretation of the kingdom was different from the plan of the Creator for they anticipated an empire, an empire governed by force and might.

The empire of which I speak is not such for it is being built and formed, developed and led by something even more powerful than force. It is being built and guided by ideas and truths that change the lives of people, giving them new directions. It is an empire that claims the hearts of people and it grows constantly and continuously, both as numbers are added to the faithful and as the commitment and faith of those who are part of it becomes more inclusive and out-reaching.

The lesson for this meditation is a blueprint for the building of the kingdom; it tells what Jesus did as he began preaching, as he called those he chose as his first disciples and as he pursued the ministry by which were laid the foundations of his kingdom. Let's look at that Empire from the perspective of our text.

The Mandate of the Charter

The word "charter" is often used interchangeably with the phrase "the articles of incorporation" when reference is made to the governing document of an entity or institution. Among other matters included in a charter is a statement of purpose or function—the reason for being. Any organization or institution, person or group desiring to do business as a legal corporate entity must have a charter that describes in general terms what it is about. It can be said that this description of purpose is the mandate.

It is not possible here to review in detail the relationship between John the Baptist and Jesus. Simply stated, John was called to prepare the way for the Messiah who was to come later. Jesus recognized the validity of John's work and was baptized by him, and when the Son of God heard that John had been imprisoned, he began to preach John's words, saying, "Repent, for the kingdom of heaven is at hand."

In those words is the mandate for the charter of the empire. Even as John the Baptist had been calling on those who listened to him to change and turn from their sinful ways, the Messiah likewise called on those who would be his followers to change the direction of their lives.

Most people dislike change; the routine is safer and more comfortable. Admit it we must; change is difficult. Many are the individuals who have taken early retirement because the computer society in which we live has drastically changed their job descriptions. Human obsolescence is becoming nearly as prevelant as out-of-date machines. Though we must have an occasional and even regular change of pace as to activity, most of us prefer to avoid abrupt changes in life-style, work habits and organizational structure.

People have always been this way and that's why many didn't like what John the Baptist said nor fully comprehend what Jesus declared as he called for those who would be followers to change their ways. That's also why you and I resist day by day turning away from the life that is self-oriented to the one that is God-oriented. We don't really want that kind of change to take place;

even if we're not having fun or aren't happy the way we are, we're too comfortable; the way to which we are called by Jesus seems too difficult, too different and too demanding. "Love your enemy. Do good to those who hate you." It's difficult enough to always love a friend and it's hard enough to find time to do good where it's worthwhile and for the deserving. But Christ sets forth the mandate clearly: Repent! Change your ways.

The empire is being built; Jesus Christ, the builder, spelled out the mandate of its charter when he began his preaching ministry; it is, "Repent, the kingdom of heaven is at hand."

The Function of the Backers

When an individual or group of people embark on a venture new to them or that is a dramatic expansion of their business operations, the question is often asked, "Who's the backer?" The query is posed in recognition of the fact that in the world of business, success is more often than not dependent upon the amount of financial resources available to the entrepreneur; either he or those who back him must be willing to invest "risk" capital or "put their chips on the line."

Among the first things that Jesus did as he began his ministry was to secure "backers." Though the venture upon which he was embarking did not demand skill on the waters, he found his first followers among the fishermen. You'll remember the text identified them as Simon, also called Peter, his brother Andrew and another set of brothers, named James and John. They were promised that they would become fishers of men if they would leave their nets and their boats.

Andrew was the first to be convinced. He had been a follower of John's and upon hearing John point out Jesus as "the Lamb of God" brought his brother Simon with the words, "We have found the Messiah." There was no doubt that they believed but they likely never expected to be called to be backers or disciples. A disciple was a close associate who would have no time to devote to any other endeavor. They were called to leave their home, their vocation, their security. They knew it was a risky venture but they also knew a backer had to go all the way.

Christ doesn't call us to a sometime thing. He refuses left-overs—whether it be left-over time or left-over commitment. Being a backer is risking everything.

The Epistle for this day refers to later backers in the movement and drives home a point that speaks to us today; the members of the church (backers) were not to be divided as to loyalty but were all to belong to Christ, the church's founder and head. The words of the lesson were addressed by Paul to the church at Corinth where the members of the parish had begun to identify themselves as being associated with one or another of the early leaders. Paul let them know in typical Pauline forthright statements that they were to give their allegiance, loyalty and obedience to Christ. No subordinate leader was important.

The empire of which we think today was and is being built by the founder, the Messiah Christ, but it has had and continues to have backers. Millions of people down through the ages have been counted among them as person after person and family after family have cast their lot, spiritually, with the Christ. They have believed and they have followed; they have been in contact through worship and devotion; they have witnessed by confession and service. They have studied the Scriptures and the implications of them; they have found the message pertinent to the lives they live and because of its significance and meaning to them, they have called and invited others to join them as backers.

The empire is being built; Jesus Christ, the head, called and still calls for backers or disciples; they were then and still are today expected to be with him, united in loyalty, and reaching out for him as they proclaim their faith and urge others to share it.

The Scope of the Operation

Not long ago, a number of us applied for a charter for a Lutheran Credit Union. It took a bit of time to get what we needed to function, for we had to satisfy the State Department of Banking that the limits of the territory the Union would be permitted to serve were realistic; the charter specifically defines the geographical area and the individuals who may be members of our credit union.

Too often the empires conceived by world leaders obsessed with power have really had no limits and therein has been their downfall. Because the logistical problems of policing the vast domains that Alexander the Great, Charlemagne, Napoleon and others wanted to control could not be solved quickly enough, their kingdoms met their "Waterloos" and eventually disintegrated. These world leaders as well as others before and since them mistakenly believed that there was unlimited strength and power in the armies and legions they commanded.

The empire of the Messiah is global as to scope of operation; it has achieved what world leaders could not, simply because it is based on something more powerful than armed force; it has its might in truth and convictions that can turn and change the hearts and lives of people. There's nothing more powerful, and because it is built on this, there are no limits to its field of service or operation.

Every era of the history of the human race has provided opportunities and challenges for the Christian faith or the empire being built by the Messiah. The one in which we now live is no exception. When people find themselves disturbed by uncertainties, beset by crises, plagued by injustice, they seem to be in a more receptive mood for the assurance of the gospel than when free from such tribulations. That gospel is the cornerstone of the empire we picture today; it was personalized by Jesus. He spelled out its thrust when he called for repentance. He described the task of his backers when he called Peter and Andrew, James and John, and the others to follow him and become fishers of men. He defined the area of operation when he went everywhere, in the little world that he knew, preaching and healing. He spelled out that territory when he commanded his backers to go and make disciples of all nations (as recorded in Matthew) and when he stated with definitiveness (as written in the first chapter of Acts) that they would be his witnesses in Jerusalem and to the uttermost parts of the earth.

Jesus preached the gospel and healed every disease and every infirmity among the people. He was not prejudicial to some of the diseases and needs; his actions give the mandate for the concern of the church today. The faith we confess, the allegiance we give, the commitment we make to him who is building the Empire must direct, dictate and define the way we pursue our vocation, utilize our leisure time and live with our families. The empire that was founded as the Christ began preaching, expanded as he called disciples and stretched out as he touched the lives of a host of people is all inclusive, both as to area and concern.

The empire is being built; Jesus Christ, the builder through the work of the Spirit still today is calling people to be followers, and by his example and word, we know its thrust and impact to be every sort and condition of human need.

And Finally

Tycoons sometimes catch competitors unawares as they build their empires; world leaders often get their empires started by adept manipulation of the constituents they are supposed to serve. The empire of the kingdom is different; membership in it comes only from conscious awareness and commitment. No one is hoodwinked into allegiance to it; no one becomes part and parcel of it by being outmaneuvered. It is being built by the changing of lives—away from ways of sinfulness to obedience to God.

The mandate of the charter is simple; it is a call to repentance from sin to acceptance of a Messiah. It's a personal decision that must be made by those who would belong to or be a part of it.

The function of the backers is likewise simple; it is to be with the builder through worship, devotion and service. It is walking on and in his way and inviting and urging others to similarly follow.

The scope of the operation is not simple; it is global and all inclusive. The gospel is for all—everywhere and for all the joys and victories, tears and tribulations of life.

The empire is being built; there's no mistake about that; it can't be counted by mere numbers though humanly speaking we have no other way to judge its size; its power comes from the lives it affects and governs as they live their days.

It's the Messiah, the Christ who is building a kingdom—he's building an empire with or without us. We pray for it everytime we pray the second petition of the Lord's Prayer, "Thy kingdom come." That kingdom is being and will be built whether we pray these words with meaning or not. Are you—am I—part of it?

REUBEN T. SWANSON
President, Nebraska Synod
Omaha, Nebraska

BEING — GIVING — RECEIVING

Fourth Sunday after the Epiphany
Matthew 5:1-12

From the time when you and I were very small until today, we have been taught to believe and feel that it is more blessed to give than it is to receive. We hear this from parents at Christmas time. We hear this from the church at stewardship time. We hear this from the Sunday school at offering time. We hear this from charities at financial drive time. All around us, from inside the church and from the outside, we hear how great it is to give. It is great to give, but this is only one side of life. There are two other sides to life—being and receiving—and they are blessed too.

These three sides, being, giving, and receiving, are strikingly proclaimed by our Lord in the passage of Scripture known as the Beatitudes. Here we find a message of real being, giving, and receiving, a message summed up in the statement: *Blessed are they who are themselves, who give themselves and their love away, for they shall be loved and filled.*

Be Yourself

As we turn to our text from the fifth chapter of Matthew, one of the first things we discover is the fact that not everyone has to be alike. There are some who are poor in spirit. There are some who mourn. Some are meek. Others hunger and thirst for righteousness. Some are merciful. Others are pure in heart. We can go on and on through the list finding nine different types of people. The Lord recognizes differences in people and proclaims that we don't all have to be the same nor do we all have to fit into the same mold. It's okay to be different, for the call of Jesus the Christ is not a call to sameness. The call of Jesus the Christ is a call to uniqueness. This is clearly seen when we stop and take a close look at those he called to be his disciples.

When we stop and take an honest look at the disciples, after scraping off all the icing and myth which has grown up about them, and begin to see them as real, flesh and blood human beings, we are almost forced to say, "Boy what a motley crew." There are all different kinds of personalities, all different kinds of attitudes, all different kinds of hang-ups, all different kinds of talents and backgrounds represented. Not everyone has hoof-in-mouth disease like Peter who's forever opening his mouth and inserting his foot. Not everyone is in the inner circle of friends like John. Not everyone wrote gospels like Matthew. The amazing thing is, though, the Lord accepted them as they were and didn't force them into the same mold. He let them be their unique selves. Jesus the Christ does the same for you and me.

When the Lord calls us to be his disciples he doesn't call us to be like Peter, Paul, or even like himself. He doesn't ask us all to fit into the same mold or have the same talents and gifts. He doesn't ask us all to speak in tongues. He doesn't ask us all to be intellectuals. He doesn't ask us all to become Lutherans, Presbyterians, Episcopalians, Baptists, Methodists, Pentecostals, or even Protestants. When the Lord calls us to be his disciples he calls us first of all to be ourselves, really, genuinely, completely, uniquely, ourselves. He calls us to be Phil, Myra, Bruce, Maggie, or Billy, and leave the rest to him. In the Beatitudes the Lord tells his disciples, then and now, *Blessed are they who are them-*

selves, who give themselves and their love away, for they shall be loved and filled.

Give Yourself

Jesus the Christ calls his disciples to be themselves, but he calls them to more than that. Being themselves is only one side of life. A second side to life is giving, and this the Lord also asks of his disciples. Jesus the Christ asks his disciples to give themselves and their love away. To do the things mentioned in the Beatitude, to mourn, to be meek, to show mercy, to be peacemakers, to be persecuted, to do all these things is really, when you get right down to the basics, to give ourselves and our love away.

There is a delightful children's book which some of you may have read out loud to your children or grandchildren. The book is *The Velveteen Rabbit.* In this book there is a conversation which takes place between two toy animals in the nursery, a new rabbit, and an old skin horse. The conversation centers on the question of what it means to be real, and I think on what it means to love and give yourself away. Let's listen in on their conversation for a moment.

> "What is REAL?" asked the Rabbit one day, when they were lying side by side. "Does it mean having things that buzz inside and a stick-out handle?"
>
> "Real isn't how you're made," said the Skin Horse. "It's a thing that happens to you. When a child loves you for a long, long time, not just to play with, but REALLY loves you, then you become Real."
>
> "Does it hurt?" asked the Rabbit.
>
> "Sometimes," said the Skin Horse, for he was always truthful. "When you are Real you don't mind being hurt."
>
> "Does it happen all at once, like being wound up, or bit by bit?"
>
> "It doesn't happen all at once. You become. It takes a long time—that's why it doesn't often happen to people who break easily or have sharp edges or have to be carefully kept. Generally, by the time you are Real, most of your hair has been loved off, and your eyes drop out and you get loose in the joints and very shabby. But these things don't matter at all because once you are Real, you can't be ugly, except to people who don't understand."

The old Skin Horse knows what it means to love. He knows

that it means giving yourself away. It means being used until the point that the hair falls off, the eyes drop out, and the joints get loose. To love means giving ourselves, all that we are, to others, allowing them to love us to pieces. It means reaching out to them at their point of need and giving them ourselves. This is what Jesus the Christ has done for us and what he continues to do.

Jesus the Christ meets us at our point of need and gives us himself and his love. He doesn't give us a bunch of pious clichés, Bible passages, or sermons. He gives us something vastly more important. He gives us himself, fully, totally, completely—even unto death.

The greatest gift you can give me is to give me yourself, your love. To give me words without giving me yourself is to leave me and my cup empty. But to give me yourself, your love in concrete human form, fills my cup to the brim and to overflowing.

In the Beatitudes the Lord tells his disciples, then and now, *Blessed are they who are themselves, who give themselves and their love away, for they shall be loved and filled.*

Receive for Yourself

Be yourself! Give yourself! These are two sides of life our Lord affirms in the Beatitudes, but there is one more side. He tells his disciples to receive for themselves.

If you look carefully at the Beatitudes, on the other side of the common, you know, after "blessed are they who," you will find that for every act of love given, something is received: the kingdom of heaven; comfort; satisfaction; mercy; the name, sons of God. For love given, love is received and received in superabundance. The cup is filled to overflowing.

Jess Lair in his book *I Ain't Much Baby, But I'm All I Got,* suggests that most of us are running around with our cups half filled wanting the other half filled, but not knowing how to get it filled. He suggests that the way to get our cups filled is both to give of ourselves and to receive for ourselves. The trouble is, though, that for so long we have been made to believe and feel that it is wrong and selfish to have our own needs met. This has been impressed on us so hard that we sometimes forget that we need to receive for ourselves.

Jesus the Christ gave himself on Calvary, but I have to receive him for myself. I can give you myself and my love, but you have to receive me for yourself. You can give me your love and yourself, but I have to receive you for myself. It's a two way street and both directions need to be traveled. The Lord Jesus affirms this giving and receiving as he tells his disciples, then and now, *Blessed are they who are themselves, who give themselves and their love away, for they shall be loved and filled.*

When we take a good, close and honest look at the Beatitudes, three things come through loud and clear. First, as disciples we are called to be ourselves. We don't all have to look alike, be alike, think alike, or anything else alike. It's okay to be different. Second, as disciples we are called to give ourselves and our love away. We are called to love people at their point of need, allowing them to love us to pieces. Third, as disciples we are called to receive love from others. Loving is a two way street. It is giving and receiving. Both sides need to be affirmed. Both directions need to be traveled.

Jesus the Christ proclaims to his disciples: Be yourself! Give yourself! Receive for yourself! God grant that we might truly be, give and receive.

PHILLIP BAKER
Shepherd of the Valley Lutheran Church
Council Bluffs, Iowa

A VISION OF GRACE AND GLORY

The Transfiguration of Our Lord — Last Sunday after the Epiphany
Matthew 17:1-9

During my childhood years I used to hear the story of Jesus' Transfiguration read aloud in church each year as the Gospel for the Last Sunday after the Epiphany, but the narrative never made sense to me. The earlier Epiphany Sunday Gospels—The Boy Jesus in the Temple, Jesus Turning Water into Wine, Jesus Healing the Centurion's Servant—these all captivated me and held my attention. But this account of the dazzling brightness of Jesus' face, the strange appearance of Moses and Elijah from out of nowhere, and finally the voice from the cloud—well, I heard it all but I didn't get it at all. Once I said as much to my father (who was the pastor of the congregation in which I was growing up); but instead of trying at that time to explain this mysterious occurrence to me, he assured me that its meaning would become clear to me in future years. He predicted that the days would come in my adult life when I would understand the significance of moments of transfiguration not only in the lives of Peter and James and John but in my own life as well.

My father was right! The days have come when I realize why Jesus displayed his glory to his disciples in this extraordinary manner. The element of the miraculous remains, of course; I still cannot comprehend *how* it happened, but I do understand *why* it happened. Jesus knew how offended his disciples would be when they saw him being taken captive, crucified, and killed. He realized that there was nothing physical about him as a human being which in any way identified him for them as the Son of God that he was, nothing to attract them to him and keep them attached to him through his awful suffering and death. So, lest they become totally disillusioned and desert him altogether, he permitted them this peek into the company of heaven—that they might know him not only as the suffering son of man, but also as the beloved Son of God.

And they certainly did remember their most holy moment with him on that mountain. "We were eyewitnesses of his majesty," Peter later wrote. "We heard the voice from heaven; we were with him on the holy mountain." That moment, coupled with their even more magnificent moments with him after he had risen from the dead, helped to transform them from wavering followers to fearless apostles. It helped to keep them going in later years when their speaking out on his behalf got them into all kinds of trouble with the defenders of the Old Covenant.

Modern Transfigurations

God still favors us, his people today, with moments of transfiguration—in order to impress his glory and his grace upon us—and in order to stimulate us to share his grace and glory with others through our work, our leisure, and our worship. But how can you recognize these moments in your own life? And why don't they come more frequently? And what happens when the same experience that is a moment of transfiguration for you turns out to be a moment of tedium or torment for your neighbor? Let me try to answer these questions one at a time.

Recognizing the Moment

How can you recognize moments of transfiguration in your own life? Any happening which compels you to confess spontaneously how good and gracious God is in all his works is surely a moment of transfiguration. It may be a moment of quiet joy in seeing your newborn child for the first time; or a moment of deep satisfaction in observing your troublesome teenager on his very best behavior; or a moment of ecstatic oneness with your spouse; or a moment of hearing your brother say he is genuinely sorry for his having sinned against you; or a moment in the singing of a hymn such as "The Church's One Foundation"; or a moment of hearing a devotionally powerful performance of the Brahms *Requiem;* or a moment of holy joy at the communion rail during the Christmas Eve Candlelight Eucharist. Every experience which compels you to sigh and say (whether aloud or silently) "The Lord is a great God and a great king above all gods" is surely a transfigured moment in your life.

Frequency of the Experience

Why don't such moments come more frequently? Maybe you need to enlarge your understanding of what such moments are. They may be experienced by others more often than you realize. During my initial years as a parish pastor I used to be much disturbed by what seemed to me to be apathy and listlessness among the people I was leading in public worship from week to week. I kept searching in vain for some magic formula by which I might be able to stir them up to a level of excitement I thought should be there, but wasn't. One day I shared this concern with a pastor older and wiser than I, and his response was in itself a moment of transfiguration for me in that it relieved me of all further needless worry.

He said to me: "How can you be so sure that your parishioners are as apathetic and listless in their worship as you say they are? If most of our waking moments as human beings were pitched to the level of excitement you keep trying to achieve, we'd all be emotionally burned out before long. Think how important everyone's daily breakfast is for their health and well-being. Yet how many people can remember later in the day what they ate that morning for breakfast? Not very many, for breakfast is rarely an exhilarating, memorable experience. But people are nourished by it anyway. So the sharing of your people in Word and Sacrament every Sunday is nourishing for them spiritually, whether or not they appear to be turned on by it. More often than not, the Spirit is at work in them in ways that are not even discernible to themselves, to say nothing of their being discernible to you."

This thoughtful response from the brother has put me at ease, content to let the Spirit hover over God's people and touch those whom he wills, when he wills, and in what ways he wills. Diligent planning and preparation for our weekly worship continue; but we depend altogether on the Spirit to breathe new life into our dry bones, in keeping with his promise to do so.

A Varied Experience

What happens when an experience that is a moment of transfiguration for you is at the same time a moment of tedium or even torment for your neighbor? This presents no problem in our private lives since each of us can go his own way. Some of you experience God's glory most vividly through a visit to the New York Museum of Natural History; others of you are spiritually recharged by a several days' hunting trip to the rugged country of northern New England; still others, like me, are carried up, up, and away by a performance of Bach's *Mass in B Minor*.

But when we come together here to worship our Lord, our individual likes and dislikes can easily become a problem. For example, you come out of church tingling with delight after having sung one of the great hymns of the church; but before you can let out with your exhilaration, you hear the person coming out of church alongside you say, in a tone of disgust: "Ughhh! The organ this morning was so loud that I have a splitting headache! Why does that organist always have to make so much noise?"

Or suppose that you love ritual and ceremony, but your neighbor finds them offensive. You respond to one style of preaching; he responds to a totally different kind of preaching. Folk music turns you on, but it turns him off. And so on. What's to be done about this dilemma? The simplest solution is for everyone to go off by himself so as to be able to do his own thing in worship, without interfering with anyone else's sensitivities. You may be one who has been tempted to do this very thing. But such desertion from the worshiping community only creates a much larger problem. For the reason we come here to worship *together* is to enable us to strengthen one another in faith and in love and in hope. If this mutual encouragement is to happen week after week, there must be a willingness on the part of every one of us to put up with one another's likes and dislikes. It is one of the marks of Christian maturity for us to recognize that a moment which may be meaningless to us may be meaningful to our neighbor and consequently to rejoice with those who rejoice —for their sakes.

God's Grace and Glory Continues

Let me say it again: God still favors us, his people today, with moments of transfiguration, not only to impress his glory and his grace upon us, but also to stimulate us to share his glory and his grace with others through our work, our leisure, and our worship. It's this latter purpose of God's which we find difficult to appreciate; we'd much prefer to enjoy our moments of transfiguration for their own sake, holding on to them as long as we can. According to St. Matthew, Peter felt the very same way. "Lord," he said, "it is well that we are here; if you wish, I will make three booths here, one for you and one for Moses and one for Elijah." He was still speaking, when lo, a bright cloud overshadowed them, and a voice from the cloud said, "This is my beloved Son, with whom I am well pleased; listen to him." When the disciples heard this, they fell on their faces, and were filled with awe.

So also, when we become too attached to our moments of transfiguration, that same voice from the cloud interrupts us, reminding us that "This is my beloved Son, listen to him!" And "listening to the beloved Son of God" means coming down from our holy mountain so as to let our light shine before men that they may see our good works and glorify our Father in heaven along with us. "Listening to the beloved Son" means giving the direction of our daily lives over to his Spirit. In short, "listening to him" means "following him."

It may be helpful for us to think of our Christian life as being an endless blessed circle. Since our days are so full of disappointment and sorrow and frustration and tedium, God gives us moments of transfiguration as booster shots for the disciplined discipleship to which we have been called. These moments, in turn, are intended to reassure us that the God of glory and the God of grace is with us, and that his Spirit will always give to those who ask wisdom and courage "for the living of this hour." I say: it is a blessed circle; I for one am happy to be caught up in it, and you may be sure that there is more than enough room in it for all of you as well.

God of grace and God of glory,
  on thy people pour thy power;
Crown thine ancient church's story;
  bring her bud to glorious flower.
Grant us wisdom, grant us courage,
  for the living of this hour.

LOUIS NEUCHTERLEIN
Cheshire Lutheran Church
Cheshire, Connecticut

HE PASSED THE TEST

First Sunday in Lent
Matthew 4:1-11

He passed the test! It was the most exacting test to which a being had ever been exposed. But the salvation of the world depended on it. This was not an academic test for an advanced degree; it was the temptation of the Son of God to prove to man who he really was.

It was our Lord's first Gethsemane. But this one was not fought a stone's throw from friends. No one except the eternal Father heard his outcries and his prayers. It was battled in aloneness in the Arabian desert. The only creatures that saw were asps slithering toward the rock shadows in the heat of the day or skittering scorpions scrambling for the underbrush. By day, vultures soared ominously in the blue and by night hyenas laughed.

Day after endless day brought wearing heat; night after night the cold east wind cut. Was this a preparation for his ministry? Did the Spirit bring him into the desert for this? Strange thoughts intruded when he was not in communion with the Father. Couldn't there be a simpler way to fulfill the Father's plan of salvation? As if in answer, the night wind raised its sad song again and the stars glinted more coldly.

The Great Confrontation

One day as hunger grew more agonizing, a lone wanderer appeared in the desert. The stranger seemed most charming; he was affable and cordial. Yet, something about him aroused immediate caution. He proved to be a remarkably fascinating conversationalist. It was as though he had lived through the ages, so well informed was he; he knew the world's great ones intimately. Detecting the hunger of our Lord, he asked, "If you are the Son of God, speak that these stones might become bread." Son of God, this must be an angel, who else at this time would immediately recognize the Son of God? Our Lord replied simply, "Man shall not live by bread alone." Yet, the visitor continued with wit and brilliance, with remarkable insights into the nature of man. This stranger implied that our Lord could have a mighty future when the people of God would be assembling in the temple of God, "Let yourself down from the very pinnacle of the temple as though you were descending from heaven like an angel into the midst of the crowd. You'll have instant success! Instant success! Too good to be true. But awareness who this person was soon become evident, yet our Lord's attitude remained firm. "You must not put the Lord your God to the test."

The stranger persisted. "Let's climb yonder mountain and you'll see great lands as far as your sight reaches, even beyond the mists of the great sea, to Rome, to Spain, to Egypt, to Babylonia, and the far north country. I'll give you these if you worship me." Only one other being asked for such complete allegiance and worship, namely, God the Father in heaven. Then, of course, this must be the prince of all evil, even though he could quote scripture by the yard. "Be gone, Devil! It is written you shall worship the Lord your God and serve only him."

So there he was, alone again, this Lord of all lords, out there in the lonely Arabian desert. He had withstood the great test. He had conquered because he had recognized who his adversary was. Here had been absolute good meeting absolute evil. It had been an earth-shaking confrontation, a warfare like the clash of two mighty armies. It was Satan himself who tempted. For this great task of confronting the Son of man, he, Satan, had to come in person. For this task he could not send an assistant, nor his executive vice-president. It had to be a personal encounter. The evil one had ruined the first Adam but he failed completely with the second. The first one was driven from the garden of bliss to the wilderness. This one was to go from the wilderness to the gardens and homes of mankind.

Evil is personal. The center of evil must reside in personality or personalities, else it could never for a moment even have aroused resistance and anger on the part of Christ our Lord. Evil is more than a force. Simply forces of themselves, like gravity or cosmic rays in the desert, would have been aspects of God's own good creation. Here was a personality, a power confronting the personality and the power of God. The Son of God conquered in this fray and thus the Redeemer was revealed.

Why Evil?

But why evil anyhow? Why in all the world and the heavens does the almighty God allow that creature of evil to hang around in the universe? He usually has his greatest influence when he persuades mankind that he, Satan, really doesn't exist. He purports himself to be a most congenial and likeable fellow, not as one hideous or repulsive. Sin has that unique faculty. Perhaps this is why sermons are preached with such titles as "Attractive Sinners and Boring Saints"!

But if evil were not around we humans would have nothing else to choose but to be God's slaves of the good. In fact, there would be little freedom, if any, because there would be nothing else to choose but the good and thus there would be no options and consequently no freedom. In being human as we are, we no doubt would complain that life would be rather restricted because we could never appreciate the grace of God properly. God would want the relationship with man to be one of genuine love, as a loving father with his loving children. We would never be able to appreciate the amazing riches of God's love until we too had wandered into the wilderness of agonizing aloneness and alienation. What joy and gratitude there is within us when, having been lost, we return home again to the waiting Father. The glory of homecoming could never prevail unless there were a far country of lostness from which a return promised utmost joy.

The eternal and loving Father had sent his son into the far country to appeal to the lost and to the lone and to the homesick. This son who was sent from the Father, was indeed the Son of God because he had the best of all credentials, the ability to pass the test of temptation in the desert, for he had been accosted by the master tempter himself. Pure gold proves it is true gold because it can resist corrosive acid and remain unscarred. The Son of God proved he was the Christ because he remained untouched by the tempter's power.

The Gamut of Temptations

Our Lord withstood the entire range of temptability. This range involved human need, the physical. It involved the ego or will, and also the spirit, which concerns ultimate allegiance to something or someone.

In the first temptation, Christ responded, "Man shall not live by bread alone." That word, *alone,* has immense significance. We can't deny the high need of bread for our hunger and all the hungers of mankind. Even in the model prayer there is a petition for our daily bread. But not bread *alone.* A sumptuous table without love is barren indeed. In whose name is bread to be given? Unless there is allegiance to God the Redeemer, all alms are empty.

A second persistent temptation for Christians is the attempt to walk the short cuts of spiritual life. Isn't it unique that most inventions in the mechanical and industrial spheres have been developed to provide short cuts? But our Lord did not yield to the idea of discovering short cuts to salvation by suddenly dropping from heaven into a worshiping crowd at the temple in Jerusalem. He rejected an immediate following by glamor-seekers of life. It's still true today that today's hit may be tomorrow's flop. There is no short cut to glory, no quickie salvation.

The temptation to the wrong allegiance is the most devastating of all temptations. Christ immediately realized the complete disaster of giving full allegiance to Satan, to power, to fame, to kingship over nations. Yet, this gnawing temptation is ever with man. I remember a young urban pastor saying that he thought seriously of leaving the church to enter politics because he wanted "clout." Clout was that to which the world listened, he thought. Clout was that which the church did not have but the world possessed. Reforms could be immediately established, even if force were necessary. Ultimate allegiance determines ultimate destiny.

The Tests of Today

With all the immense advances in technologies for earth and space, it is amazing that man has become less conscious about guilt, about his soul, and thus his need for the grace of God. It seems that man has lulled himself into believing that if he can control so much of time and space and resources, he will soon be able to devise gadgets to regulate his spiritual life. And the devil is already celebrating the victory!

Another area where the captain of evil seduces the spirit of man is to convince him that guilt is only a very private matter, that there could be no community or national guilt. But there is community guilt; we become involved by collusion with others. If we keep out a neighborhood health facility, a necessary school improvement, or if we gang up on a minority, or stand idly by when crime is committed, we can't escape responsibility by implying, "The community did it."

And surely there is national guilt, too. After every war our nation experienced a vast burden of conscience for having fought a war, for all the hatred exhibited, the killing, the lying, the greed. After the Civil War we attempted some sort of self-cleansing via the great revival movements. After World War I our nation adopted the Eighteenth Amendment, Prohibition. We felt very righteous until we discovered that we couldn't make man moral by law. After World War II we were appalled at the horrendous genocide of the Jews by the Nazis; thereupon we assisted in establishing the nation of Israel. Colonial powers suddenly felt guilty about imperialism and many new nations were given their freedom. Thus the third world was born.

After the Korean and Viet Nam wars, upheaval in society in the late Sixties caused a massive sense of guilt toward the treatment of the minorities and the disadvantaged. Almost a religious fervor prevails in an effort toward a self-cleansing process by pummeling leadership, especially leadership in government. Our offended moral standards demand more stringent election laws, and we have Watergate!

Perhaps the very fact of sensing a national or a community guilt indicates a growing brotherhood among men, a feeling of responsibility in community and nation. Indeed, it is our earnest hope that out of such guilt constructive actions toward society and the nation will eventuate.

Victory

With all of his tools, his works, and ethical fervor, man cannot devise his self-redemption. He must come as he is to the throne of grace through the credentials of faith. For the Redeemer has been certified, revealed, authenticated as the redeemer indeed. True, the early Christian spent much time in debate whether Christ was temptable or not, whether as Son of God he could even be capable of being tempted and yield. But man as a whole has preferred to accept him in the terms of the writer of Hebrews, "And now he can help those who are tempted because he himself was tempted and suffered . . . but did not sin." And that promise suffices! Truly, he is the King of kings, the Lord of lords. He understands us. He went the same route of trial. He prevailed out there on that day in the Arabian desert. He passed the test.

WALTER M. WICK
President, Indiana-Kentucky Synod—LCA
Indianapolis, Indiana

GOD CAN'T BE LIKE THIS — UNLESS . . .

Second Sunday in Lent
John 4:5-26

Surely John must be mistaken about this story. God can't be like this, acting the way Jesus does with this woman of Samaria. The whole purpose of John's gospel is to say, "Jesus is the revealer of God!" "He that has seen me has seen the Father." John does a great job too . . . usually . . . but here?

Caring About Anyone and Everyone

God can't be like this . . . being interested in and caring about anyone and everyone, even the not so nice. I mean really. This lady is almost too much, isn't she? She is even rude to Jesus. "How is it you, Jew, ask a drink of me, a woman of Samaria?" "How can you give me water? You don't even have a bucket." She misunderstood everything he said. She is the wrong religion and her morals? Five marriages and a "shack-up"!

God can't be like this *unless* he has an overpowering desire to love us all, down to the last one and to save every mixed up one of us. He can't be like this *unless* he has something up his sleeve that can handle the likes of the worst of us as well as the best of us. God can't be like this *unless* he is a God who would call an unknown guy by the name of Abraham and to suffer through his problems just because the world was a mess and he wanted to make it well again. He can't be like this *unless* he is a God who, as this strange Paul claimed, is a God who justifies the ungodly, and gives life to the dead . . . all kinds of dead, and calls into existence things that do not exist! But this is exactly who he is!

A Word of Promise and Not of Judgment

God can't be like this because Jesus' first word to this mess of a woman is a word of promise and not of judgment. He spoke a promise and not a command to change . . . an invitation which was not first a checkup! Before God will do anything for us we have to shape up first, right? Did you hear that promise? "Woman, if you only knew how much God has to give and how much he wants to give it and who I am for you, all you would have to do is to ask and I would give you water to make you alive. If you have it you will be satisfied forever because this water will be inside you—a never-ending source of the power of life." What a promise! And to someone not pious or even very good.

God can't be like this *unless* he is bound and determined to give himself, for no other reason than that *we need him.* God can't be like this *unless* he is willing to give his gift of life just for the asking. Why one could even baptize an infant and dare to believe Jesus claiming him to be a receiver of his gift of life before that kid could do a thing except cry and eat and wet. And so it is true. Do you like this promise?

A Personal and Embarrassing Word

But just when we think God may be like an over-indulgent parent (in idea we could accept I think) we are astonished again.

Out of the blue Jesus says to the woman, "Go call your husband." We know what she had to admit, don't we? God can't be like this. That would make him get too personal, forcing us to see what's really inside us and face the mess we fear but don't want talked about. Can't you imagine how she felt . . . helpless and undone. God wouldn't get that intimate with people!

God can't be like this *unless* that promise of his power within us means a love so great that we can afford to be honest before him and ourselves. God can't be like this *unless* he insists on a cure for what really ails us rather than what we may think may be our problem. What ails us is that we really thirst for God himself although we probably don't know it. This woman was hardly aware that she even had a problem, let alone what it was. She wasn't looking for God. She didn't know she needed him but he found her.

Jesus always gets personal. That is what makes him a true Lord. For so many of us our ideas about our weaknesses, problems and sin are pretty conveniently hazy and general. But when the living Lord zeros in he touches us in our vulnerable spots like our incorrigible jealousy, or incredible need to always be on center stage, or our pathological fear of different people. He gets very personal and very embarrassing. This is how we know that it is the true Lord who is dealing with us. In fact, he kills to make alive. It is the truly dead that he raises! God can't be like this *unless* he wants to make us all really well! And he does!

Religion Is Not Where It's At

If we needed final proof that God can't be like Jesus here we surely have it now. Jesus says that religion is not where it's at. What kind of a God would say that? This embarrassed but impressed woman finally gets around to asking a religious question. . . . *The* religious question. "What is the true faith? Is it yours, Jewish man, or is it mine? Perhaps it is that I just have to do it better?" She is following in the steps of many people who want to get their life together. They are convinced that the answer to their problem is to find the true religion and all will be well and all their problems solved. She asked the religious question, "What should *I* do?" And did she get an answer! Jesus said, "That's neither here nor there! *The question is not what you should do but who God is!* Do you know who he is? He is the God of the present moment. He is the God who is not of the hazy past of religion nor in the far distant future after a life of religious devotion. He is the God who breaks into the present claiming you for himself. The time is *now.* The place is here! God is real and he is for you."

"You mean like you are here standing before me, giving to me, Jesus?" "Exactly!"

God can't be like this *unless* he insists that the issue is never one of whose religion is right or whose church is best. The issue is that every moment and every place is pregnant with the reality of God reaching out to touch you where you are and gather you in and make you well and get you going. This issue is not that you should find God. That is the concern of all religion. Rather, it is that he finds you. That is why Christianity has to be an evangelistic faith which goes out and finds people. We can't sit back and say, "Well, when people are really interested in finding God they'll come here." The Good News is that even when people don't want to find God he finds them! That's what Jesus is all about!

There is no escape into the yesterday of religion or into the tomorrow of pious hopes. The time for God to touch you is always and only a NOW. It is living water time and isn't that great? In the end the key is not what you must do but what has happened for and to you.

Let's get down to it. God can't be like this *unless* in fact he is Jesus! That is, Jesus is the one who makes it all come together. He is the one to whom we are privileged to say, "My Lord and my God." That means taking him at his word when he says, "My friend, I am the one for you."

How Does the Story End?

This story really doesn't have a very good ending. We really don't know what happened to this woman. Is the story a tragedy or a comedy? Does it have a happy ending or a sad one? Was she really changed? Did she really make it? Did she buy in on the promise so freely offered? There is really no answer. It is good that there is no answer because it is really not so much a story about the woman as it is a story about Jesus. It is not so much a question of whether or not she makes it as it is "Will *we?*"

Will we hear the words of Jesus, "I am the one for you," and so know that we are found anew by God? Am I willing simply to ask and receive the unfathomable offer of pure grace? Can it be that you and I, just as we are, can in fact be the possessors of "a spring of water welling up to eternal life?"

God can't be like this. It would be too good to be true. But it is! It is!!

WAYNE WEISSENBUEHLER
Christ the King Lutheran Church
Denver, Colorado

AN IMPORTANT PERSON—YOU

Third Sunday in Lent
John 9:1-41

A number of years ago a pastor wrote an intriguing series of Lenten sermons. He gave that series this title: *Little People of the Passion.*

Standing in the shadow of the Cross on this Third Sunday in Lent, I would like to talk to you about *big people of the Paraclete,* about persons who are spiritual giants because of the Holy Spirit, about men and women and children who are spiritual Goliaths because of the Son of man. Such a spiritual seven-footer am I; and you are one, too.

Never could you have possibly dreamed it! Neither did the Master's disciples dream it when they stared one day at a poor, blind beggar in the Jerusalem ghetto. They almost failed to see the pearl in the oyster and the lily bulb in the mud. They almost failed to realize that they were looking at a miniature Israel who had been miraculously freed from the Pharaoh of human sin and divine punishment.

A Delivered Person

"Now who was the culprit who committed the colossal sin which caused this man's blindness? His parents? Or he himself?" They point long, sharp fingers at the little man as they make their inquiry.

With the fellow or his parents accused and condemned, Jesus reaches out to rescue all three of them from the accusations and condemnations. "An extraordinarily enormous sin lies on the doorstep of none of them," he cries. "The man is stricken, but not because he has been found to be a monstrous transgressor! The man is pounded by problems and burdened with blindness, but not because he is being punished by the hand of an angry God!"

These words of our Lord we need to hear. For often, when life deals its below-the-belt blows to us, as it dealt a below-the-belt blow to this Jerusalem charity case, we conclude, as the disciples did, that intense *suffering* presupposes intense *sinning*, that we who groan in agony must of necessity be experiencing the disfavor of a displeased, inflamed, aroused, and enraged Deity. But for children of God this is by no means true.

We are not colossal sinners; we are forgiven saints. Though the word *sin* has been written by ten million devils—or by ten trillion pens of our own—upon the slate of our hearts, the red cloth of Calvary has run over the word, has totally erased it, has completely obliterated it. The blood of Jesus Christ, God's Son, still cleanses us from all sin, even in this current year and even in this present moment.

Therefore God is not an angry judge or a pursuing punisher. Disheartening reverses do not presuppose divine wrath. Postage stamps are licked, placed upon envelopes, and pounded by fists—not because someone is angry with the postage stamp and is determined to punish it, but because someone simply wants the postage stamp to stick to the envelope and to perform a mission. It is to carry that envelope and its letter to some friend in a far-off city. God frequently allows life to lick us with its lamentations, to lay us down upon its crosses, to pound us with its blindnesses and cancers and cataracts and calamities and adversities—not because he is angry with us and is determined to punish us, but because he wants us to stick more tightly to his love and to perform for him an important mission. We are to carry the good word of his marvelous grace to all who see us suffer and to any who hear us groan.

We are important people—because we are delivered people. God has freed us from the horrible thoughts which we have about ourselves when we find ourselves suffering. God has rescued us from the terrible thoughts which we have about him when we find ourselves troubled.

A Selected Person

But I am more than a delivered slave. I am a selected instrument.

Over the dirty streets of the Holy City the soft voice of the Holy One whispered: "This affliction was allowed so that God might affirm his power! This blindness was permitted so that I might affirm my love! Upon this blind man I will perform a miracle so that men may see who I really am. Upon this sightless beggar I will perform a wonder so that others may learn what I can really do, not only for the beggar, but also for them. This mendicant, you see, is my instrument. And so are you disciples. *We,* I and you Twelve, must work the works of him who sent me before the whistle blows and the working-day is forever ended. In spite of the bad condition of your hearts, in spite of the sad condition of his eyes, you and the beggar are in mission with me!" What an honor!

That honor has not bypassed *us.*

God forgave Saul of Tarsus—to show me that, if he forgave a man like that, he can also forgive me. Saul of Tarsus became God's instrument.

Christ restored sight to this man who was born blind—to show me that, if he helped this mendicant in his dilemma, he will also help me in mine. The mendicant became Christ's instrument.

Jesus raised Lazarus of Bethany from the dead—to show me that, if he could raise from his coffin one who was interred four days, he can also raise from our graves my departed loved ones and me in the hour when he returns in the majesty of his glory. Lazarus of Bethany became our Lord's instrument.

The very same Savior uses our troubles, our trials, our lamentations, our lives, to show other people what kind of a sustaining God he is, to point out to other people what kind of wonderful works he does for his children—and will also do for them, if they will but come to him. As car dealers select certain cars to be used as demonstrator-cars by which they hope to show the public what Fords or Buicks or Pontiacs are like, God selects certain people—*us!*—to show the world what his grace and peace and love and hope and power are like.

A V.I.P.—*a very important person—you are! You have been selected by Christ to be his instrument! You have been chosen by God to be in mission with his great Son!*

A Protected Person

Marvels roll like waves over marvels. Honors literally heap themselves upon your head. For in the sight of God you are a dignitary, a president, a king, and are therefore surrounded, as it were, by secret service agents who perpetually protect you.

The Jerusalem beggar was a kind of jewelry box into which the Holy Spirit had deposited the Kohinoor Diamond of a fantastic faith.

A silly act it seemed to be! A blinding mud-plaster laid on eyes which had already been blinded on the day when the chap was born! And that was supposed to help!

A silly word it seemed to be! "Wash in Siloam Pool, and you will come back seeing!" And that was supposed to work!

But the silly act was accepted and the silly word was believed. The blind one washed in Siloam Pool—and came back seeing! A marvelous miracle—and a phenomenal faith!

A similarly phenomenal faith has been deposited by God's Spirit in the hearts which we own. Blood stains; but staining blood is to remove sin-stains! Calvary blood, smeared over consciences, is supposed to cleanse! And you *believe* that! What a miracle! "Wash in the Golgotha Pool, and you will come back justified!" And you *believe* that! What a wonder! What a fantastic trust!

That fantastic trust our Lord is determined to safeguard and keep.

Neighbors might run the beggar in and turn him over to the Pharisees, incensed because the miracle was performed on a Sabbath Day. Parents might let the beggar down and leave their son like a prey at the mercy of the church officials, fearing lest they be excommunicated from their parish. Theological bigwheels may damn the beggar to a thousand hells, call him a sinner, and brand him as illegitimate. But they are unable to excommunicate him from his faith or to destroy his trust. He continues to crown Jesus as a man who is sent by God, as a Prophet, and finally as the very Messiah himself! The erstwhile blind one is brought to a highway and a path which he did not know; darkness is made light before him; crooked things are made straight—redeeming the pledge which was made in today's Old Testament Lesson. For many years in darkness, he was now—in more respects than one—"Light in the Lord," as today's Epistle insists that we also are.

Such gleaming candles of faith God shields. Such people with spiritually seeing eyes the Holy Spirit safeguards and keeps.

You are a very important person—because you are protected by God's Secret Service Agent, the Holy Spirit who is determined to preserve your faith!

An Invited Person

Will you fall into a faint if I dare to declare that God's wonderful description of you is not yet completed? *You are also an invited person. You have been requested to appear in the presence of the King to behold the face of the Son of God!*

The boom was lowered, and the Jerusalem beggar was taken from his church's roster and ousted from his parish's membership.

I think I see him as he sits on the cobblestones of one of the winding streets. The Preacher from Galilee has found him in the shadows. The sound of his voice lifts the opened eyes of the frightened fellow: "So you can see, my son?"

"Oh, yes, yes, yes!" The tone of the beggar's response brings a smile to the Preacher's lips. "For the first time in my life, sir, I can see a mountain, a lake, a cedar, a song-bird, a trellis, a tree—a man! The hair! The eyes! The cheeks! The chin! The smile! The face! A Man! A Man!"

And the man said to the beggar: "What about the Messiah, son?"

And the beggar said to the man: "The Messiah! Of course! Who would not look upon the face of the promised one? But has he come? If so, where is he? And who is he, good friend?"

And the man said to the beggar: "*Where* is he? Right here! *Who* is he? You are gazing at him! He is talking to you!"

Then the beggar rose to his feet, studied the strange man who was standing before him, peered into his eyes, and knew that he was beholding—the Son of the living God! And he worshipped him.

In spite of the fact that one of his hands has been amputated, a very talented artist—who lives in Winston-Salem, North Carolina—was invited to the palace in London to have an audience with the queen, to paint her portrait. We have been invited to the palace in Paradise to have an audience with the King, to look into the eyes of Jesus, to behold his beauty, to sing his praises forever and ever!

When the sea of life has become as smooth as glass, when the last roll of thunder has died in the distant hills, when the glow of the sunset has faded and the evening star has appeared, when the tents on earth's plains are being folded up while the drawbridges over heaven's moats are being let down, when the drums of earth are no longer played while the trumpets of eternity begin to be sounded, God's people will be ushered by angel-bands through the *Arc de Triomphe* of the Celestial City, down Radiance Avenue, up the glistening steps of Glory Mansion, into the Golden Room of God Eternal, to see the face of the Savior—to behold the countenance of the King! For that never-ending audience with the Redeemer *you* have been given a ticket. To that never-ceasing celebration in Paradise *you* have received a personal invitation.

You are a V.I.P.! You really are! So am I! So are all of the Christ's redeemed!

"You are an illegitimate no-count!" That's what the Pharisees screamed—when they stared at the trembling beggar. He wasn't that at all. He was a crown-jewel in the diadem of the king of the universe! So are we all!

Maybe a mirror should be hung on the wall of our chancel, then, so that every time you approach our Lord's altar to partake of his Holy Supper, you might look into it earnestly *and see a very, very special person*—a very, very special person who happens, by the grace of God, to be *you!*

L. A. WOLF
St. John's Evangelical Lutheran Church
Winston-Salem, North Carolina

SOME QUESTIONS FOR LENT AND LIFE

Fourth Sunday in Lent
Matthew 20:17-28

He was thinking about going to Jerusalem . . .
They were thinking about going to heaven.
He was thinking about giving his life for the world . . .
They were concerned about getting a favored position for themselves.
He said that to be great is to be a servant . . .
They didn't really understand.

There are two main parts to the gospel text for this day. The first part is a third recording in Matthew's gospel of Jesus' announcement to his disciples that he was going to Jerusalem to die. The second group of verses deals with the request of James and John to sit at either side of Jesus in his kingdom (Matthew says that the request came by way of their mother).

Between these two parts of the text there is a great gulf—not in space but in spirit. There are almost two religions involved—at least two conflicting interpretations of what true religion is. There is God's way—and there is our natural human way, and they often do not coincide.

Let us reflect on the meaning and message of this familiar excerpt from Matthew's gospel in the framework of a few simple questions.

Where Are You Going?

Matthew tells us that Jesus knew where he was going. Though it involved suffering and probable death, Jesus faced the journey to Jerusalem as a part of his God-given purpose and he could not be dissuaded. He had a goal, a work to do, a mission to perform—all related to his very reason for being here.

Matthew wants to be sure that his readers understood what this purpose of Jesus was. He begins his gospel with a genealogy—showing Christ in the role of fulfilling the promise to Abraham and continuing the line of David. Jesus is the promised child whose birth announcement calls him the Savior who is Christ the Lord. Jesus goes about teaching, healing, training his disciples—all that the world might know that he has come to redeem them from their sin, from their lostness, from their bondage, from their separation from God. Matthew implies that Jesus is trying to tell his disciples that his impending death is not the triumph of man's way but the revelation of God's way—in contrast to man's common way of hate and revenge and destruction there is the divine way of love and forgiveness and redemption.

So Matthew could have joined John in saying that the reason his book was written was that his readers might believe in this Christ—and that believing they might have life in his name. That is also why the church is still telling the story of this Christ. That is still the good news—at Christmas and Epiphany and Lent—and throughout the church year.

That was Jesus' purpose in life. That is why he came and why he died and rose again.

But what about our purpose? What is our goal in life? If you reach the destination you are heading for now, where will you be? If you become what you are now becoming, what will you be? If you amass all the treasures you are working so hard for now, what will you have?

When your life is over and you reflect on what you have been and done, in spite of failures and sins, will you be able to say in some significant measure: It is finished. . . I have accomplished the work that God has given me to do. . . I have fought the fight, finished my course, kept the faith . . . ?

Or are you drifting—pushed around by others, your goals determined by their mad rush for things, your morals determined by the cheap standards of the contemporary world—and are you a victim rather than a victor?

In the New Testament the most common word for sin means

to miss the mark. And the word for repentance means to be *turned around.* In this Lenten season let us evaluate our lives in terms of our purpose and direction. As we hear again of Christ's life and mission, let us ask ourselves about our goal in life: Where am I going?

Why?

Matthew wants all to know that there was a redemptive purpose in Christ's life and death and resurrection. He gave himself *for the world.* He came, not to save himself but to save *others.*

The disciples and their mother come through with a different concern. They are out to take care of themselves. They are politicking—seeking to get a commitment from Jesus that would guarantee their own future status and enjoyment.

It is almost scary, isn't it, to think that a mother can let her love for her children become selfish and perverted, and that disciples of Jesus can want to go to heaven and "be near Jesus" for the wrong motive, and that Christian people can try to use religion to gain status and authority, and that even prayer can be perverted by wrong motivations?

Whether scary or not—it ought to be thought-provoking and heart-searching.

How do we use the authority that we have—for self-aggrandizement or for service? Why do we want Christian assurance—for the selfish satisfaction of our own desire for power or for strength to minister to others? How do we look on the gospel—just for ourselves or for the whole world? How do we look on our own congregation—as a favored place for us "to sit next to Jesus" or as a place where we can be recipients of his love so that we may share that love with others? If we have a position of significance—in the church or the community or government or the family or in our circle of friends—are we using it just as a status symbol or have we learned to use it as an opportunity for service?

Years ago I read a story of a man who bought a little grocery store and worked hard to make it go. He put in long hours to get the business started, and things went very well. But he became so engrossed in his business that it soon became the passion of his life. He had no time for his wife and children. He never saw his friends. He dropped away from church. One day he had a heart attack and died and one of his friends suggested sadly that they put on his gravestone: "Here lies . . . born a human being—died a retail grocer."

The peril of forgetting the question "Why" in our life is very real for all of us. What have we learned about the symbolism of wanting to sit at the head table, or of being willing to wash the feet of the disciples? What have we absorbed of the spirit of him who came—not to be ministered unto but to minister and to give his life a ransom for many? What is our definition of greatness—closer to that of James and John or to that of Christ?

The Lenten season ought to make us pause to consider. Let not this Lenten season pass without a genuine prayer from us: "Search me, O God . . . know my heart . . . renew a right spirit within me."

How Much Are You Willing to Pay?

Matthew is eager to have his listeners understand that Jesus went to Jerusalem with his eyes open. He wasn't trapped into going there, nor was he surprised at what took place. Three times Matthew tells of Jesus' announcement of his death. He anticipated it; he was dedicated to doing his Father's will whatever the cost. Though the price was high in terms of personal, human suffering and the struggle within him was intense—his love for his people prevailed.

As Matthew wanted his readers to understand that Jesus willingly paid the price, so Jesus wanted his disciples to realize the cost to them of following him. He warned them of what was to happen to him *and to them.* He never promised "cheap grace." He never suggested that the Christian life was to be one of ease, of universal acceptance, of freedom from suffering and pain. He did say that the servant was not above the master and warned that the reception which he would be receiving would not be very different from their lot.

Of course, he was not suggesting that this is the good work that permits us to earn our way to salvation. But he was saying that the person who honestly seeks to follow him will have to take up his own cross—and pay whatever price is necessary for being faithful to Christ.

And so the challenge comes to us—his present-day followers, who know the Lenten story so well. It is easy to recount the events of the passion of Christ. It is easy to talk of the values of Christianity. It is easy to claim the promises of God, and to rest secure in the assurance of his love and providence. But that is only part of the story. The other part is that God calls us to the same witness and to the same struggle that Christ had.

We are called upon to take up our own cross and follow him. We are to witness to our own church, our community, our nation, our "sphere of influence" as to God's will and purpose, and whenever that runs counter to the prevailing mood and power structure a cross will be formed, and a modern Gethsemane created for us. Lent is not only a time of remembrance—it is also a time for rededication of ourselves to God's will and way.

Of course, we live in a different world, a new culture, where circumstances are different. We can rejoice that no one is listening in on our worship to betray us for confessing our faith (or can we be sure?) We are not threatened with death because we confess that Jesus is Lord. We can go to church without fear.

But this is an oversimplification. For the expression of the Christian faith is not limited to our gathering for worship. It includes our attitudes and actions in every situation in life.

It involves that we stand for *truth* instead of falsehood, whatever the cost. The basic question is not whether or not there is legal evidence that we have been guilty of perjury or wrongdoing, the basic question is whether or not we have been honest, have acted out of integrity and whether or not we will witness to the truth whatever the price. The world is crying for that kind of honesty—and let your Christianized conscience examine your own life and witness.

It involves standing for and working for justice for all of God's children—no matter how prejudiced our friends or our communities are. Do we have the courage to be criticized and defamed—because we fought for racial justice, equal opportunity for all, fairness for the underprivileged, equal rights in the courts for rich and poor—or do we "chicken out" lest someone think us a bit extreme?

It involves loving our fellowmen, which exacts its price on our selfishness, our pride, our covetousness, our smug satisfaction with the status quo as long as we get what we want.

The challenge goes to all of life—but the question is still: He gave his all, himself—will you?

Arthur O. Arnold
Lutheran School of Theology
Chicago, Illinois

THE LAST MIRACLE OF JESUS

Fifth Sunday in Lent
John 11:1-53

There is a sense in which the raising of Lazarus could be called the last miracle of Jesus. At least it can be called that in the context of the Gospel According to John. When St. John set about telling the story of Jesus he arranged the material in such a way that it is possible to call part of his gospel "The Book of Signs." It is that part which begins with the miracle at Cana of Galilee and ends just after this last miracle. Here the public ministry of Jesus is recounted, and it is done in terms of signs, miracles, which pointed to who Jesus was. This thinking then is on *The Last Miracle of Jesus:* It sets the last stage and it meets the last need.

It Sets the Last Stage

This is an uncommonly long gospel reading, fifty three verses. The temptation is strong to make it two separate stories, the raising of Lazarus, and the meeting of the Sanhedrin. Yet the two are intimately related.

As John tells the story of Jesus the raising of Lazarus is what finally provoked the authorities to action. For them it was bad enough when the people heard what Jesus had to say. Although what he had to say was unique, different from what others were saying, it was not unusual for persons to come along who were teachers. It wasn't unusual for them to gain a following. It still isn't. With some frequency there still come persons who are like comets in the ecclesiastical skies. They flash briefly, attract some attention to themselves, and then disappear.

You recall that even John the Baptist wondered whether or not Jesus was one like that. He sent his disciples to Jesus with the question, "Are you he who is to come, or shall we look for another?" And then Jesus sent the inquirers back with the evidence, "Go and tell John what you hear and see: the blind receive their sight and the lame walk, lepers are cleansed and the deaf hear, and the dead are raised up, and the poor have the good news preached to them. And blessed is he who takes no offense at me."

As long as Jesus taught he wasn't too much trouble. It was when he continued to implement his talk with action that there began to be some concern. It was this which set the last stage for his ministry, that which is before us next Sunday in Passion Sunday, and in the events of Holy Week.

"What are we to do? For this man performs many signs. If we let him go on thus, everyone will believe in him, and the Romans will come and destroy both our holy place and our nations." It was the last miracle of his public ministry that caused Jesus this trouble. He not only talked about life, he gave it.

It is ironic that Jesus' gift of life to Lazarus leads to his own death. It's a kind of irony in reverse that the words of the high priest turn out to be the ones that interpret the meaning of Jesus' death in a far different way than he intended. . . . "It is expedient for you that one man should die for the people, and that the whole nation should not perish."

This apparent "common sense" bit of political expediency was just his way of setting the stage to get rid of Jesus lest, as one more of a series of revolutionaries, this troublemaker provoke the Romans to action against the puppet rulers who were supposed to keep a captive people in check.

Caiaphas could not have begun to suspect that he was right. The death of Jesus would save the nation from destruction. But he was right in a way that he never knew. To the perceptive ear, such as St. John had, Caiaphas was echoing a traditional saying of Jesus himself: "The Son of Man came . . . to give his life as a ransom for many."

This sort of reversal should not surprise us. If we remember the reversals that are spoken of in the beatitudes, if we remember the reversal that was associated with Jesus' birth, if indeed we remember the reversal that sets the stage for this part of the text, then we ought not to be surprised when the power of God also reverses the results of the intentions and the meanings of the words of Caiaphas.

That is an encouragement for us. God rules. He rules over his own and he overrules those who resist him.

Does this lead to a kind of quietism, "God's in his heaven, and all's right with the world?" No, it is rather an encouragement as we carry on the ministry of Christ in the world today. As we meet with discouraging results that sometimes come because not all welcome the gospel, it is well to know that God works not only through those who willingly follow him, but even through, and in spite of, those who oppose him.

That is what is seen in one of the consequences of the last miracle of Jesus. It set the stage for the last scene in his earthly ministry. It was the stage on which was enacted the drama of the cross, his death, and ultimately the resurrection. It was that resurrection which gives meaning to the other part of this long text, the raising of Lazarus.

It Meets the Last Need

The last miracle of Jesus meets the last need, and that means not only the last need of Lazarus, but the last need of us all. As was the case with the first miracle of Jesus in the Fourth Gospel, it took place in a home at one of those decisive times in life. In the miracle of Cana, turning water into wine, the wedding merely provided the opportunity for the miracle. But in this one, the death of Jesus' friend Lazarus, not only is the opportunity provided but it is directly with that death that the miracle is concerned. It says something about the gospel with regard to death. It is death which St. Paul described as the last enemy to be destroyed. It is death which provides the last need of every one of us.

Death isn't talked about very much. We all know that it is "out there" for us somewhere. But somehow, no matter what has preceded death, it is always sudden. We are never quite ready for it. That is understandable. For, at least as we experience it, death is not what God intended for us. It is an intruder. Death remains, therefore, a difficult experience. When Lazarus was ill Mary and Martha sent for Jesus. But he didn't come. Their implied prayer for healing was not answered. Which of us has not had that kind of an experience? We pray, and the prayer seems not to be answered. Lazarus died.

And, if we are honest, which of us has not felt as Martha did, "Lord, if you had been here. . . ." Somehow we wonder where God is when the tragedies of life beset us.

Perhaps what she did suggests a good way to handle such feelings. How do we handle yesterday's tragedies? That is important, because what we do with them shapes what they do to us. The simple advice, "Take it to the Lord in prayer," may indeed be too simplistic. But if it is an honest prayer, such as Martha's, "Lord, if you had been here, my brother would not have died," then the possibility for something happening is opened. There is resentment there, honestly expressed, and graciously dealt with.

The word to her is, "Your brother will rise again." That word brings forth a confession, "I know that he will rise again in the resurrection at the last day." That confession brings forth the confirming word of Jesus. "I am the resurrection and the life; he who believes in me, though he die, yet shall he live, and whoever lives and believes in me shall never die."

This is the word that is for the last need of us all. It is the word of the resurrection to eternal life. It is a word which is spoken to faith, and which builds on faith, and which develops faith.

When that word had been spoken I am sure that Martha thought that was the end of things. Some day there would be a resurrection, she had known that, and had been reassured of it. Now Jesus would seek out Mary, and minister to her.

But the story doesn't end there. Jesus went to the grave, and bade Lazarus to come forth, and the evangelist says that he did. What happened? I don't know, not really. But then this is a story for faith. It is addressed to faith, it builds on faith, it develops faith. Faith comes primarily as a response to what God shows and tells us about himself.

What was that resurrection like? What really happened? What will the resurrection be like? What will really happen? I for one would not be too sharp in defining. Those who were "most certain" as to what God would do in the coming of the Messiah were the very ones who set the last stage as a result of this last miracle. They couldn't believe that it was happening the way it was, and therefore were men of no faith at all.

The response is not "I can't believe it," and therefore setting the stage for the death of faith. The response is rather, "Yes, Lord, I believe that you are the Christ, the Son of God, he who is coming into the world."

It is then that this last miracle of Jesus speaks to your last need, the need that comes in your death. For through his death Jesus speaks, and to your death he speaks, "I am the resurrection and the life." And to your faith he speaks now, in this last miracle, "Do you believe this?"

STANLEY D. SCHNEIDER
Lutheran Theological Seminary
Columbus, Ohio

LET'S PLAY IT AGAIN

Sunday of the Passion — Palm Sunday
Matthew 26:1—27:66

Would you suppose that from a group of 300 persons you could select and organize the cast for a passion play? Say, yes, and add that your script should be St. Matthew's account of the arrest, trial, and crucifixion of Jesus. There would be characters enough and scenes enough in that account for dramatic effect.

However you would agree that the story behind the story would have to come through, otherwise why have the play at all.

Today is Passion Sunday. The suffering and death of Jesus Christ is the theme and message of the day. The time has come "to play it again." At no time in our life of faith in what God has done and is still doing *for* us and *through* us in Jesus Christ will the events of our Lord's passion become old hat and drained of meaning for us.

Here's the Cast

In choosing the cast, I think you would choose a quiet, devoted woman who would ignore the indignation of the disciples when she anoints the head of Jesus in the home of Simon the leper at Bethany. You would select a man able to portray a boasting and cowardly Peter, yet one struggling to become what Christ had called him to be. You would be concerned about a crafty, yet confused and dispairing Judas. Caiaphas you would want to be officious and plotting and oozing with stuffed shirt piety. You would seek out a young and steady John. A wishy-washy and compromising Pilate would be found. Your selection of supporting characters like Barabbas, Malchus, Simon of Cyrene, the centurion, and Joseph of Arimathea would follow. Then you would pick the other disciples, also the maids and bystanders who challenged Peter in the palace courtyard, then the Pharisees and scribes and other accusers, the mockers, the soldiers, and the women who stood at the cross, including the mother of Jesus. "All the rest of you people will furnish the crowd of spectators," you would say. "We'll use you to stand around the edges or push in or follow along. Okay?"

But What About the Ending?

As we study the script, you note that the play ends on Good Friday evening and the last scene is a closed and sealed tomb guarded by Roman soldiers. The iron spikes are pounded through the hands and feet of this gentle Jesus, nailing him to the wood of the cross like one would nail a board to a fencepost, and he dies and is buried—and it's all over. What do you make of that? Is Jesus some blythe martyr who endures suffering and death with stoic calm? Is this the point of it all? Hardly. How will you point up with convincing force that this was God's own Son becoming obedient unto death on a cross? How will you develop the thrust of the whole scene so that it becomes a clear signal which no one can miss that "The Son of man came not to be served but to serve, and to give his life as a ransom for many?" Does the script furnish the lines that give the whole event special and unique meaning? Suppose we see.

We See No Hapless Victim

Just a few days before it all happened, Jesus was telling his disciples about the last days and the coming judgment. "When the Son of man comes in his glory," he said, "And all the angels with him, then he will sit on his glorious throne." He then describes the last judgment which it will be his to make. And then he says, "You know that after two days the Passover is coming, and the Son of man will be delivered up to be crucified." He was no hapless victim. He went to Jerusalem and walked into the trap that was being set for him with his eyes wide open. Didn't he say, "This woman has done a wonderful thing for me, she has poured this ointment on my body to prepare me for burial?" Of course he knew what was coming. "Truly, I say to you, one of you will betray me. . . . The Son of man goes as it is written." So he knew he was to die and why.

We Hear "This Is the New Covenant . . ."

The words of Jesus in the Upper Room give us a sure signal about something special happening. He was saying farewell to his disciples, yet he was looking forward to the heavenly feast when he would be with them again. "Take eat," said Jesus as he gave bread to his disciples, "This is my body." During the time of the separation, they were to remember him by eating together and the promise was, "I will be with you to the end of this age. Take and eat bread and believe that you will have me with you." In the same way, after the Passover Supper, Jesus took a cup of wine and said, "Drink of it all of you; for this is my blood of the covenant, which is poured out for many for the forgiveness of sins. I tell you I shall not drink again of this fruit of the vine until I drink it new with you in my Father's kingdom." This cup is to be for the disciples the visible, tangible promise of their share in the new covenant, established and sealed in his death.

God had acted in Christ to bring forgiveness and peace and renewal to all people. We may believe that when we "eat this body" and "drink this cup" we share in the promise that rests upon God's faithfulness in offering mercy to sinners through the atoning sacrifice of his Son. God wills that people shall live—

and that they live in hope. Jesus knew himself to be the central actor in his Father's outpouring of love and the one through whom God would satisfy his justice over against sinful humanity without in any way denying himself. God was going to make life possible through the victory of his Son over death, and Jesus knew this. The ransom for many was to be paid. The old covenant has passed away. "This is the new covenant in my blood."

We Note the Failure of the Disciples

The way in which the disciples "blew their parts," as we say, is very sad. Their lines aren't very praiseworthy all the way through and their actions aren't to their credit either. They question, they sleep, they flee, one betrays, another boasts, strikes with a sword, and later turns coward. John is the only disciple present at the trial and at the cross. Jesus knew that they would fail and told them that they would all fall away because of him that night. But Jesus willed that they should not evade this failure but face it and taste it to the full. They would aways be beggars, as they and all people should be, needing forgiveness, and they most of all.

We Can't Miss the Majesty of Jesus in His Suffering

Although the central figure of the drama says very little after his arrest, his quiet majesty heightens his devotion to his task and we catch the message that his Father's will is being fulfilled in what was happening to him. He was the victim, but he was in control of every turn of events. He went to Jerusalem, he went out to meet his captors, he was calm at his trial, he said not a word when soldiers mocked him. At the cross he spoke words that wrung from the centurion, "Surely this was the Son of God!" Do we not realize that this is the shepherd giving his life for the sheep? Do we not know now that this was the great high priest offering himself to God as the sacrifice for all men for all time? Is this not the new Adam in action, the man in the form of God emptying himself and becoming obedient unto death? There is no reaching out to grasp equality with God, like the first Adam who reached for the fruit of the tree of the knowledge of good and evil. This one wins the victory of God for all humanity by his obedience unto death. God's dominion in and through his creation is operative again in Christ. The kingdom of power and grace has come and people are able to live forever within his purpose and plan worked out in Jesus Christ.

We Surely See God at Work Here

The men who wrote the accounts of the Passion saw, in retrospect, when the Holy Spirit came and made them able to see, that God the Father had led his Son into the depths and that step for step his suffering and dying was God's way with him, the obedient Servant. Judas witnesses to the innocence of Jesus, as does Pilate, Pilate's wife, and the Centurion at the cross. To the disciples, the purple robe, the scepter, and the crown were not symbols of mockery but signs of his lordship. The predictions and claims which Jesus made all came true. The titles given him by God are heard again. The total passion history adds up to the arm of the Lord being revealed. And when Jesus died, the sun was darkened, the temple veil torn in two, from top to bottom, and graves were opened. These happenings attest that the new age of God's ransom from death and the promise of life had begun.

We've Seen It All Again, So?

Are we not convinced again that our blindness, our meanness, our self-indulgence and self-seeking, our refusal to trust God, our indolence—it won't be difficult to make a list—were operating in the hearts of those who crucified Jesus? We share in the criminal actions that killed him. He died on a cross made by us. But that's not the full message. The full message is that his forgiveness is what we need. The fact that he stands by us in our sin and bears it for us and pleads mercy to a righteous Father is almost too good to be true. And when we come to realize that God's mercy in Jesus precedes any movement on our part to ask for forgiveness, that actually he comes to meet us while we are yet sinners and reconciles us to himself, we almost gasp at the greatness of the mercy of God.

We need the words of St. Paul to express what we feel and believe. "Let us give thanks to the God and Father of our Lord Jesus Christ, the merciful Father, the God from whom all help comes. . . . He died for all men so that those who live should no longer live for themselves, but only for him who died and was raised to life for their sake" (2 Cor. 1:3; 5:15)

Harry G. Coiner
Ebenezer Lutheran Church
Greensboro, North Carolina

HE TOOK A TOWEL

Maundy Thursday
John 13:1-17

He took a towel
That night before the Passover was to begin,
Stripped off his clothing, filled a basin with water—
And washed his disciples' feet before their last supper;
An act done out of time, an act repeated at the wrong time,
Stirring up memories of an enslaved people,
The land of Egypt,
And the Passover that set them free from Pharaoh's bonds,
Only to face a watery wall, which God opened up for them—
A door to the wilderness and a 40 year struggle that seemed worse than slavery.
The Promised Land with its milk and honey was a fanciful dream in those days.
A towel . . .
ensign of the servant,
symbol of the slave doomed to a life of menial service,
a kind of living death.
The slave knew his future, his fate—
to be turned out when his usefulness was ended,
to wander and beg for food, remembering how good his master had been to him,
until he lay down in weakness and dried up in the desert,
returning unnoticed to the earth,
dust to dust.
A towel . . .
so out of character for the Son of man, the King of kings—
to do for others what had been done for him a few short days ago in a house at Bethany,
When a jar of precious ointment was opened, evoking memories of the birth of a child,
and the visit of Wise Men bearing gifts of gold, frankincense, and myrrh.
No manger here, no mother's loving arms;
This was the beginning of a wake.
One who sought refuge from sin and guilt shed copious tears,
washed his feet in a torrent of remorse,
and wiped them with her rich, luxurious hair, wrapping them in a shroud,
as if to hide them from the world, or make them impervious to nails, and the sting of death.

A towel . . .
Such a humble act; a step toward the cross.
The disciples should not have been surprised.
They were with him as he entered Jerusalem on the lowly beast of burden.
The Prince of Peace went through the Golden Gate of the City of Peace in character—meek and lowly and sitting upon a colt, the foal of an ass.
Despite the acclaim of the crowds,
the palm branches, the flowers, and the clothing spread in his path, and even the Hosannas,
That's when the let-down, the end, began.
Perhaps some began to think that a stronger man would have to take over the leadership of the little band,
make it into an effective instrument of power and pressure;
The Passover message had to be reframed and sent to Rome,
"Set my people free!"
Only a real man, a genuine king, could lead this movement;
a servant armed only with a towel—and words—eliminated himself. He was politically dead already!
A towel . . .
It had to be done before supper,
before his suffering began at that table,
When he had to tell them what he knew of one's betrayal,
a sellout for the price of a slave.
He was acting out his fate; Judah had already doomed him to the ultimate slavery, death
His fate was sealed.
He would not be whisked off to Egypt
as Joseph had been when his brothers stripped him of the coat of many colors and sold him into slavery.
He lived to forgive his people and feed them in a foreign land when famine threatened them with extinction.
He gave them a new life, refuge for the exiles,
and the hope of return to the land they loved.
But this Servant could expect no sojourn in alien territory—
only a cross—to show the world what happens to revolutionary slaves.
A cross—warning to all to accept without question the power of princes and rulers.
A servant-slave makes no protest; he simply accepts his fate in silence.
The towel told the world that Christ had learned the lesson
which the Romans would teach the world—

Caesar is king! Long live the king!
Death to all who would make the earth a place of peace
and freedom for all.
He had come just for this, to serve God and to suffer for it—
to set men free from sin and death,
to show what incarnation really means when God becomes
man and lives and dwells among men on his good earth.
A towel . . .
such a lesson—
"Not my feet only, but also my hands and my head."
But that towel tells us what we can expect on this night
when we remember and relive the Last Supper
and celebrate the New Passover, the Passover of gladness.
The Present One, the living Lord, Host at this table, is
the Servant,
who did this for us, for the forgiveness of our sins.
He offers us the only food he had to give them—
himself—
Bread—his body broken
Wine—his blood shed for all
the true staff of life,
and the key to a life of loving service of God and man.
And when we have eaten our fill this night—at his table—
he clearly says,
Take a towel
and follow me!

GEORGE M. BASS
Northwestern Lutheran Theological Seminary
St. Paul, Minnesota

THE CROSS AS MIRROR AND WINDOW

Good Friday
John 19:17-30

At the heart and center of the Christian faith stands a particular symbol. It's one that graces every church, usually at the most prominent of places. At our church you see it by the altar, in the narthex, in the chapel and at the top of the tower. The symbol of which I speak is the cross.

Other systems of thought, other movements, have their symbols. Judaism its Star of David; the United States its stars and stripes; Communism its hammer and sickle; Nazism its swastika. But the church's symbol is a cross. And, not only is that our main symbol, that's at the heart of what it's all about; that reminds us of what we stand for and tells much about how we see things. So central is the cross that when we lose touch with it we grow weak and lose our way. When we renew contact with it, we regain our strength and direction.

To some, this is a strange idea. And, when you stop to think of it, there's something about it that *is* strange. We love life, but the cross speaks of death. We're success-oriented, but the cross speaks of defeat. We seek peace and harmony, but the cross reflects conflict. Why, then, do we still give the cross its place of honor in the church? Why is it still the central symbol of the faith?

I believe it's because deep down we know it speaks the truth. The truth about ourselves and the world in which we live. And the truth about God and his love for us.

In a sense the cross is like a diamond with many facets, each of which conveys something. But there are two images which I think summarize the meaning of the cross, two images which reflect why the cross is at the heart of our faith: The image of a mirror and image of a window. The cross is something like a mirror and something like a window.

A Mirror to Reflect

The cross is like a mirror because it tells us about ourselves and our world. Though we love life and strive for success and peace, we all know a full measure of their opposites: conflict, failure, and death. Moreover, as with the apostle, the good that we would do, we often do not do. The cross at this point confirms our human experience.

But the cross as mirror helps us look more carefully at ourselves, helps us look deeply into our souls. Helps us see through our concealment and self-deception, revealing how things really are with us and how we stand with God.

We who love peace and life and success, yet know conflict, failure and death—what are we like? This discrepancy between what we strive for and what we finally produce—what causes it?

The mirror of the cross is not complimentary at this point. It tells us that while we are capable of heroism, self-sacrifice and idealism, we are equally capable of envy, brutality and injustice. It reveals that the best within us and the best we can produce is shot through with flaws.

Consider, for example, some of the people who were present on that first Good Friday. Were they unusual people? Especially corrupt? Godless? I don't think so. I see their faces as being all too familiar. Judas loves God; the trouble is he loves his nation a fraction more. Peter is a man of sincere faith; he only miscalculates the power of temptation. The scribes, priests and Pharisees seek to preserve the truth, but they are too sure of themselves to consider a new idea. Pilate wants to maintain the peace—but he chooses the wrong strategy. And as for the crowd, all they want to do is get involved; so they stop thinking for themselves and believe and repeat the propaganda they hear.

Familiar faces, aren't they? Ordinary people. The kind of people you and I see when we look into the mirror of the cross.

When you continue to look carefully into that mirror, you begin to see more than individual people. You see what people build—their governments, their cultures, their religious systems.

Pilate, remember, represented the best government the world had ever known—a government based on law. And he did his best to administer justice, saying again and again, *"I find no fault in him."* But in the end, Pilate illustrates the perennial corruption of justice for the sake of political expediency. A government of law is shown here for what it is—susceptible to corruption by those who administer that law.

There was at least a touch of democracy at work that day, too—decision-making by consensus, you could call it. It's common to think of the crowd as a group of fickle people—anxious one day to make him king, anxious the next to have him lynched. But is that really so? Was this crowd distinguished by its fickle-mindedness? As unflattering as it may be, weren't they a rather ordinary crowd—made up of well-meaning people who tend to be short-sighted and who quickly lose their perspective? Democracy may well be the best form of government there is, but in the mirror of the cross democracy, too, is judged and found wanting. For the verdict of the majority was: *"Crucify him!"*

Or take the religious leaders who were there—the scribes, the priests and Pharisees. They are not wicked men. On the contrary, they are genuinely concerned for the things of God, looking out for the welfare of the people, convinced of the truth of their position. But this has something to say to us too. Religion can be a shield we hold up before God, a disguise we wear before men. Some of the cruelest of acts and the most malicious of gossip have worn pious masks of religious concern. Some of the bloodiest of wars have been fought in the name of religion. Racial prejudice, social injustice, character assassination have all been cloaked and justified by religious people for supposedly religious reasons. At the cross even our religion is brought into question, measured and evaluated.

The cross as mirror is a depressing image. Accurate but depressing. For it shows us ourselves. It brings home the tragic mixture in every one of us—the tendency toward evil that permeates and accompanies every tendency toward good. At the cross Jesus is ostensibly on trial, but in reality we are. The world is in the dock! And, if you stand in our narthex studying Paul Granlund's sculpture, you are struck by the tragic necessity of it, you get the point. For in the mirror of the cross the verdict is clear. We are guilty.

A Window to See Through

But think goodness there's another image! The cross is something like a mirror, but it's also something like a window. And as you look through the cross as window you see God at work, revealing himself and redeeming the world.

From the cross our Lord spoke seven "words," made seven statements—three of which are reported by John. The first two express concerns that are very human. His mother is there, and so is his good friend, John—both of whom would need the care of another. So our Lord commits them to each other: *"Woman, behold your Son!" — "(John) Behold your Mother."* He then asks for water. It had been eighteen hours since his last supper. He had endured the agony of Gethsemane, the betrayal, the arrest, the cross-examination, the trial, the scourging, the weary walk to Calvary, the crucifixion. His request for a drink is a simple announcement: *"I thirst."*

But the big word from the cross is the last one John records. His mother is cared for, his thirst is quenched. He has assured the thief of paradise, asked the Father to forgive them, cried out in despair. And then, just before commending his spirit into the hands of God, he says: *"It is finished."*

Don't misunderstand this saying. This is not the resignation of a martyr, the surrender of a well-intentioned but futile effort. This is a shout of victory! Jesus died knowing he had achieved something! His mission is fulfilled! He has finished the work he was given to do!

And the "Work," remember, was to bring us back to the Father —to reconcile and restore us. Now, says the cross, that is possible. The way is clear. We need no longer be strangers, alienated and cut off. The work is finished!

But how? What, in more precise terms, did this man's death accomplish? Why do we call this "Good Friday"?

Staying with the image of the cross as window we look through it and see three New Testament pictures—each of which describes the work that was finished.

The first of these sees the world as a scene of conflict between God and evil. Men are enslaved by evil; their minds and hearts are darkened and overcome. It's as if they are in the prison of evil. But God does not remain aloof. In Christ he enters the battle; in Christ he sets out to defeat evil and set men free from its prison. And through the life and death of Christ that's what he does; he defeats evil and transfers us into his kingdom. *"He has saved and redeemed me,"* said Luther, *" . . . he has freed me from sin, death, and the power of the devil . . . that I may be his own, (and) live under him in his kingdom and serve him . . ."* Looking through the cross as window we see evil defeated; and now we are freed of its powers!

The second picture sketched in the New Testament is quite different from that. The scene is a courtroom—a judge, a defendant and a law to be administered. The judge is forced to pass sentence on the defendant, even though that defendant is his own son. The son's guilt is unquestionable and there is no doubt as to the punishment which the law demands. The sentence is death. But then, as the judge pronounces the sentence, he leaves the bench, goes to the prisoner's dock and takes the place of his condemned son. That is another way of understanding the death of Christ. God is the judge, we are his guilty son and our sentence is death. But in Christ God has left the bench, has taken our place in the dock and has borne the punishment. We are acquitted!

Looking through the cross as window we see a third picture. Theologians call it the Moral Influence Theory. Someone else has aptly described it as the Magnet Picture. What we see here is God's love—outgoing, immeasurable, unending. The shepherd seeking his one lost sheep—that's God! The father forgiving his wayward son—that's God! The "only begotten son" going all the way to the cross—that's God! He is the seeking lover. His love knows no bounds. The cross shows us God's matchless conquering, irresistible love! And like a magnet, that demonstration of love pulls us out of our ignorance, our apathy, our fears. Now we dare to come home. We know he will receive us. Like a magnet, "love so amazing, so divine" draws us back to the Father!

"In the Cross of Christ I Glory"

The cross as mirror and the cross as window—a mirror reflecting ourselves and our world and a window through which we see God, his will and his work. That's why it's central to Christian faith and life. That's why it's displayed so prominently in our churches. That's why in losing touch with it we grow weak and lose our way and by renewing contact with it we regain our strength and direction. "In the cross of Christ I glory" because the cross is at the heart of what's it's all about between us and God!

HARRIS W. LEE
Lutheran Church of the Good Shepherd
Minneapolis, Minnesota

RESURRECTION — FEARFUL DOUBTS OR EXCITING FAITH?

The Resurrection of Our Lord — Easter Day
John 20:1-9

Celebration Today

What a festive atmosphere of celebration we have here in our church this Easter Sunday morning—happy faces, stirring music, resounding hallelujahs; all together creating an exhilarating mood of joyful worship.

I like this. There springs up in me a great urge to lead a procession through the sanctuary out into the streets and then out into the highways and by-ways of the world, shouting "He is risen! Hallelujah! He is risen, indeed!"

I would find that exciting, but I am not so sure it would do a great deal of good, for too many would focus on us and perhaps there would be a few news stories about a bald-headed preacher and his congregation doing something radically different on Easter Sunday, and the Resurrected Savior would receive little notice.

It is best, therefore, that we celebrate here in the sanctuary with our hymns and psalms, with Word and Sacrament, building each other up in the faith and glorifying our God for all that the Easter message means to us.

May the Holy Spirit rule strongly in our hearts and help us as we permit the Easter message to come through to us.

In Jerusalem— Doubts and Faith

The faithful followers of Jesus must have been emotionally drained after the traumatic experiences of that last Friday of crucifixion and death and their agonizing pain of loss and loneliness on Saturday as they contemplated their shattered hopes and dreams. They just could not understand it all. Their one thought as they waited for Sunday morning was to go to the tomb and pay their last respects and perform a last, loving service for him whom they had called their Lord.

Our text reports that Mary Magdalene came to the tomb early on Sunday morning. Other accounts make it clear that she was accompanied by Mary, the mother of James, and Salome. What a surprise for them as they approached the tomb and saw the stone removed from the entrance! What consternation when they discovered the body of Jesus was missing!

Mary Magdalene's reaction shows what fearful doubts gripped their hearts. She hurried to tell Peter and John, "they have taken the Lord out of the tomb, and we do not know where they have laid him." She, with the others, surely believed that the Lord's enemies in their hateful opposition to him stole his corpse and hid it from his followers.

Peter and John had no reassuring word for Mary Magdalene. They, in great anxiety, quickly ran to the tomb to see for themselvest. They entered the tomb and found it empty and at that point were filled with fearful doubts, wondering just what had occurred.

These followers of Jesus probably felt crushed with additional sadness as they thought that possibly the body of their beloved Master was being desecrated by unscrupulous and callous people. They did not realize that the very people they were accusing in their thoughts were people who were filled with more frightening doubts than their own. The people who had plotted against Jesus and had successfully insisted on his crucifixion before Pontius Pilate, as well as the guards stationed at the tomb, must have been terrified by the events on Easter morning. What fearful doubts must have seized their unbelieving hearts and minds.

In all that is reported in our text there is just one little expression of faith. It is reported that John, after he entered the tomb and observed the linen cloths and the face napkin carefully placed separately, believed. This is the one word of faith mentioned in our text. The text explains that the lack of faith in these disciples was because they did not yet know the Scriptures, that he must rise from the dead. Even though Jesus had clearly predicted his resurrection on the third day after his death, it was reported at that time and became evident on Easter Sunday morning, that "they understood none of these things; this saying was hid from them, and they did not grasp what was said" (Luke 19:34). Thus, Peter, John, Mary Magdalene, and the others did not have a spectacular celebration of the resurrection, but went back to their homes.

Today — Fearful Doubts or Exciting Faith?

This morning I have a pastoral concern that we not just take an apathetic glance into the empty tomb and return to our homes in an indifferent mood, and possibly be filled with fearful doubts. Perhaps as I state such a thought, you may be filled with resentment. How could I even suggest that Christian people can be indifferent to the resurrection of Jesus Christ and live in fearful doubts?

Permit me to say it clearly and emphatically that when there is lacking in our hearts an exciting Easter faith, there is inevitably an indifferent spirit and there will eventually be doubts not only about the reality of Christ's resurrection, but also about the validity of our Christian faith and commitment, as well as a disturbing dimming of our hope for eternal life and our own resurrection. The Apostle Paul spells this out in the fifteenth chapter of First Corinthians, and makes it clear that a negating attitude toward the resurrection of Jesus Christ really cancels out our faith, the forgiveness of sins, and the Christian hope. That's why it is true that people who have only a thinly coated veneer of personal Christianity, and not an exciting faith in the resurrection of Jesus Christ from the dead, are most miserable of all people, filled with fearful doubts.

There seems to be much evidence in our society today that people really can't be sure about anything. It is difficult to trust people. We have come to be inclined both in the nation and in our church to view statements of assurances with a great deal of skepticism. Our intellectual climate has developed an attitude in many people to question everything that had been held as truth in the past. We find that those who have become adept at debunking the respected personages in our history have found gullible audiences and a ready profit. When we add to all of this overwhelming influence of science and technology in our culture, we can begin to understand how difficult it is for many to hold on to any kind of assurances that have to do with things that are spiritual and eternal. All this breeds fearful doubts in the hearts of people.

It is not surprising in this kind of atmosphere to find many timid, fearful people when it comes to proclaiming in strong and meaningful language the glorious resurrection of Jesus Christ from the dead. Somewhat unsure of their own understanding, and fearful of being put down by the wise of this world, it is quite possible that many are overcome with fearful doubts, and therefore find little joy and meaningful excitement in the Easter celebration.

This is tragic for us as individuals and for the cause of the gospel in our cynical, superstitious, and frightened generation. Our world needs the bold and joyful proclamation of the resurrection of Jesus Christ from the dead, and of its great significance for our Christian faith and for victorious living the one little life we have on this earth.

When we Christians take in the full scope of the reality and the theology of Christ's resurrection, we not only celebrate with excitement the Easter festival, but we will live strong Christian lives in the full assurance that our Redeemer lives and that in his resurrection we can celebrate our own victory over sin, death, and Satan. In this Easter faith, under God, we can bring hope and deliverance to our confused and hurting generation.

How good it is, therefore, for us to celebrate this Easter festival with a living, exciting faith here in the church this morning! How challenging it is for us to continue our celebration out in the world day after day as we live in close fellowship with the resurrected Christ, demonstrating to people all around us in transformed lives and in a Christian hope that shines through every dark hour, that it truly is great to be a Christian here and now and forever in heaven. Hallelujah! Christ is risen, indeed! Amen.

CARL A. GAERTNER
Zion Lutheran Church
Dallas, Texas

JUST AN ORDINARY GREETING

Second Sunday of Easter
John 20:19-31

Shalom, and again he said, *Shalom.* "Peace be with you." It was just an ordinary greeting, much like our greeting of "hello" or "have a good day." Just an ordinary greeting, but on the occasion reported in the gospel, it had an extraordinary meaning.

The disciples were huddled together behind closed doors; afraid, scared because of the authorities. Would they arrest the disciples? Would they execute them because they had befriended the man who was killed for being a traitor and a heretic? (Jesus, killed for being a traitor and a heretic. Have you ever thought of him in those terms?) And the rumor was about that this man was alive again. Stamp out the rumor by rubbing-out the disciples. A sensible strategy. It always has been—even today. (Consult the newspaper and you may detect how often authorities try to stamp out rumors by eliminating or discharging friends—even today!) So, the disciples were huddled together in fear. There were grounds for it, make no mistake about that.

And there are grounds for our fears, too. Who among us is eager and willing to tangle with the authorities—to press deliberately for moral integrity in persons holding high offices and low; or to protest against the common notion that the end always justifies any means—lying, wiretapping, skewed advertising, you name it; or to challenge such matters as unjust zoning regulations in your neighborhood or unequal law enforcement; or to question the priorities and practices of some businesses, and even some of our churches; or to step forward and befriend the outsiders in our community, yes, the people who live on the other side of the track? Let's face it, and I suspect that most of us have already, there's a great deal of sound and fury these days which is fear creating. Maybe that's why we often huddle behind closed doors and make our houses and churches huts of privacy instead of havens of hospitality.

From "The Wounded Healer"

But it was precisely to his friends huddled together behind closed doors that Jesus came and said to them, *Shalom*, "Peace be with you." Then there follows in the text those incredible words: "He showed them his hands and his side. Then the disciples were glad when they saw the Lord." The disciples were glad when they saw the Lord, and they recognized him as Lord, as *Lord* mind you, by the *wounds* and *scars* on *his body!* Even a week later Thomas will acclaim Jesus as Lord when he sees the wounds and scars on his body!

A mighty strange combination of encounter and response. The disciples recognized Jesus, the Lord, by the wounds on his body. Not the most pleasant way to identify a person—by his wounds and scars.

Moreover, it is precisely this wounded man who says *Shalom*,

"Peace be with you." And the disciples are glad. A mighty strange combination of encounter and response.

So what does *Shalom* mean when it is heard from lips of this wounded man? Certainly it doesn't mean the absence of conflict, of struggle, of pain and defeat. Jesus, the wounded man, spoke the word.

No. *Shalom* doesn't mean the absence of struggle and pain. We know that in our own lives. But it does mean the presence of love in our wounded lives. The presence—not the absence of anything—but presence of love in our fear-riddled lives. That's what the greeting of *Shalom* means when Jesus speaks it. And this meaning and presence we may not know so well in our own lives.

In part, because we may suppose that his presence and love should alleviate our fears and heal our wounds. And that isn't what we have experienced in our lives—at least not many of us. We may expect his presence to make us courageous, take away our fears, make us whole and healthy so that we won't be bothered and plagued by tension and pain.

Instead, Jesus shares his own pain and wounds as a sign that we need not try to escape our fears and pains. We can share our wounds, our weaknesses and our fears with him and with one another. And in this mutual sharing, the paralyzing effect of fear and pain can be arrested. Moreover, this mutual sharing of weakness can alert us to the signs of hope in God's promise of coming strength, his promise of *Shalom.*

Perhaps it was something of this shared life that the ancient prophet had in mind when he said of the suffering servant of God, "with his wounds we are healed" (Isaiah 53:5b). And maybe it's a clue to St. Paul's unusual retort, "I will all the more gladly boast of my weakness, that the power of Christ may rest upon me. For the sake of Christ, then, I am content with weaknesses, insults, hardships, persecutions and calamities; for when I am weak, then I am strong" (2 Cor. 12:9-10).

Meant for Us

It was this discovery and recognition—that weakness is borne but not eliminated—that led a woman who suffered polio as a child into a deeper awareness and appreciation of the *Shalom* of God. As a result of her illness, one leg grew shorter than the other and finally created problems in her spinal column. A fusion was done, bringing temporary relief, but other symptoms and problems developed. Through the repeated heartbreak of raised hopes followed by repeated disappointments, she finally concluded that all the future held for her was a life of diminishing activity.

Through this ordeal, she continued to trust in a good and gracious God. Moreover, she found that she had time to do things she had always wanted to do, but hadn't. The words of Jesus to the effect that life is more than food and clothing became verities. She had life and life was good. One day she said to her pastor, "I thought of faith in God as meaning that God would always make everything come out all right, as I conceived of all right. Now I have found that God cares for me even when things don't come out all right. This is my God."

Long before the woman lived and died, our wounded healer confirmed this truth. Jesus didn't get wealthy, but he found God cared for him in his poverty. His own family questioned his sanity; his friends betrayed him. He asked to be spared from a death, but he had to endure it. Things didn't turn out all right for him. Yet he endured. His life confirms that the *Shalom* of God means that "God cares for me even when things don't come out all right. This is my God."

Do you begin to see why we will know what Christ's greeting of peace means only as we refrain from letting his wounds scare us, only as we refrain from letting his wounds intimidate us, only as we refrain from letting his wounds make us feel guilty? We will know what his greeting of peace means only when we let those wounds indicate that there is one who is radically *partisan towards us,* One who is *totally for us* (as no other person can be in life and in death), one who is complete *with us in spite* of our weakness and strength. We will know what his greeting of peace means only as we risk being sent on a mission as he was sent, only as we risk serving and loving and probably fail at both. For as one man has said, "A person who risks and fails can be forgiven. But a person who never risks is already a failure."

So, have a good day. Have a good day. I know that's only an ordinary greeting, but it can have an extraordinary meaning for us. For the *Shalom* of God which passes all understanding keeps your heart and mind in Christ Jesus, our Lord.

Amen.

Morris J. Niedenthal
Lutheran School of Theology
Chicago, Illinois

HIDDEN IN A WORD

Third Sunday of Easter
Luke 24:13-35

Despite pious claims to the contrary, I wonder sometimes if the experience of God's absence isn't a lot more common to us than the sense of his presence. There are times, to be sure, when God seems frighteningly or uncomfortably near. But there are times on the other side as well—maybe most of the times—when God seems to have gone on vacation, when he seems to have disappeared completely and left us hanging. It can be worse, too. There are times when he not only seems gone but when it looks like everything godly has been defeated. Then if he's not gone he's hidden, hidden where only faith can hear or see him.

Shattered Disciples

If Cleopas and his partner would have had any say in it, the story would have had a different ending, one without suffering, a cross, and a grave. "We had hoped that he was the one to redeem Israel," they said. That would have been a different story entirely. Then the Palm Sunday parade would have continued, swelling into a crescendo of triumph. There would have been a new exodus, only this time the Romans would have left town to escape, leaving Israel in a glorious kind of freedom. Cleopas and his friend might have had their sights set a little higher, too—the redemption not only of Israel but of the whole creation, God overthrowing all the humdrum, all the ordinary, all the suffering, to take up permanent residence with men and wipe away every tear.

Instead they saw suffering and finally an agonizing defeat. It was the one thing that neither Cleopas, his partner, nor any of the other disciples were prepared to stomach. Redemption, liberation, victory over all that ailed them they could buy in on but somehow suffering and worse yet, an ignominious death, was not a part of the bargain. When Jesus was arrested in the garden, all the disciples "forsook him and fled," Mark says (14:50), every last one of them. The cross shattered every hope, dream, or illusion they might have had about Jesus. Seeing it coming, hearing of it, they dropped Jesus like a bad bet to get out while the getting was good.

There was nothing that could hold Cleopas and his partner in Jerusalem, either: not Jesus' own word that he would suffer, die, and on the third day arise; not the word of some women that the tomb was in fact empty that morning; not word of visions of some angels. Like the other disciples, "these words seemed to them an idle tale," Luke says, "and they did not believe them" (24:11). The God who had seemed so overwhelmingly close in the presence of Jesus had disappeared. It was all over—there was nothing left, no hope remaining. For all they could see, Jesus was washed up —one more promising hope trounced. So they were leaving, going home maybe, or perhaps escaping, looking for a good place to lick their wounds and figure out what went wrong.

Maybe our hopes are a little bit more modest than the dreams and visions Cleopas and his partner entertained. There don't seem to be many people on tiptoe, necks extended, ears cocked waiting for some ultimate kind of release. The world has grown more comfortable now. But still there always seems to be someone or something around promising some kind of redemption—freedom from what's ailed us, triumph over the ordinary, deliverance from suffering. And whether grand or modest, they all seem to meet the same fate, never quite being able to deliver.

It happened in the government. The slogans of the sixties and the seventies have been promises of redemption: "the new frontier," "the great society," "a generation of peace." One by one they've been proclaimed to us, each one offering its own special brand of hope for a new world: the elimination of poverty, pestilence, racism, a world without war—cold or hot—for at least part of a lifetime. One by one the slogans, the promises, have bit the dust, maybe causing more suffering than they've cured. "We had hoped. . . ." It got trounced again.

It has happened in the church, too, over and over again. Somehow it always seems so simple. "If only we could get hold of the gospel, if only people would really hear it and take it to heart" then the church would be redeemed—set free from teachers and preachers who ask embarrassing questions and acknowledge the possibilities of doubt; set free from sagging finances, empty pews, pernicious anemia; set free from self seeking leadership, and programs that never seem to work. Maybe new attitudes, new bishops, new pastors, new programs will do it. . . . But it never seems to work. The purges in some churches have brought destruction, weeds and wheat burning and being burned together. The firecrackers of renewal have turned out to be duds. The programs fail. New leadership either patterns itself on the old or can't make any headway. We are right back where we started from—hopes raised, trounced again.

It looks like the ordinary, our everyday struggle, has got a hammerlock on us. There are those moments, to be sure, when

God seems to have moved right in to stand next to us—a great concert, a magnificent sermon, a time when the community has gathered to support a family in grief or trouble. And there are times when redemption seems just around the corner—when the government finally breaks through momentarily to make some progress, when the church rises to the occasion and temporarily hits its stride, when we really feel like we have broken through. But it's always so temporary, always for the moment. Then it's back to business as usual, Monday morning with its alarm clock waking us up to the humdrum. Then God seems to be gone again and worse yet, our every hope of godliness—progress against social maladies; a church that does its job; our resolves to somehow improve ourselves and do better—seem to get defeated. Then like Cleopas and friend, there seems to be nothing left but to pack our bags and go—to try something else, to get out, to forget about our hopes, to lose ourselves in the routine of daily life and let the world go its merry way.

In the Depths

But maybe there's something here to hold us. When Jesus finally found Cleopas and his partner, he interpreted the Scriptures for them. "Was it not necessary that the Christ should suffer these things and enter into his glory?"

That, you remember, is the one thing the disciples were not ready to stomach. When the suffering started, when the cross loomed over them, they pulled stakes and took off. And that's just what all our own hopes for some kind of redemption promise to remove from us—suffering. There are some kinds of suffering, you know, that are polite, that have a moral to them. When they're over we can dress them up and talk about suffering being a good teacher. But the pious sighs afterwards don't do much to make us eager pupils. It's the elimination of suffering that tickles the fancy, that gives us hope, that makes us willing, even after being broken again and again, to go back and give a new promise another try. "We had hoped that he was the one to redeem Israel." Then the pain would have been over. We had hoped for a new frontier, a great society, a generation of peace, to secure a meaningful future. Then the suffering would have been finished. We had hoped for renewal, for a church on its feet and moving, for new leadership, a stronger impact, better results. Then the struggle would have been ended.

It is as Luther says in his commentary on the Magnificat. "This we experience every day. Everyone strives after that which is above him, after honor, power, wealth, knowledge, a life of ease, and whatever is lofty and great. On the other hand, no one is willing to look into the depths with their poverty, disgrace, squalor, misery and anguish. From these all turn away their eyes. Where there are such people, everyone takes to his heels, forsakes and shuns and leaves them to themselves. . . . Therefore to God alone belongs that sort of being that looks into the depths with their need and misery, and is near to all that are in the depths."

Sometimes, maybe most of the time, God seems absent. Maybe it's because he is absent, because he removes himself from our every attempt to make the world our oyster; from our every attempt to somehow take hold of his word and manage and manipulate it to our own ends, making him a means to serve our own purposes; from our every feeble struggle to stand on our own, calling ourselves self-made, self-sufficient. He is the God of the first commandment who jealously refuses to allow us any other gods, who will not have us fearing, loving or trusting anything else—be it government, church, our own piety. He's the one who breaks our phony redeemers to smithereens and casts them to the four winds. He's the one who turns earthly promises of redemption into lies. He will liberate us, redeem us, take care of us, give us everything good. No one else can, or will.

That's what we're made for—to stand naked, empty-handed, defenseless, poverty stricken, in the depths; to live where there is confusion, doubt, despair, emptiness and longing; where there is suffering, helplessness; where we can't seem to get control, have nothing to lean on, but only the promise that he will be our God. That is where Jesus came: not on the heights but in the depths, not in glory but in humiliation, not in power but in weakness, not to full course dinners where he was one plate among many but to empty tables where he was the only possibility. And that's where he comes now: not with spectacular manifestations of power, not with signs and wonders, but in the most humble, common, and hidden sorts of ways—in the word, in the water of baptism, in the bread and wine of communion.

In a Word

That's what finally broke the secret for Cleopas and his partner. As long as they were looking for him in the heights, in a spectacular liberation of Israel and all the earth, they couldn't recognize him. But when Jesus preached the word to them and then sat down at the table and broke bread with them, they saw him. As soon as they saw him, he disappeared. Israel still lay in its bonds; the world wasn't changed. But they had what they needed—his word, the sacrament—and they took off on a dead run, not to escape this time, but to find the others, to shout, to tell.

Sometimes when we are scanning the heavens or searching the heights for signs of redemption God seems terribly absent. Sometimes, too, it seems like everything that we regard as godly is being defeated. Sometimes even when he comes we can't see him, feel him, or find any sign of his presence. But he is here, with us, in the depths where there is brokenness, pain, disillusion, helplessness against the old Adam's wiles and ways. God is here, with us, in a word. He is here, with us, in his sacraments, to wash, to break bread with us. Listen. Eat and drink. Fight. Struggle. He's here. He's coming soon. You can bank on it, bank on it because he alone is faithful—faithful to the cross and death, faithful to the depths, faithful to raise you and yours from the dead.

JAMES A. NESTINGEN
Editor, Curriculum Development—The ALC
Minneapolis, Minnesota

WHAT IS A SHEEP WITHOUT A GOOD SHEPHERD?

Fourth Sunday of Easter
John 10:1-10

Have you ever seen a mangy dog running around the neighborhood and wondered why its owner didn't take better care of it? It makes a lot of difference to a pet as to whether it has an owner who cares about it and for it or whether he just sort of lets it run wild.

Nature in the raw is pretty rugged and takes its toll on an animal in spite of many of our romantic notions of how "nice" nature is. When left to themselves, animals can have a pretty rough time in the "dog eat dog" world of nature's wilderness. There is substance to the idea that nature tolerates only the survival of the fittest.

The Good Shepherd Who Cares for His Sheep

A good shepherd is that kind of difference to his sheep. There is a considerable difference between the lives of sheep who run wild and sheep who have a shepherd. This is the thought concentrated in that beloved twenty-third psalm: A sheep with a shepherd is blessed indeed!

The author of that psalm proposes to be the sheep who benefits from the care and concern of a good shepherd. The shepherd finds food and water for the sheep and examines it carefully lest something harmful should be present. "Thou preparest a table before me in the presence of my enemies" probably refers to the way the shepherd carefully examined the ground he wanted to use for grazing his sheep. The table is prepared by examining the area for harmful and poisonous weeds that wild sheep might otherwise unwittingly eat without a conscientious Shepherd to watch out for them. When the good shepherd "leads me beside still waters" I can let the worry and concern rest on the shoulders of the shepherd while I safely graze under his watching eye. That is why the sheep of our text follow with such confidence when they hear the voice of the good shepherd calling them by name and leading them out.

Should they stumble into brambles or bruise themselves on some rocks on the way, the shepherd who leads them is always ready to anoint their heads with oil. The loving touch of the shepherd's hand with the healing ointment assures the sheep that the troubles into which they have gotten themselves are always under the scrutiny of him who is in charge of the sheep. The good shepherd makes a good life possible for the sheep under his charge.

Dangers are always near. Wild animals are apt to separate sheep from the flock and destroy them. How comforting, then, to know that "he who enters by the door" has a rod and staff to comfort me. This shepherd wields the blows of his staff when my enemies come around and he curtails my wandering with his long rod so that I am returned safely again to the center of the flock. And at night the comforting surroundings of the sheepfold with the watchman at the gate permitting nobody to enter who might mean harm makes it possible for me to lie down to sleep with the confidence that nothing can approach me for ill. Should even a thief climb over the wall to invade this fortress, the club of my shepherd will be my defense and shield.

It is to the shelter of this sheepfold where my shepherd will hurry me if storm clouds darken the horizon. In those hours when lightning and thunder strike fear in my heart and make me rush about without any thought with all the attendant dangers that I may in this mad dash rush headlong over a cliff to my destruction . . . then the doors of this place of safety will be open to me and the shepherd will stand near-by calling me by name. And his voice will soothe me and comfort me until all is again calm and peaceful.

That is what it means to have a good shepherd. He calls us by name, and we follow with confidence, knowing that our food and our drink will be provided and all our worries cared for by him. He protects us from all our enemies and binds up all our wounds. They are not our worries. He has taken them upon himself. No wonder the sheep with a good shepherd are so much better off than those left to themselves!

The Sheep Often Do Not Know When They Are Well Off

But it doesn't always *appear* that way on the surface, does it? The sheep who has the run of the range, who doesn't have to feel bound in by a shepherd's direction and who finds his own place to sleep at night is the one who appears the freest of them all, does he not? That's the way the prodigal son felt about it, at least. He saw the father as a terrible shepherd because he placed restrictions on him. He insisted that he couldn't eat off just any pastureland and told him that he could not go into certan craggy areas where he might get lost and injured.

Or must we speak of the prodigal son? Is not this the very essence of what we call sin? We all want our freedom! Like the prodigal son or a sheep under the restrictions of a shepherd, we feel "bound in" by all our duties. The God who promises to be a Good Shepherd to us appears to hamper our freedom instead, to hold us back from our fanciful flights into adventure and fun! "All we like sheep have gone astray; we have turned every one to his own way," Isaiah describes the situation of human life. As a sort of test question against which to ask if Isaiah is on target, inquire of yourself just why you sin if it is not because your freedom from the Good Shepherd seems so desirable. A good short definition of sin is: A straying away from the one who wants to care for us. We think we know better than the Good Shepherd what is good for us. The grass looks so green in the forbidden pastures where poisonous weeds grow. It is so tempting to explore the dark passageways of the dangerous areas where the Shepherd knows wild animals lurk. Like little children we ignore the concerned eye of the Shepherd and go our own way.

So the question of life is: Under whose care will we place ourselves? Will we let the fickle fates of nature be our guard and caretaker, hoping to find our way through the forbidding passageways of the valley of the shadow of death as we scrounge for grass in any pasture we choose, slake our thirst from any water we happen across, let time heal our wounds and trust that our own judgment will find a safe hiding-place for the night? Or will we trust the Good Shepherd's judgment for all this and be free of all the worries and concerns that attend such a so-called "care-free" life?

When all is said and done, the sheep who has a good shepherd has the best life by far. That sheep is the freest of all who needs not worry about poisonous plants and brackish water and wounded bodies and destructive enemies. In its captivity it is free from those threatening dangers that engulf all animals left to the whims of nature!

The Key to Life Is to Have a Good Shepherd

The secret, of course, is in having a *good* shepherd. There are those, indeed, who would use and abuse the sheep, seeing in them only a means to gain a profit. There is no guarantee whatever that giving yourself into just any shepherd's hands will bring freedom. It could well be that your enslavement will be the greater in wrong hands than it would be if you just ran wild.

The difference, then, lies in how the shepherd views his sheep. That is where the crux of the whole matter lies. The welfare of the sheep depends on knowing who the shepherd is.

In a book called *The Little Prince* a conversation between a fox and a little boy is recorded in which the fox says, "I have no need for you. And you, on your part, have no need of me. To you, I am nothing more than a fox like a hundred thousand other foxes. But if you tame me, then we shall need each other. To me, you will be unique in all the world. To you, I shall be unique in all the world. . . ." Or, as the fox puts it even more briefly a little later on, "Men have forgotten this truth, but you must not forget it. You become responsible, forever, for what you have tamed."

It can't be put much better! That's what has happened in the form and person of Jesus Christ. The one who put in his claim to be our Good Shepherd is the one who has "tamed" all the forces that once held us captive and then "tamed" us so that we "might be his own and live under him in his kingdom!" The very fact of the cross tells us something about our Good Shepherd so that we can know whose voice to follow. And if he has tamed us, he has taken upon himself the responsibility, forever, for what he has tamed! We can follow his voice with confidence that he will always "be on our side."

It Is Important to Know the Voice of the Good Shepherd

There are so many voices who call us to follow them, though! There are even thieves who jump the fences of our lives and forcibly attempt to make us follow them. It isn't hard to get confused amid the swirl of so many voices. There is the voice of worry and fretting over a broken relationship between parent and children; the voice of sorrow over a fractured marriage; the voice of concern over financial problems; the voice of fear that the world will errupt into an atomic holocaust of violence. It is so tempting to follow the voice that leads to financial security at the compromise of integrity or the voice that leads to an apparently secure emotional involvement in a clandestine love affair, or even on occasion the voice that looks to death by suicide as a "way out of our trouble." Voices of all kinds pound our ears and the cross becomes obscured as other forces come to play on our life, virtually drowning out the one voice that really can and will lift us above all this and sustain us with firm foundations.

That is why a merely casual and passing acquaintanceship with the Good Shepherd will never do. If that is all we want, then we will never be sure who is calling or whether we should follow when all the other voices whir in our ears. That is why faith is not and cannot be nourished only in a casual fashion or by a sort of informal agreement to hear his voice "when we feel like it" or worshiping when there's nothing better to do or receiving the holy supper only when it is conveniently offered in one of our infrequent forays into the sheepfold to see how things are going!

This seems all right so long as the weather is clear and we are relatively free of injury and we don't happen into the poisonous patches of grass. But when things turn on us and we desperately need and want the comforting care of the Good Shepherd, we must know his voice through an intimate acquaintanceship fostered in the good days as well as the bad. For the voice of the thief the one who will do the sheep harm, will ring in that day across the dark night of our souls alongside the voice of the Good Shepherd. And if we have not learned well to distinguish between the two, that is a perilous night indeed! It is finally among these voices crying our name that we must choose when death, the dark night that follows all lives, comes calling for us. Then, most assuredly, we must know the voice of him who watches over us even in that dark valley with his rod and staff protecting and guarding us. If in that moment we cannot recognize his voice, the panic of having to follow another shepherd will stampede us through those dark doors into eternal ruin.

So now is the time to know the Good Shepherd. He has called you by name. In your baptism he has called: "John . . . Mary . . . Frank . . . Hilda . . . Mark . . . Martha . . . come follow me." We are here this morning as part of our response to that call, to be with him who knows where the good pastureland is where the still waters flow, where the dangerous places are so that we can avoid them, to walk through the dark valley of the shadow of death and see the bright sunshine of resurrection on the other side. We are here to once more listen to the voice of him who says, "The thief comes only to steal and kill and destroy; I come that they may have life, and have it abundantly." As today's Epistle puts it so well: "By his wounds you have been healed. For you were straying like sheep, but have now returned to the Shepherd and Guardian of your souls."

HUBERT BECK
University Lutheran Chapel
Texas A and M University
College Station, Texas

GO WITH THE GUIDE!

Fifth Sunday of Easter
John 14:1-12

Sometime ago I bought a swing set. It was the kind you put together yourself. It didn't appear complicated to assemble, so I quickly laid out the parts and pieces in the back yard. A cheering section of smiling children soon gathered to help fit piece to piece. I was putting it together from memory of the one in the store. Then it happened. The piece that should have fit next was not it at all. Suddenly, nothing seemed to work. Were there pieces missing? Or was my memory slipping? I was about to take it back to the store amid the disappointed looks of the children when a booklet slipped out of the packing box. Across the front in bold type it read: INSTRUCTIONS: IF ALL ELSE FAILS, FOLLOW THESE DIRECTIONS! At once I started over, following the directions. Every piece was there and the swing set was assembled with ease.

There is something about us that likes to figure things out for ourselves. Whoever wrote the directions had not only a sense of humor, but insight into our human make up.

Missed Directions — Misled Lives

In a much deeper sense, it is the very nature of sin to want life on my terms and according to my directions. We want to lay out our course. We'll figure things out for ourselves, that is, until we hit snags and dead-ends. When things don't fit, we wonder if we have all the pieces required to put life together. That's when we begin looking for more explicit directions.

The psychiatrist, C. G. Jung, assessed that about a third of the people who came to him for psychological help were not suffering from any clinically definable neurosis, but from the senselessness and aimlessness of their lives. He described this as the general neurosis of our age, which especially afflicts people in the second half of their life.

T. S. Eliot said it in poet's prose—

As we grow older
The World becomes a stranger, the pattern more complicated
Of dead and living.

If we count on ourselves alone, if we try to rely upon our own memory and wit, eventually we encounter missed directions and the specter of a misled life. As much as we want to feed our pride of self-accomplishment, that eludes us more and more in our complex world. The longer we live, the more nagging the prospect of being misled. We are easily haunted by the notion of having come all this way—only to have followed the wrong directions.

How Can We Know the Way?

We are not the first people to wonder if we have missed a clue that could help us get our bearings. Look at the conversation of Jesus and the disciples in our Gospel reading today. They were huddled together on Passover eve for supper. There had been mounting opposition to his ministry. It was becoming more difficult to be one of the inner circle. They were more dependent than ever upon his presence—and just then the Lord began to talk of going away.

> Do not be worried and upset. . . . Believe in God, and believe in me. . . . I am going to prepare a place for you. . . . And after I go and prepare a place for you, I will come back and take you to myself, so that you will be where I am. You know how to get to the place where I am going (John 14:1-4—TEV).

Thomas found no comfort in those words of the Master. Instead of quieting his fears, they stirred to the surface all his uncertainty. His saintliness, under this lens of apprehension, is shrunk to midget proportions. He didn't know which way to turn. He had to be more sure of himself and his Lord, and cried:

> "Lord, we do not know where you are going; how can we know the way to get there." Jesus answered him, "I am the way, the truth and the life; no one goes to the Father except by me" (John 14:5-6—TEV).

Getting Our Bearings

How can we know the way? How can folks like you and me, who get detoured and trapped in dead-ends, get our bearings? The words that directed Thomas' groping and uncertainty also direct ours:

I am the way, the truth and the life!

But just as they were not immediately helpful to the disciples, they may not be immediately helpful to us in our searching and seeking.

Perhaps we are looking for a map with more explicit directions. "Do this . . . do that . . . turn here . . . go left there . . . watch for clear signs along the way." That would satisfy the curiosity we have about our journey. When we become desperately anxious about the future we almost demand a well-marked map. But God gives us no map of our future. We have no step by step directions. Even Christians have to admit at times, "We do not know," just as Thomas confessed. But acknowledging we don't always know the direction to go doesn't mean everything is up for grabs. We are not without a rudder to guide us on our way.

You see, while we have no map for our life's journey, we nevertheless have guidance. It is not the kind of guidance you get from a travel agency—complete with descriptive folders, historical sites to visit, helpful hints on making change in a different currency and a quick language course on how to ask life's six most important questions! Rather, it is simply that Jesus is our guide. He is the way!

There will be no peek into heaven to catch a glimpse of the great mansion and our own room. We are not even going to see the Owner just yet, because, "Whoever has seen me," said Jesus, "has seen the Father."

Martin Luther once recalled, "In times past a pious hermit, St. Anthony, admonished his brethren as he spoke of the young and inexperienced saints who want to be smart enough to fathom God's inscrutable counsel and everything with their thoughts:

'If you see such a young saint clambering heavenward and planting one foot into heaven, pull him down posthaste, before he can set his other foot up there too and then plunge down head over heels!' This is well spoken against the fluttering spirits, who like to speculate about sublime matters, who would like to bore a hole through heaven and peek in to discover what God Himself is and what He does, meanwhile ignoring Christ as superfluous for that purpose."

Go With the Guide

Jesus doesn't say, "I'll show you the way." Rather he embodies the way. Our destiny is tied to our living Lord, not some mechanical formula or pre-charted route. He doesn't show us the way to the Father, he takes us there. He is indispensable to true human life. "No one goes to the Father except by me." You and I are invited to go the way with Christ as our guide.

There have been many persons throughout history who sought to lead men and women into what they saw as humanity's destiny. Only Jesus endures after all these centuries—as this poem makes clear:

I saw the conquerors riding by,
With cruel lips and faces wan,
Musing on kingdoms sacked and burned,
There rode the Mongol, Genghis Khan.

And Alexander, like a god,
Who sought to weld the world in one;
And Caesar with his laurel wreath,
And like a thing from hell, the Hun.

And leading, like a star, the van,
Heedless of outstretched arm and groan,
Inscrutable Napoleon went,
Dreaming of Empire and alone.

Then all they perished from the scene,
As fleeting shadows on a glass,
And conquering down the centuries came
Christ, the swordless, on an ass. —Anonymous

He endures because he is still with us, risen, victorious Lord and Savior. He helps us find the only way for us to go, if we are to arrive at our God appointed destiny, by being the way.

For, when people like you and me go with the guide, we are challenged at every turn. He lays claim to our futile attempts to go it alone under our own directions. The Master's way was full of heartache as well as joy. There was discipline and disappointment. There was a cross as well as a crown. His way is still demanding, still strewn with hurdles requiring tough decisions. Those who go with the guide discover he doesn't change all that to what he might want—

I said, "Let me walk in the fields."
  He said, "No, walk in the town."
I said, "There are no flowers there."
  He said, "No flowers, but a crown."

I said, "But the skies are black;
  There is nothing but noise and din."
And He wept as He sent me back,
  "There is more," He said, "there is sin."

I said, "But the air is thick,
  And fogs are veiling the sun."
He answered, "Yet souls are sick,
  And souls in the dark undone."

I said, "I shall miss the light,
  And friends will miss me, they say."
He answered, "Choose tonight
  If I am to miss you, or they."

I pleaded for time to be given.
  He said, "Is it hard to decide?
It will not seem hard in heaven
  To have followed the steps of your Guide."

I cast one look at the fields,
  Then set my face to the town;
He said, "My child, do you yield?
  Will you leave the flowers for the crown?"

Then into His hand went mine,
  And into my heart came He;
And I walk in a light divine
  The path I had feared to see."

—"Obedience," George Macdonald

HARVEY L. PRINZ
President, Central States Synod, LCA
Kansas City, Missouri

EMPOWERED TO LIVE!

Sixth Sunday of Easter
John 14:15-21

How timeless the Christian venture! Each generation of spiritual pilgrims tends to feel its struggles are unique: at no other time has it been so difficult to "keep the faith"—to carry on the mission of the church. And our generation is no exception.

The Dilemma of the Desolate

We would quickly grant that the life of faith was never meant to be easy. But at what other juncture have the people of God had to handle in depressing succession such dire proclamations as "living in the post-Christian era," or "God is dead," or "the emergence of secular man:" all of its apparently documented with discouraging statistics of declining church membership and participation in corporate worship. If we are easy prey for pessimism, we have no trouble finding food for our mood.

But now listen to the Master as he relates to that first generation of followers: "I will not leave you desolate." What prompted that note of promise?——unless he perceived the uneasiness, the uncertainty, the fears, the pessimism of his friends as they groped with the prospect of their Master's pending departure. What then? An abrupt end to this inspiring, invigorating relationship with one who had lifted them out of drab routine into dreams and hopes which made their inner spirit come alive?

The Deliverance of the Divine

In such traumatic setting, the Lord of the church gave a timeless prescription for power available to Christians of every generation—the assurance of remarkable resources with which to live victoriously, whatever the odds.

The first resource: "I will pray the Father, and he will give you another Counselor" (the Holy Spirit). . . . The familiar name of the King James version is good: *Comforter.* But for modern-day Christians, the Revised Standard name is better: *Counselor.* For one thing, we are well versed in the function of counseling. But beyond that, we have need for the strong impact of the original Greek: One who is not only tender and patient—but one who comes to rally our spirit, put us up on our feet, and face tomorrow unafraid. Defeated as we may have been today, to quote John Masefield,

But tomorrow,
By the living God, we'll try again.

A second resource for the embattled Christian: "the Spirit of truth"—the kind of Counselor who will give guidance where the way is difficult, the crossroads puzzle, and hearts are at a loss. Pontius Pilate may have been reacting with scorn; but his exclamation could be the wistful plea of a bewildered twentieth century America, "What *is* truth?" To what can I fasten my mind and devotion, with a clear confidence that this is the same as it was yesterday, and will be the same tomorrow as it is today? Is there any great central reality around which my life can orbit, something which will unlock the mystery of existence, and offer a trustworthy beacon for the paths I travel, wherever they lead?

"Yes," comes the solid reply of the Master. "I am the way, the truth, and the life"—"When the Spirit of truth comes, he will guide you into all the truth . . . for he will take what is mine and declare it to you."

As if this were still not enough to reassure his distraught friends, the Master comes with a third resource: "I will not leave you desolate; I will come to you." Beyond the crucifixion, there would be another day! I assume the enemies of our Lord came down from the hill of Calvary well satisfied. They had put an end to this upstart reactionary from Nazareth. There would be no more of him. How little they could foresee the millions today who live in daily communion with the one they crucified—speaking to him—communing with him—drawing inspiration from him. It is because he lives, that they really live!

Like the poet:

Loud mockers in the roaring street
Say Christ is crucified again.
Twice pierced His gospel-bearing feet,
Twice broken His great heart in vain.
I hear and to myself I smile
For Christ talks with me all the while.

The Direction of the Devoted

Yes, how timeless the Christian venture! The needs of God's people matched with the resources of God, whether it be in the first century or ours. So, if like those first people in the Way, we are inclined at times to also feel "desolate," let the full thrust of the scriptures we handle come home—with all their strong, renewing implications:

God is present and active in his world. In times of discouragement we are apt to forget that this is God's world. Many drift into a mood of despair, as though the world were a marble which had dropped out of God's pocket. We are prone to believe that only secular forces control the day. The scriptures affirm another power-structure: the Creator God at work through the Holy Spirit, the Counselor and the Spirit of truth. The great God of the universe present in our affairs through his Son. The God who in the beginning created the heavens and the earth is still creating. This kind of faith lifts the chin of a Christian. It puts tension back into his spiritual muscle.

God is present and active in his church. If we lose track of that, we are in danger of falling into mechanical routines which leave no place for "the rush of a mighty wind."

I recall from my boyhood how announcements were often made in my home church. "God willing, we shall have services as usual next Sunday morning." Or, "the regular meeting of the Ladies' Aid will be held next Thursday afternoon." In retrospect I would question those terms, "as usual," or "regular." If the church is the fellowship of God's people, touched by the Counselor, even the Spirit of truth, a company with whom Christ has assured his presence—then there can be no worship "as usual" or "regular" meeting of the faithful. For given the resources we have named, any worship runs the potential of being highly unusual, and a fellowship group most irregular.

The Christian church in the world picture has always been a minority. She remains that today. In some places it seems like a pitiful minority. But the minority factor should leave us with no delusions. As far as we can measure, God has always acted through a minority. Wherever there is the contagion of one glowing heart to another, wherever here and there a person is brought into allegiance to Christ—there is big business, the world's biggest business. The man faithfully teaching a class on Sunday morning is a "big business man." The woman bringing her love and skill into the work of the church is a "big business woman." For what business compares with working in tandem with the living God, his very presence assured in the life and work of his people!

Some in our society are quite unimpressed. "So you have a few million members around the world—what are they among the teeming millions of mankind?" "So you have multi-million dollar budgets—what is that as the world measures investments?" Not much maybe—except for the brilliant potential of Christ present in his church—the Holy Spirit giving counsel, and desire, and will to lift a people far beyond what they ever dreamed for themselves.

And the beautiful thing about it all is that now we are empowered to live—to live as God meant us to live. His commandments no longer come across as dreary duty or confining regulation. Rather, they become guidelines, the marks of a dynamic love-relationship. "If you love me," begins our text, "you will keep my commandments." Not surprisingly, the text closes on the same radiant note: "He who has my commandments and keeps them, he it is who loves me; and he who loves me will be loved by my Father, and I will love him. . . ."

How long can any Christian be "desolate"—with such a prescription, and promise, and power for life!

MAYNARD IVERSON
Bethlehem Lutheran Church
Minneapolis, Minnesota

THE SAME ROAD TWICE

The Ascension of Our Lord

Luke 24:44-53

Travelers with some experience on mountain roads know that, if you want to catch all the scenery, you'd better travel the same road twice—once going "that way" and once coming back "this way." Some say it's the fact of concentrating "the first time through" on every turn in the road. Some say it's the obsessive desire to avoid spilling off the road at those sheer drop-offs. Others indicate that the scenery is just too expansive. Whatever the reason, when driving in the mountains, travel the same road twice—once "that way" and once "this way." The second time you'll see everything from a new perspective, noticing vistas you might think were not there the first time.

A New View

Considering the record of our Lord's ascension at the end of the Gospel of Luke gives us a chance to travel a road twice and see things we never saw before. That is one meaning which the ascension event had for the disciples. Jesus' ascension became for them a U-turn, a chance to turn around, look again at events just experienced, and come to new understandings about Jesus and his mission.

That is the same meaning which the remembrance of the ascension can have for us today in this service. It can be an opportunity for us to make a U-turn, to walk again past those events in our Lord's life which we have recently commemorated, and to find in them a meaning we missed the first time through.

Why do we make this use of the ascension account? Certainly, not because the ascension doesn't have other meaning. The church has always found cause for celebration in the ascension, because this event marks the visible return of Jesus to the Father, his return to a position of undiluted honor and unimpeded power. There is no denial of that understanding and meaning in this sermon. What there is, however, is the desire to ask: Can the ascension cause us to remember more? I believe it can. I see it in the fact that we heard the ascension event recounted twice in the readings of this service. Both accounts are written by Luke. In the Acts account, which we read first, Luke uses the ascension story as a starting point. In Acts the ascension becomes the springboard from which the reader walks forward into a consideration of the events of the early church. But in his gospel account, Luke tells of the ascension as the concluding act to a series of events. It is the U-turn for viewing those events in a new way. It is our opportunity to do what the original disciples surely must have done—turned around and in their minds traveled the same road twice. The ascension of their master became a U-turn experience from which they could look at his ministry, suffering, and death and see in them meaning they never saw before.

The First Time Through

Before we look at those new things they never saw before, we can profitably recall for a moment how those events looked "the first time through." Can you recall, for instance, the first time Jesus laid on his disciples the same words which he gives to them again on the occasion of his ascension? At the very moment when Peter had openly confessed that Jesus was "the Christ of God," Jesus told him and the other disciples, "The Son of man must suffer many things, and be rejected by the elders and chief priests and scribes, and be killed, and on the third day be raised" (Luke 9:22). From Mark's Gospel (Mark 8:31-33) we know how the disciples responded "the first time through." They found his words unthinkable. Peter literally scolded Jesus for such talk. Peter wanted Jesus to know as emphatically as possible that his ministry as Messiah was not going to end up in such a disaster.

"The first time through" every event after that moment seemed to hurdle them pell-mell downhill. There were those experiences of their own making. They—the ones who had followed Jesus for three years and had heard him teach again and again—had run away in a most crucial hour. Peter—their strong man—had denied him. There were the injustices perpetrated by others who might have made it go differently. Pontius Pilate—the one who symbolized the justice of Rome—defaulted in a critical moment and caved in to a lynch mob. Herod had dangled the possibility of freedom before the eyes of Jesus as a way of blackmailing him to perform tricks and magic.

Then there was Jesus himself . . . the unresisting victim. It appeared he didn't even try to fight, to take charge, at least to escape. And then the cross . . . the naked ignominy of the cross. The whole rush of events "the first time through" seemed to admit of only one interpretation: It was a time of pure disaster —pure, unadulterated disaster. It was a time in which the noble and mighty endeavor which they had envisioned for Jesus had been washed down the drain. It was a time when his whole ministry had been reduced to zeroes and negatives.

The Second Time Through

On the occasion of his imminent ascension, however, with the knowledge of his resurrection also fresh in the disciples' minds, Jesus helps them go back through it all again. He jogs their minds with words that must have seemed familiar. Luke tells us, "He opened their minds to understand the scriptures, and said to them, 'Thus it is written, that the Christ should suffer and on the third day rise from the dead!' " It is obvious now that the way the disciples saw things "the first time through" must give way to a new and ennobled understanding. They must travel the road of those events twice to see, not a Jesus reduced to weakness, but a Jesus manifesting his power and pursuing his purpose in ways so strange that they cannot understand without his help and explanation.

As we stand with the disciples in the moment of Jesus' impending ascension, can we turn around too and look back through the resurrection to see Jesus' suffering and death in a new way? Can we for a moment look at his suffering and death and see in them, not a Jesus shredded, pulverized, and debilitated, but a

Jesus actively exerting a power over human affairs in ways unexpected and unforeseen, and therefore difficult to detect? To be sure, he is a victim of events which seem to crush him, wipe him out, and reduce him to a jumble of bones. But when looking again, when traveling the road of those events twice, when seeing them through the resurrection, when sensitized by the instruction of the one who is about to ascend to the right hand of his Father, we begin to see, in fact, one who is manifesting great power. Quietly and inconspicuously he shows that power as he sets his face against the chill winds of friendships grown cold and against the hot winds of men angry with hate.

Consider what would have issued from those events had Jesus displayed his power in any other way. If in power—as we normally think of it—he had slapped those who slapped him, there would have been no chance for his reconciling power to regain those men. If he in power—as we normally understand it—had denied those who denied him, there would have been no way to draw them to himself again. If he in power—as we normally describe it—had spit at those who spit at him, had lashed at those who whipped him, and finally, had even killed those who killed him, there would have been no power—manifested in any manner—which could have become a reconciling force among men.

We are not looking at a weak Jesus. We are not looking at a scared Jesus. We are not looking at a Jesus who can't help himself. We are looking, rather, at a Jesus who displays a power almost beyond our detection, because he displays his power in ways we don't consider normal. He is facing people and events with a power by which there can ultimately be rescue and reconciliation and restoration between God and people, between one person and another person.

A Power to Forgive

Because of such power, exerted in uncommon and unexpected ways, the ascending Jesus can make to his disciples a most uncommon and unexpected announcement: "It is written that the Christ should suffer and on the third day rise from the dead, *and that repentance and forgiveness of sins should be preached in his name to all nations, beginning from Jerusalem.*"

We all know from our own experience what power it takes to forgive. Thus, when we talk about a forgiveness that comes from God and issues to all nations, that forgiveness must be backed by a power which has experienced the worst humans can offer and still not quit. Jesus fashioned that kind of forgiveness and he did it by exercising a steady, quiet, inconspicuous power in the face of whippings, tongue-lashings, sufferings, and even death.

When we travel the same road twice and see our Lord manifesting such power and understand the necessity of it all, then we, too, are prepared to accept from our ascended Lord the power which he was shortly to give to his waiting disciples and still gives to us today. Luke records Jesus' parting words: "Behold, I send the promise of my Father upon you; but stay in the city, until you are clothed with power from on high."

What sort of power was this to be? How precisely we can give an answer! It was the power to understand clearly the meaning of his suffering, death, and resurrection! It was the power to share a message, a message dubbed as scandalous by some and snubbed as foolishness by other. It was the power to forgive the sins of others on earth. It was the power to approach people in love. It was the power to know right from wrong, the power to give up that which hurts and pursue that which helps, the power to avoid that which destroys and to commit oneself to that which builds up. In short, the power which was to come from on high were the gifts of the Spirit of God, all given so that God *through people* might continue to change others with his unexpected power. Listen to the gifts of power which God gives: Love . . . joy . . . peace . . . patience . . . kindness . . . goodness . . . faithfulness . . . gentleness . . . self-control! (Gal. 5:22)

What power is evident in those gifts! . . . the very power which we as Christ's church need and can have to carry out his mission on earth. It is that steady power evident within Jesus when he said to those who nailed him to the cross, "Father, forgive them, because they don't know what they are doing!" It is that awesome power present in the heart of Stephen when he prayed in the midst of stones crashing about his ears, "Father, forgive them, because they don't know what they are doing!" It is the power which the Apostle Paul knew followers of Jesus could count on when he give them this advice: "Ask God to bless those who persecute you; yes, ask him to bless, not to curse. . . . If someone does evil to you, do not pay him back with evil. Try to do what all men consider to be good. Do everything possible, on your part, to live at peace with all men" (Rom. 12:14-18; cf. Luke 6:27ff.).

The call of our ascended Lord to understand his power, to see his power, to receive his power, and to use his power becomes plain to us as we, in concluding this sermon, pray the words of an individual who understood well the work God had given him:

Lord, make me an instrument of your peace.
Where there is hatred, let me sow love;
Where there is injury, pardon;
Where there is doubt, faith;
Where there is despair, hope;
Where there is darkness, light;
Where there is sadness, joy.
O Divine Master,
grant that I may not so much seek to be consoled,
as to console;
To be understood, as to understand;
To be loved, as to love;
For it is in giving that we receive;
It is in pardoning that we are pardoned;
And it is in dying that we receive eternal life.

(Francis of Assisi)

RICHARD T. HINZ
Southeastern District, LCMS
Washington, D.C.

THE CHURCH HAS A FUTURE

Seventh Sunday of Easter
John 17:1-11

Last Thursday we celebrated Ascension Day. While the event of Jesus' ascension occupies only a few lines at the end of the Gospel of Luke and in the first chapter of the Acts, it has a double significance. It marks the end of the earthly life of Jesus of Nazareth and the beginning of the reign of Christ, his coronation as king.

This Sunday, which immediately follows Ascension Day, is known in the church as Expectation Sunday. Jesus has ascended and his disciples were left alone. He had blessed them and left them. Before their eyes he was lifted up into heaven.

We would expect that seeing him leave would fill their hearts with sorrow and dismay. Not so! Instead they return to Jerusalem with great joy and they remain in the temple praying and blessing God.

Their Master had told them to wait for the coming of the

Holy Spirit and they waited. They believed in the promise so they obeyed. What has happened is that their eyes have been opened. They know their Master lives, that he reigns, and that he is at the right hand of God, and this joyful certainty is stronger than separation and waiting.

The apostles have learned to look at Christ rather than at themselves. What the promised Holy Spirit meant, they did not know. What they did know was that they had witnessed Jesus' death on the cross, that he had risen from the grave, and that he had shared the risen life with them.

Fear had been dispelled and confidence restored because "he had shown himself alive to them in many ways and appeared to them repeatedly," and had talked to them about his future and their future.

Jesus' Future

Jesus said, "My work is to do the will of my Father" and "I must work the works of him who sent me." That was his passion. And the passion to do the work the Father gave him to do led him to the cross. Indeed, the climax of his work was the cross.

Rather than deny the cross, he gloried in it. The high priestly prayer which is the Gospel for today, is a song of praise, adoration, and thanksgiving. There was no other way for Jesus to be glorified, so he prayed, "Father, the hour has come; glorify thy Son that the Son may glorify thee."

Eight separate times the word "glorify" or "glorified" or "glory" occurs in this prayer. It runs like a thread of gold that holds the prayer together. Here is no unwilling victim dragged to the altar; but one who offers himself freely, holding back nothing, making no conditions.

Jesus makes two requests of his Father. The first that he may so meet the hour that has come that his Father might be glorified through him. And, the second that through him the legacy of eternal life might be left to those "you have given to me."

These two requests were enjoined with four claims Jesus makes for himself, as he gives account of his stewardship to his Father:

—I have made known your name to the men whom you gave me.
—I have taught them all I delivered from you.
—I have protected by the power of your name those whom you have given me.
—I have given them your word.

Jesus came to announce the fact of the Father, to reveal the Father's love and to be the Father's grace to man. He sought no credit line for himself. It was credit enough—yes, his joy—to make known the Father's name, to teach what he had received, to stay by those the Father had given him, to make sure they received the Father's word, and to be assured that his work would go on.

Without the cross Jesus could not have said "Mission accomplished." Without the cross there would have been no return to the Father. The Cross was the way back. The last two words from the cross were, "Mission accomplished" and "I am coming home."

In exalting Jesus to His right hand the Father placed all the future in his hands. "Therefore God has highly exalted him and bestowed on him the name which is above every name, that at the name of Jesus every knee should bow, in heaven and on earth and under the earth, and every tongue confess that Jesus Christ is Lord, to the glory of God the Father" (Phil. 2:8-11).

The Disciples' Future

Today's Epistle gives us a picture of the apostles looking into heaven just after the ascension. But two men in white robes send them back to their work in the world. Earth rather than heaven is the place where they are to witness and live in obedience.

The apostles who are assembled in the upper room after the ascension are not yet the church in the full meaning of the word. To become the church, empowered and equipped to do their work, they must receive the outpouring of the Holy Spirit.

The apostles were well aware of this. They remembered their master's word of promise and his ringing voice of confidence in their future before he ascended, "You shall receive power when the Holy Spirit has come upon you; and you will be my witnesses in Jerusalem and in all Judea and Samaria, and to the end of the earth."

We have seen God humble himself by taking the form of a human being and concealing himself under the figure of the suffering and crucified servant. And we see him now humbling himself and allowing his disciples to represent him and be his witnesses. His story would be their story.

Jesus never doubted they could carry on the work he gave them to do. Ordinary men they were, to be sure, but ordinary men imbued with the power of the Holy Spirit.

What a story theirs is in word and action and obedience and sacrifice, as St. Luke tells it in the Acts of the Apostles. They were indeed his men who had in their hearts and hands "the harps of God," were joyous in their calling, were scarred but victorious, wounded but radiant.

They were well aware of how weak and unworthy they were of themselves but they staked their future on him who was their Lord. Come what may, nothing could separate them from the love of God in Christ Jesus. He gave them their future! And they pressed on to the high calling that was theirs!

The Church's Future

There are those who ask, "Why does the Acts of the Apostles end in the middle, with St. Paul in prison awaiting sentence?" We like success stories. Undoubtedly, St. Luke ends the story where he does because he wants to make known that discipleship is costly and because it is a continuing story until the end of time. Until he comes again the story must read, "to be continued."

Jesus has entrusted his work, not to the disciples only, but to the church that came into being with the outpouring of the Holy Spirit. Until the end of time Christ continues to act through the ongoing life and witness of that body which he claims as his own.

But one thing is certain, the church never has and never will *possess* the Holy Spirit. It can only keep praying that God will give it the Spirit. It can only wait for the Spirit in faith, knowing that without the Spirit its preaching, its work, and its witness are all in vain.

And no guarantee of perennial existence is given to the historical churches. They can be rejected and die. All we know is that God's plan, God's unfolding purpose, cannot be thwarted because of human unfaithfulness. He will not leave himself without witnesses. He will lead history to its ultimate fulfillment through the church, which is Christ's body.

In his Letter to the Romans, we find St. Paul asking what it means to be part of the Church. It means, he says, being received into the death of Christ in order to walk in the newness of life. It means being transformed through self-loss into that body which is indwelt and ruled by the Holy Spirit. It means crisis, a costly change. It means the battleground of the human soul, whether God shall be God or man shall be his own God, has been fought and won. It means the Holy Spirit has had his way with them. It means unconditioned surrender.

"Present yourselves as alive from the dead," says St. Paul, "and your members, all that you have, and every bit of you, as instruments and tools in his hands for his purposes." That is St. Paul's standard of churchmanship. That is the kind of life into which he conceives his converts are baptized—and there is something vigorous about it. As Daniel T. Niles, of blessed memory, put it, "We are witnesses of God primarily by being part of the evidence ourselves."

We build up the church best, not by mere restructuring or reordering of priorities, desirable as this may be, but by opening ourselves more and more to that Spirit God who is among us as one that serves and reaches out through his church in witness and service to all men everywhere.

If we roll up the talent of love in a nice white napkin of piety and put it safely out of the way, sorry that the world is so hungry and thirsty, so sick and enslaved, and leave it at that, we may have to discover at the crucial moment that we are spiritually bankrupt. From him that has shall be taken away even that which he has. History bears witness to what happened to a self-serving church.

It is a critical moment now for the church of Christ; and that means for each Christian, because we are the church. At the same time it remains one of the most encouraging and uplifting things in the world, that Jesus put his trust and confidence in people like ourselves. We dare not disavow that trust and confidence. In spite of human weaknesses and sins we go forward under his high command.

But always we must remember that the reality and future of the church do not abide in us. The church is not a spiritual Rotary Club. The church's reality and future abide in the one God, whose triune Spirit fills it by filling each one of its members.

The church has a future!

The important question is: Are you and I living members of the church which is his Body? Do you and I have a future?

THEODORE E. MATSON
President, Wisconsin-Upper Michigan Synod—LCA
Milwaukee, Wisconsin

PEACE AND POWER

The Day of Pentecost
John 20:19-23

Do you think you can identify with the ten disciples who were hiding for fear of their lives? Try to enter into the midst of their concerns. Whenever we read the Bible we should try to make it our story. "To make it my story means I do not have any neat little immunities. I cannot like Dante in the *Inferno,* be unsinged by the fires, or like an astronaut, walk around in a space suit. The Bible becomes me" (Karl Olsson).

Let me give you an example. A few years ago Oswald Hoffman, "The Lutheran Hour" preacher, came to Kansas City and was interviewed for the six o'clock news. My phone rang. The voice on the other end of the line asked if I had heard what Dr. Hoffman had to say about black people and white people learning to live together. Before I could respond, the caller launched into a racist tirade. When he paused, asking my opinion of his remarks, I replied I hadn't heard anything so un-Christian for several days. Bang went the receiver. But he rang right back saying (and I'll edit out the part I don't want you to hear), "1 John 1:5, God is light and in him is no darkness."

By way of contrast, one Saturday I heard Eddie Hargett, quarterback for the Houston Oilers, speak a few words about his faith at a Fellowship of Christian Athletes breakfast. As a boy he was afraid of the dark. When he would go to the barn to tend the stock or fetch an armload of wood, he kept one eye on the light shining from the kitchen, in which he knew there was safety and love. Eddie Hargett likened his days before he was a Christian to a fearful groping in the dark. And he quoted 1 John 1:5—"God is light and in him is no darkness." That young man tries to make the Bible his own story. The other man tried to make his own story read like holy scripture.

So, if you can place yourself in the story you are more likely to find the gospel there. There are two gospel words that come to us from the compassionate Christ. The first is

A Comforting Word

When Jesus suddenly appeared to his fearful followers it was a thrilling moment of confidences restored. What a strong, saving word for them to hear: "Peace be with you." From that moment on the Master would resume his power in their lives. The glorified Lord would use them and succeeding generations of fragile human beings to extend his love to all mankind.

Imagine how they must have been nearly out of their minds by the dramatic turn of events. The cross was not the end after all, it was a beginning. Now the lessons they learned about feeding the sheep and forgiving 490 times began to make sense.

They could see by the disfiguring hands and speared side that he was the crucified one. He had, in fact, conquered death. He was back with them, just like old times. Except he was now glorified and powerful. His word of comfort overcame their crisis of confidence. His claims were right; his teachings were true. The powers of sin, death, and despair had been overcome by the certainty of love's way and eternal life. A miracle happened that night. Ten spiritually exhausted men, for all practical purposes dead, were brought back to life by the compassionate Christ.

I hope you can see yourselves in these verses, because there is a word of comfort for anyone whose confidence is shaky, whose doubts are large and faith is small.

Peace Be With You

Especially if you have lost a family member recently. How can you cope with this awful emptiness, this silence, this vacuum, this despair which flattens you?

Someone here this morning is not well, and is thinking: "For too long I have been incapacitated, resting and waiting for my body to mend. But I can't take it much longer. I hate being on the shelf. I want to be useful." Waiting to get well is wearisome.

Perhaps you face an important decision. How do you get your head on straight so that your own selfishness does not impede doing the right thing? It's not a matter of black and white; not everybody can win. But one direction has to be more right than another.

You are dying. You know it. Your doctor knows it. Your friends suspect it is so. Medicines are less helpful. So is therapy. Oh, for an injection that would take away the pain of irreversible dying.

Someone in our midst is losing love. The person you want to live with more than anything is slipping away before your very eyes. Can anything pull it together again? Your heart is heavy with guilt. Your enthusiasm for divorce is zero.

So you've been fired! Literally had the rug pulled out from under you. It's like falling down a well, grasping for something to hang onto. Your pride is squashed. How easy it is for others to say it's but a temporary step toward something even better.

You're fed up. Why does it always have to be me who has to set the example? Why expect me to be the one with the patience of Job? It's somebody else's turn. I'm at the end of my rope, tired, kaput.

Are you able to find a place in the circle of disciples whose confidence was shattered? Then surely there is a word of comfort for you. God loves you. He wants to come to you and bless you with his Spirit.

Suffering Love

The root of the matter is a very simple, old-fashioned thing—it is love. Nathan Söderblom said, "The cross unveils, in its divine brutality, nothing less than God's own love." Jesus died a malefactor for all to see. What is unseen is the heart of God burning with desire to save us all. What is unseen and yet can be trusted is the will of the compassionate Christ to take hold of every man, woman, and child who suffers or is afraid.

His "Peace be with you" is a confidence restoring Word. It gives you something to believe in. His love is stronger than your unbelieving heart. It alone can conquer the forces of cunning and confusion that threaten to rob you of your life.

It is the loving God who redeemed, bought, and won you, from all sins, from death and the devil's power, not with gold or silver, but with his holy and precious blood and his innocent suffering and death; that you might belong to him, live and have your being under him in his kingdom, and serve him in eternal righteousness, innocence and blessedness, even as he is risen from the dead, and lives and reigns forevermore.

A Commanding Word

The second word from the compassionate Christ is a commanding word. Jesus breathed on them saying, "Receive the Holy Spirit." The chosen apostles were given a new power—the power of the Spirit—which changed every situation in which they were placed. The word from the Lord today is this—the same supernatural power is your inheritance and mine.

"It is this power and only this," writes Evelyn Underhill, "which can bring in the Christian society of which we hear so much." We ought to pray for it, expect it, and trust it. If the Christian Church wants to do something about its own confidence problems, it will not be by better organization, but by power. Do you remember the *heart* of the account of Pentecost? Was it wind and fire and speaking in tongues? No, it was power! It was a power that captured the apostles and sent them out as victorious witnesses to the saving love of God.

Perhaps you prefer the comforting word but not the commanding one. Well, no matter how earnest you may be about receiving the Holy Spirit, little actual power will be given to those who have cold feet about going where the Spirit leads. Colin Morris says it straight: "True conversion ought not to waft the convert away on pink clouds of religiosity, but transform the pressure points of his daily life." The comfort and command of Christ go together.

You probably know there is a good deal of interest in the Holy Spirit these days. In fact it has grown in scope to what is called the neo-Pentecostal movement. While there is much that is to be commended in this movement, a glaring weakness is apparent. Seekers and doers of pentecostal things often sail away on pink clouds of religiosity and give little attention to putting their gifts to work in ministering to the people for whom Christ died. So if the pentecostal movement declines it will be because the followers forgot about proving the love of Christ by serving others.

The gospel is God's love for you, that's true. But it is more. It is God's love for the entire world. He loves this suffering, despairing, unconverted world so much that he gave his Son for it. To you who have been baptized, who have received the promised power for confident living, who trust in God for forgiveness and life eternal—to you is also given a great commission: Go, witness, love, serve; shepherd the scattered sheep; transform the pressure points of daily life. Peace and Power. Amen.

JACK F. HUSTAD
First Lutheran Church
Fergus Falls, Minnesota

THE TRIUNE GOD — PRESENCE, PURPOSE, PROMISE

The Holy Trinity — First Sunday after Pentecost
Matthew 28:16-20

I'm quite sure that no one has to convince anyone today of the importance of energy, for industry, defense, business, home, and transportation. Energy is vital, indispensable.

Naturally, then, it is vital and indispensable to find new sources of energy, and people are working around the clock to do just that. Once we have to say that there are no more sources, that's it, friends. We walk again.

Physical energy is important. Society recognizes its need for all that it can offer to life and activity. But it can't begin to compare with the spiritual energy that saves life. Because it does just that—saves life, makes life possible, tolerable, and eternal—it is the most vital and valuable energy of all.

Where do you find this energy? In yourself? Hardly. In science? No, as the bromide goes, we can get to the moon, but we can't quit smoking, drinking, or eating ourselves to death. We can fly to the moon, but we can't live with our husbands and wives. We can't raise our kids to live full, rich lives, above delinquency. We can get around in space, but we can't keep the water pure, the atmosphere breathable, or the world at peace. We don't know how to live.

Where do you find the life-making, life-saving energy? In occultism, in astrology, in the gurus and maharajas of today's hottest fads? In a god, in some gods? Well, now we're getting remotely close, at least to the concept.

Obviously, there's only one source of this kind of energy, and that is the true, triune God. From him and him alone comes the power-pak that creates and sustains life that is. This is Trinity Sunday, and the reality of the only God, the true God, Father, Son, and Holy Spirit, is and always will be the greatest lift available to our lives. Let's talk about our God as the producer of the power-pak that saves lives.

The Presence of Jesus

The first facet of the power-pak is the powerful presence. It is the presence of Jesus of Nazareth, who was crucified, dead, and buried. Yet, here he stands and says, "All authority in heaven and on earth has been given to me," and also, "I am with you always, to the close of the age." His followers had exclaimed about his presence on a number of occasions. What manner of man is this whom even the wind and waves obey! What manner of man who drives out evil spirits! Who raises the dead! Now they are faced with the manner of man who himself is raised from a death that was for them and for all people. What kind of presence is this? Presence to save and restore! This is the living presence that can do what no force on earth can do—remove the stain of sin and guilt from any and all—forgiving the Peters and John Marks, the fearful and traitorous, the self-sufficient, the selfish and materialistic, removing their guilt and waiving their punishment, because this Presence became guilty for them and died to absorb their punishment. This presence rose again to prove beyond doubt that he had been successful.

As a result, this familiar Presence was a totally new Presence and conveyed the assurance that he had done what no amount of political maneuvering could do, namely, reconcile an angry God to an ungrateful and rebellious world. None of the big wigs, the kings or emperors, could arrange this. The man who suffered and who died innocently was the one who could, and his resurrected Presence said that he did.

This Presence was able to do what no human institution could even begin to do—change a man and his way of life. The most immediate and notable example of this were his followers—once wavering, fearful, undirected—now solid, full of conviction, loyal, completely sure of themselves and where they were going.

And, finally, this Presence could and did do what no psychotherapy on earth could do—give total happiness to his people. He had said, "You will grieve when I die, but when you see me again, your joy will be full." As he stands with them on the familiar hill in Galilee, and even after he ascended back into heaven, there was nothing missing in the completeness of their happiness. He went on high, but he left them high, and they stayed high with him the rest of their lives, no matter how rough their everyday adventure in his name turned out to be.

The powerful Presence was and is able to bless and protect; to bless with all that God is and has to offer and to protect against all threats and enemies in all of life's complex situations. No matter if the world misunderstands and rejects; no matter if the price of the Christian life is high; the Presence says, "It's worth it." The Presence says, "Right on."

The Presence says, "Don't worry." "You've got me! We've got it all together! It's all ours! My Father confirms it! The Spirit proclaims it! Believe it! Enjoy it!"

The Presence sustains and transfigures. The road is long and hard. The Presence helps us press on, reminding us of the great goal, giving us the mountaintop experiences, showing us his glory, promising us the ultimate in beauty, satisfaction, and fulfillment in the life to come, transfiguring our weakness to strength, our fear to confidence, our unimportance to the greatest meaning, and our defeats to victory. "All authority is mine," says the Presence, "and the Father, the Spirit, and I will never leave you."

A Sense of Purpose

The second facet of the power-pak is a sense of purpose. One of the differences in the followers of Jesus Christ after his resurrection was this sense of purpose, something they didn't have before. Purpose is power. A well-aimed and purpose-directed life is potent stuff. An aimless life, even with all kinds of gifts and abilities, had no punch. This is what St. Paul meant when he wrote: "I don't just shadow-box when I fight." In other words, he knew what and where to hit and he did it hard and constantly.

The purpose, of course, is life itself—to display it, by word and example, and to share it by urging others to accept it and become followers—disciples, to celebrate it together in gatherings, as church, the body of Christ.

The powerful purpose offers its powerful instruments to our life and work—the means of God's love, the Word, "all things which I have given you," and the Sacraments, notably Baptism in the name of the Father, Son, and Holy Spirit. Using these instruments, one can't fail in accomplishing his purpose, which is to spread the power around which helps people to recognize and celebrate the presence.

The Powerful Promise

The third facet of the power-pak is the powerful promise. There is the promise of the name, the name of the true and living God. God's name is his reputation, justly earned over centuries of mighty acts, centering around his greatest act—the redemption of all people through Jesus Christ. The Father made the world and made the plan to restore it when it became corrupted by sin. Jesus, the Son, came down to this earthly workshop in the work clothes of our nature to hammer out the product of salvation by living, dying, and rising again for us.

The Holy Spirit brings the impact of that plan into our lives by the gospel and helps us accept it and be personally reconciled. These are his mighty acts. This is his name. A Christian is saturated with that name, literally, in Baptism. He is wrapped in those mighty acts by the inspiration of and instruction in the gospel which sustains faith in the mighty acts. This is a daily promise. These acts will come through for you, on Monday morning, Thursday afternoon, and Saturday night, not to mention Sunday! This name will bring you all the good it has delivered to all those who rested on, trusted, lived, and died in it. No one who has ever called on the name has been disappointed in it.

There is also the promise of the imperative. Go—make disciples. Jesus Christ never told anyone to do what can't be done. If he says "Do the impossible," it will happen! You can't do it alone, but, then you are never alone.

And that brings us the final promise: the promise of the involvement. When Jesus Christ says, "I am with you always, to the close of the age," he's not just saying that he'll be there to watch, or even just to encourage. He'll be there as an active participant. You won't be alone, witnessing to his presence— he'll be giving you the words. You won't be alone, convincing anyone of his sin; his spirit will. You won't have to convert anyone to faith. He'll take care of that. This is sheer power, this promise.

Our true, triune God is alive, active, and powerful beyond imagination. What a joy that we can pray, "O Lord, who usest Thy power chiefly in showing mercy!" Make full use of the powerpak of your faith in the living, triune God. Amen.

EUGENE F. GRUELL
St. Matthew's Lutheran Church
Miami, Florida

IN NAME ONLY

Second Sunday after Pentecost
Matthew 7:21-29

Please note at the outset that this is the concluding portion of that section of scripture known as the Sermon on the Mount. This sermon will concentrate on the first few verses of the section, beginning with the twenty-first. "Not everyone who says to me 'Lord, Lord' shall enter the kingdom of heaven, but he who does the will of my father who is in heaven. On that day many will say to me 'Lord, Lord, did we not prophesy in your name, and cast out demons in your name, and do many mighty works in your name?' Then I will declare to them 'I never knew you. Depart from me, you evil-doers.' "

It's a difficult text, particularly this first portion, and I want to speak to it at the risk of producing what might appear to be an almost totally negative sermon. "On that day many will say to me, 'Lord, Lord, did we not prophesy in your name, and cast out demons in your name, and do many mighty works in your name?' "

The first question which comes to mind is: "How can someone who does mighty works, even casts out demons, in the name of Jesus Christ be excluded from the very kingdom of our Lord?" Of all people, isn't he *doing* the will of God?

To begin with, perhaps that's the wrong question, and we need to be reminded that for the wrong question there is no right answer. When you have trouble solving problems, you might first ponder, "Am I asking the right question?"

I would like to suggest that perhaps the right question might be: "What did Jesus mean by using this illustration in relation to a concept of salvation? Why did he pick this illustration and what did he mean?" We cannot assume that he meant good works were unimportant. We cannot assume that he meant it was okay to be passive in one's Christian faith. So let us tackle the problem. What did Jesus mean by being so specific and direct in talking about works and salvation?

I would like to offer three ideas. First: Everything that's done in the name of Jesus is not done because of commitment to the will of God. Secondly: the right thing done for the wrong reasons does not enhance the kingdom of God. Third: not all activists, automatically, are examples of disciplined disciples.

Nominal Commitment

Speaking to the first idea, trying to focus again on this particular concern of Jesus, I'd like to say that there are many things done in the name of Jesus that are just nominal, and nothing more. It is possible to be related to a person, or to a group, or to a situation, or to an activity, *in name only*. As I read the scripture it appears that one of the favorite tricks of the Pharisees was to hide behind their ancestry. When confronted with the truth by Jesus, which demanded a response and a commitment, they would hide behind the statement, "We are Abraham's children," and resent his confronting them. Or, as you recall, they said, "Moses is our father," and made it clear that they didn't need Jesus.

You see, I believe that a child can bear the family name and not the family will. I believe that there were people in Jesus' day who were children of Abraham in name only, and that's what Jesus was trying to say. In the course of events there may be things done in the name of someone, something, some group, and that's all. It is possible to be related in name only. I am suggesting that this applies to some "Christians" and to the work they do.

Many people have a nominal—that is, in name only—relationship to the church of Jesus Christ and believe that that fact assures their salvation. They forget that salvation is by grace alone to which the Christian responds in worship. The name-only membership is meaningless.

Thinking churchmen have always questioned such things as

the efficacy of baptism, which is done only in the name of Jesus. Baptism according to the will of God, in my reading of the holy scriptures, is the result of commitment and obedience. It is closely related to worship and to the sacrament of Holy Communion. Parents who bring their children for baptism only because they (the parents) were once baptized, and who think their child's baptism is the parents' only responsibility to their offspring, need to be confronted with this idea. Pastors who perform baptisms for non-worshiping "Christians" need to interpret this passage in light of their ministerial act.

Thus it is possible to do something in the name of Jesus, something good like baptism, and still not be in the right relationship —that is, the faith relationship, the grace relationship—with our Lord Jesus Christ. So the first idea: everything done in the name of Jesus is not done because of commitment to the will of God.

The Right Thing—The Wrong Reason

The right thing done for the wrong reason does not enhance the kingdom of God. By that I mean that motivation has many roots. Personal ambition can cause a person to join a church. Institutional preservation, including the self-preservation of a fellowship become corporation, can push people to give. Cultural tradition motivates some and patriotic loyalty others. These I submit have all been used wrongly as a means of doing things "for" God. How many crimes—and how clearly history records them!—have been committed *in the name of* Jesus Christ! And conversely—how many outwardly good deeds have been wrongly done—that is, without the saving relationship! It is possible to do the right thing for the wrong reason, but that does not enhance the kingdom of God or fulfill his will.

If selfishness in the form of greater profits or more business causes me to perform an act of kindness, the recipient of the kindness is helped, but the kingdom of God is not thereby enhanced. When fear or publicity causes me to do a deed of helpfulness, I am not thereby relating myself through that deed to the kingdom of God.

Many things are being done, people are being helped—but not all helpful acts are Christian. It's not things and deeds—but the kingdom—that need attention. Heathen humans can be helpful. But "on that day" the question is one of relationships (the right reason) producing the fruit (the right act) for the purpose of the kingdom.

Not All Activists, Automatically . . .

Now the third idea notes that not all activists are automatically examples of disciplined disciples. I am very sensitive that this not be misunderstood. Someone may think again that one can be a Christian without being active. Perhaps our way of life tends to encourage salvation by doing, by busyness. And how often our cultural way of living determines our Christian life style!

But the point still remains that just by being active, by being a do-gooder, one is not necessarily to be called by the name Christian. To do good is not an end in itself. "A good tree *must* bring forth good fruit," Jesus says—even if it rots. So then the relationship is as important as the product. To be a disciple means to be in a particular relationship, and the relationship does produce fruit.

Even in the Old Testament (in Deuteronomy 11) we read that the Word of God was to be a part of life in many ways—worn as a frontlet, spoken of in the family, read on the streets—literally to be "lived." Though the acts could be perverted and performed only for their own sake, the purpose was to infuse them into the life style of the chosen people.

So all of the active "run-around" people are not necessarily disciples of Jesus Christ. It's not a two-way door. This is difficult with our Aristotelian logic, but true according to the scripture as I see it. It is possible to have, as Elton Trueblood says, a cut-flower civilization—where we see the result and want to hold it to ourselves, selfishly forgetting the root. And the relationship has to be that of the tree and the fruit. The relationship has to be between the root and the flower.

Discipleship as a Christian relates a believer to Christ as his master—the discipline of the mind—of the spirit—of the emotions. Christ went regularly to the temple—for reading, discussion. His was a life of prayer, private and corporate. His discipline of emotion was not to submerge feelings but to channel them—his compassion on the crowd, his weeping over Jerusalem, his sweat in the garden. He did act—helpfully toward people, but relationally toward his Father. And we who bear his name must be disciplined as his disciples.

Thus it was natural for Jesus to state plainly that salvation and entrance into the kingdom were a combination of hearing and doing. He went on to relate the story of the two houses—a sermon for another time. I believe we can be motivated positively, even by the negative illustration of our Lord. By understanding Christ's judgment on those who twisted and perverted the meaning and the means of salvation, we are reminded of the goodness and grace of our relationship.

When writing to the Roman Christians, Paul emphasized the grace of God as a gift—apart from works and deeds. "Then what becomes of our boasting?" he asks. Was he perhaps thinking of those who would say, "Did we not do this and that for you—in your name?" We are justified by grace as a gift, through the redemption in Jesus Christ.

My hope and prayer is that you and I will be encouraged to do what we hear because of what we have been given in our baptism by God's grace. That's what makes it joyful to be alive and to move out into the adventures (which include some of the storms) of life, but knowing that our relationship is secure and our actions are fruitful—for the kingdom.

"Not everyone who *says* to me, 'Lord, Lord,' shall enter the kingdom of heaven, but he who does the will of my Father who is in heaven."

T. A. YOUNGQUIST
Faith Lutheran Church
Glen Ellyn, Illinois

SO CLOSE AND YET SO FAR

Third Sunday after Pentecost
Matthew 9:9-13

Some time ago I came upon a man and overheard him praying: "Lord, at times you can be so close and then again at other times you can be so far away. Does it have to be this way? Lord, teach us the meaning of this tension." Our theme is rooted in our text, and the words of this prayer are the immediate occasion which triggered it.

Why So Many Churches?

You live in a typical American community with many churches in your neighborhood or city. You have visited them on occasion at weddings, funerals and public services. You have sensed differences and diversity among them. How would you characterize the diversity which you have observed? I would suggest that two emphases are basic rallying points. Some of them take seriously that God comes to us through earthly elements. In other words, God is close at hand and comes to us through the words of an old book and through water, bread and wine. The language of the

Bible is that God comes to us through the medium of flesh. Sometimes we give a technical name to this emphasis and call it the sacramental principle.

When you have visited other churches, there is little to suggest that God comes to us through earthly elements. In times past, the simplicity of the altar has been a reminder that the Lord is distant. As you listened to their sermons and sang their hymns, you were reminded that the only way you could lay hold upon the Lord was through personal faith. At the same time, you felt that this Lord was very distant. In the event you learned to know some of these neighbors as persons, you may have discovered that the Lord was hidden in them and that they could be a kind of sacrament.

Similar Differences in Old Testament

In our first lesson, Hosea is speaking to this same issue. In the name of the Lord, the prophet asserts: I "desire love not sacrifice; I desire knowledge of God and not burnt offerings." Hosea lived and worked in what was called the Northern Kingdom. By the time Hosea came along, lots of water had passed under the bridge. One might say that many salient events had taken place. For example, Jacob and his sons had gone down to Egypt where they became a nation and a threat to Pharaoh. This led to their oppression and they cried unto the Lord for liberation. The Lord raised up Moses to lead them out of Egypt. At Mount Sinai, the Lord entered into a relationship with them which is called the covenant. The wilderness journey continued for the better part of forty years, and Moses died in the land of Moab. Joshua took over and was the leader in the next event, the conquest of Canaan, where the people settled.

Many of these people settled around Shechem in the north. After some time Shiloh and then Bethel became the central northern place of worship. Their priests were Levites, who took seriously the covenant which their fathers embraced at Sinai. Their motto was the word, which Moses had spoken in the name of the Lord at Sinai: "You have seen what I did to the Egyptians, and how I bore you on eagles' wings and brought you to myself. Now therefore, if you will obey my voice and keep my covenant, you shall be my own possession among all peoples; for all the earth is mine, and you shall be to me a kingdom of priests and a holy nation" (Exodus 19:4-6). This meant that they understood their relationship to God in conditional terms and that every member of this community thought of himself as a priest and as accountable to God. This did create a democratic spirit and may explain in part why the monarchy never caught on in the north. Hosea was a northerner, and he sensed something of the infinite distance which separated himself from the Lord.

Sons of Aaron as Southern Priests

Another group of people settled in the south at Hebron, where Abraham had lived at a much earlier time. God had entered into a covenant with Abraham, and it had a different emphasis. Genesis 12 and the chapters which follow make it clear that at the heart and center of this covenant were promises which created a sense of undying hope. Moses had a brother by the name of Aaron whose sons took over as priests at Hebron. Numbers 25 affirms that the sons of Aaron understood this covenant as a relationship which was made first with them as priests. This tended to transform them into authoritarian priests, and in a sense this helped to prepare for the monarchy in the south. It was here at Hebron that David began to rule. These sons of Aaron took their functions seriously as priests at Hebron and later at Jerusalem. This meant that they gave instruction and made sacrifices.

One of the most readable books on this topic is *The People of the Covenant* by Murray Newman. This author makes it clear that the whole assumption at Hebron and later at Jerusalem was that God was close at hand and pleased with these sacrifices. In the temple at Jerusalem, these sacrifices became more and more complicated. This posed the temptation, as time went on, to make them into an end of their own. God intended them to be equipment to serve a more ultimate purpose. In order to see and sense the subtle human tendency to make idols out of religious institutions, one needs a more ultimate perspective. The covenant which God entered into at Sinai gave these people a more ultimate perspective and was the basis of the reformation movements which the prophets championed. This is what Hosea is trying to point out when he challenged the people with the demands that the Lord wanted devotion and love, and not sacrifices. The purpose of God is to create a holy nation and a kingdom of priests. The sacrifices are means which the Lord will use unto this end. The criticism of the prophet is that the people have made them into an end and that, as such, they deflect from the more ultimate purpose.

Our Lord Identified as Prophet

In our Gospel text, our Lord called Matthew to be a disciple. He even entered the home of this social outcast who was a tax collector. The Pharisees, who were well meaning in many ways, objected. The reply of Jesus to them was that they who are whole do not need a physician but only those who are sick. Then our Lord quotes from Hosea these familiar words: "I desire mercy and not sacrifice." Furthermore, our Lord comes not to call the righteous but sinners to repentance. By these actions, Jesus placed himself in the company of the prophets and shared their ultimate perspective.

It is easy for us to take something which is good in itself and make it into a kind of idol. However, in order to see the full ministry of Jesus in perspective, we must remember that he instituted sacraments. In the words which are the basis for the Lord's Supper, he reminded the disciples that he intended to remain close at hand and that flesh and blood continue to be the medium of spiritual life.

We return again to the words of Jesus that they who are whole do not need a physician but only those who are sick. What then is this sickness? I am a victim of it and at the same time I am blind to it. This sickness is rooted in my relationship to God, who is the ultimate and distant one who made me. The Lord created me and is the source of my existence. He wants me to be with him forever and as such is the true end of my existence. In my rebellion, I have made myself into an end of its own. This is my sickness to which I am blind. This vertical relationship affects my horizontal relationships. When I cut myself off from my real and authentic security, it is inevitable that I try to create my own little securities. This leads to subtle and unending competition with my neighbors and brothers.

In our Epistle, the Apostle Paul shares this same prophetic perspective. He remembers that Abraham took God at his word, being "fully convinced that God was able to do what he had promised." Then he points out that faith in the gospel means faith in God's ability to do for us what we cannot do for ourselves. This faith encounters us at the very point of our rebellion and begins to restore us day by day to what God intended us to be. I am intended to be responsible before God and at the same time dependent upon him. This is why faith as dependence constitutes my true existence as a believer.

Prophets and Priests Are Still in Tension

The late H. Richard Niebuhr wrote a small book which he called *The Purpose of the Church and Its Ministry*. He pointed out that in the long history of the church there has been this emphasis on priests and sacraments. This tradition is informed by the conviction that God is close at hand and that he comes to us through the medium of flesh and blood. At the same time, there is prophetic criticism like that of Hosea, Jesus, and Paul in our texts. This tradition affirms that God is the ultimate and distant one who sits in judgment on our tendencies to make idols out of what may be good in itself. Prophetic criticism is directed against the tendency to make priestly activity an end of its own. In other words, God does not intend that we should escape from the tension between these two traditions. Rather we are to learn to live in this tension.

There is another significant book which relates to our topic. It is called *Obedient Rebel* by Jaroslav Pelikan. It is a study of Martin Luther in terms of these two traditions. As a young prophetic reformer, Luther rejected the tradition of the church and its emphasis upon the sacraments. At Worms, Germany, he took a firm stand for the authority of the Scriptures and our individual freedom to interpret them. Pelikan points out that to Luther's credit, he soon saw the dangers of individualistic interpretation. Tradition never again became a principle of authority for Luther. The Scriptures alone remained the normative authority. However, he returned to the tradition of the church in its long historical continuity as the necessary context in which biblical interpretation must take place. This tradition of the church included the sacramental life of the church. In this way, Luther began his work as a rebel and ended as an obedient rebel.

What Does This Mean for My Life?

Within the pages of the Bible I have met the Lord of heaven and earth. How can this Lord become concrete in history so that I can worship him? At the same time, he must retain for himself the ultimate qualities. If the Hebraic and Christian faith is to retain its integrity, it must sustain its sense of the ultimate. The God of the Bible spoke and through the medium of his Word created all that is. The entire creation is dependent upon him who acted through his creative Word. It is this Word which has become flesh and dwelt among us. The author of our Epistle calls this something new which has entered into this world of horizontal time a *new creation.* Paul also contends that baptism is God's act of incorporation and that his *new creation* is hidden among real people. There is a biblical exhortation which is rooted in this act of God in Christ. I must become in life what I am already in Christ. This kind of exhortation possesses a ring of authenticity. What has entered into this world and become concrete in history remains ultimate.

This is why the sacraments which Christ has given to us can not become an end. In baptism we are united with Christ in his death. His life does not end with death. In baptism we are united now with Christ in his resurrection. My baptism propels me to strive to become what I am already in Christ. My only hope is expressed in our Gospel. Our Lord says that he came not to call the righteous but sinners to repentance. In this life of striving I can appropriate this promise of forgiveness without feeling that I am a fake.

Baptism not only unites us with Christ; it also unites us with each other. It becomes the basis for a new community. My life is not complete apart from this community. In this community, I participate with others in celebration and I share their guilt and they share my guilt. This community was not very old when it began to make this confession about Christ: "He ascended to the right hand of God." This is not a place but a biblical metaphor for the power of God. As our brother, Christ is true man and is now at the root of power which upholds the universe. Christ has joined heaven with this earth. The ultimate One has become concrete in history.

Striving to become what I already am, is not a matter of climbing a ladder to a spiritual world. Rather in my rebellion, I have turned God off. Now God wants me to realize that here Christ is in, with and under bread and wine as I participate with the community in the celebration of the Supper he has instituted for us. These words of institution make personal the words of our Gospel which are their counterpart: "I came not to call the righteous but sinners to repentance." As he instituted this sacrament, our Lord said: "Given and shed for you for the remission of sins." These words—*for you*—pull back the veil so that we get a glimpse into the mystery of this sacrament.

God in Christ wants to meet us and raise us up into newness of life. On the one hand you can turn to Christ as you are; on the other hand he will never let you remain as you are. This is the nature of his presence among us.

John V. Halvorson
First Lutheran Church
Brookings, South Dakota

LET'S GET GOING

Fourth Sunday after Pentecost
Matthew 9:35—10:7

Why should we care what others do with their life? Why not let everybody figure that out for himself and reap the reward or take the consequences?

The parental adage is familiar: "I can't live your life for you. You yourself will have to make those choices—spouse, career, habitat—and live with them." Does that view also apply to religion?

Parents do, of course, subtly or overtly influence the choices their children make. Their own lives provide a likely pattern for their offspring to imitate. Deliberately and consciously most parents try to shape their children's attitudes towards life and help them build a perspective within which acceptable choices can be made. But wise parents try also to let each child make its own choices in significant matters.

Even when we grant this delicate balance between control and free choice in the relationship of parents and children, we have not thrown much light in the initial question when it is applied to those outside the family. Why should we care what others do with their life?

We will grant, of course, that teachers should care about their students' goals; employers should care what kind of conditions their employees live under; and governments should care about the citizens who are their constituency.

So the circle of care and concern broadens and widens. Where does it stop? The Christian view is that it does not stop. It encircles everyone. The demands of caring by one individual for others vary according to the relationship involved—that is, they are not identical simply because we care. But Christians, like Jesus Christ, want to care about everyone.

Today's epistle states Christ's concern and care for all people in sacrificial terms: He died, Romans 5 says, for the wicked; he died for us when we were yet sinners. By that death we are reconciled to God. Now it is up to us likewise to care about others actively, that is, not just in feeling concern or talking love but in care shown by action.

It's Time to Get Going

Our text sets Christian caring in a wide perspective. Jesus sent out his disciples to help people physically and spiritually.

Chiefly they were to help people free themselves from sickness and from spiritual ignorance and unbelief.

The time had come, Jesus indicated, for them to be more than disciples; they were to become teachers and doers of what they had themselves learned. The instruction Jesus gives them as reported by Matthew is extensive and detailed. They were to be alert, compassionate, ready for danger, and willing to be supported by others.

The immediate motivation for the directive from Jesus to his 12 disciples, who are carefully named, was that Jesus had himself just completed a tour of preaching and healing in many villages and synagogues. As he did this he realized the tremendous need of so many people, and he felt sorry for them.

His word to the 12 disciples was: "There are so many people who need help, and there are so few people who can help them who care about them. Pray God for helpers."

And then Jesus sent them out to do the work that needed doing: "Proclaim the good news," he said, "and help them in their human needs." Jesus told them it was time now to get going. They were not to wait for people to come to them; they were to seek them out in order to help them.

That's not the ideal counseling situation. But it is the work of evangelism. The Christian church is not just a city on a hill that cannot be hid and therefore attracts people. Individual Christians are not just to get their opportunity to help those who have seen their lives and actions and ask for help. They are to seek out people who are in spiritual need and do not know it, who are burdened with life's problems but do not go to God for help.

For the Christian every place and time affords its own special opportunity to glorify God. Whatever age he may be, whatever the condition of his health, whatever his education or job responsibility, he can look at life as a trust, a gift from God which provides his individual and unique opportunity. For that reason it's always time to get going for the Christian.

With such a view of life: as always ripe for harvest, always a time of opportunity. It could be that Christians would feel harassed and pressured. It is part of Jesus' instruction to his disciples to warn them that they will encounter misunderstanding, antagonism, and even violence when they live as he directs. But he assures them they need not feel unprotected because the Father's hand is over them, and he will supply the words they need.

The people without trust in God have reason to feel harassed and helpless; whoever knows Jesus Christ and trusts him has a true hold on serenity and peace within himself.

Believers Draw Strength from Jesus

The film and the book, *The Exorcist,* dramatized the horror of unchecked evil. Perhaps the film used some of the devices of terror in an exploitive way to impress people where they are most vulnerable still to shock, but the contrast between the effect a real devil produces and the results of the power of God could not go unnoticed.

When we are told in the first verse of our text (Matt. 9:35) that "Jesus went round all the towns and villages teaching in their synagogues, announcing the good news of the kingdom, and curing every kind of ailment and disease," the concept we get hold of is that of God intervening in human lives with goodness, order, and enlightenment. Jesus brought understanding, hope, and relief to people who felt oppressed by life.

The words and actions of Jesus were not pretentious, though they often effected radical change. He was not averse to drama, excitement, or confrontation. But he sought none of these for exploitation; nor did he use them to glorify himself or to gain corrupting power over people. He simply did and said what the good of people and the glory of God required.

Consequently, when those more devious than he, looking out for popularity and power, faced Jesus, they had to suspect, oppose, and condemn him. They did not believe his good news. It can scarcely be surprising that Jesus tells those who follow him, his 12 disciples and all believers, that they may expect the same when they are faithful to their discipleship.

Jesus felt compassion for people but never in such a way as to minimize the accountability of human weakness or to lessen the importance of God's holiness and his requirement of perfection for real human fellowship with him. So the cross and grave were for him inevitable by both human need and divine righteousness. The perfect Savior became the victim of the sin of those he came to save. But his death atoned for human sin and opened a clear path between every person and God.

That is why the time of harvest is here ever since. Pray God for laborers willing to bear the heat and burden of the harvest. Not only pastors and full-time church workers are needed, but also people who love God and serve people in diverse occupations and roles, never forgetting they are messengers and workers for God.

Perhaps the Old Testament lesson for today roots our concept of this effectively in God's own promise: It says (Exodus 19:5): "If you will obey my voice and keep my covenant, you shall be my own possession among all peoples; for all the earth is mine, and you shall be to me a kingdom of priests and a holy nation."

It's Always Time to Get Going

Our faith becomes our way of life as Christians. When we see clearly, undeterred by human weariness, weakness, or worldliness, we know that because of Jesus Christ, life in all its ramifications and variety is always an opportunity.

Slow and weak as we often are to live by that vision, nevertheless God's Word and sacraments strengthen and equip us peculiarly and uniquely for that precise end: to grasp our opportunity to glorify God by what we do for people in all of life.

Evangelism becomes a broad description of how we feel about life: that we share the burden of every other person and of all humanity. For this is exactly what Jesus Christ did to perfection, and this is what he sent his 12 disciples to do and, eventually, what he sends us to do.

We take that burden not like those who have no burdens of their own, but as those who have found help and hope in Jesus Christ and now joyfully share it. No age or place or time excludes us from this opportunity. It is part of our peculiar view of life as Christians. In it we walk by faith, never fully vindicated in that view until the last day when every knee shall bow and every tongue confess that Jesus Christ is Lord.

Of that final victory we already have the first fruits in the resurrection of Jesus Christ from the dead, which becomes the strongest prop to our hopes when they sag and which is the bedrock on which our faith rests. Since that resurrection is true and real, much is possible.

Time, however, moves on. The urgency to use our day of opportunity daily weighs down upon us. For Jesus says that the crop is heavy and the laborers are scarce. There are great things to be done in Jesus' name. He has sent his Holy Spirit, who still comes freely and with power to make us able and faithful witnesses, to work the miracles in people's lives which only God can do.

It's always time to trust God, to care about people, to glorify God. It's always time to seek the Holy Spirit, to witness to Jesus Christ, to be serene because God is in control. It's always time to do evangelism. Let's get going. Amen.

OMAR STUENKEL
Lutheran Church of the Covenant
Maple Heights, Ohio

LANDLORD TO A GHOST

Fifth Sunday after Pentecost
Matthew 10:26-33

The major evangelistic effort, Key 73, taught us something about evangelism, but it taught us even more about our own fears. People didn't mind learning about evangelism; they didn't worry about attending classes on "How to be an evangelist"; but when it came to sitting down and talking to someone else about their faith, many folks said, "I'm scared!"

There are many reasons for this reaction. We are afraid that we'll sound "pious" or even "phony." We worry about what people will think. We fear ridicule or argument. So we remain silent, too timid to speak.

Today's Gospel addresses precisely this fear. Like us, the disciples had been summoned to spread the good news of God's kingdom. Jesus warned them that opposition would arise. He spoke of floggings, court trials, family conflicts, and even death. In fact, the deadly persecution faced by those first disciples makes our own fear of ridicule look—ridiculous.

Get Your Fears in Order

"Have no fear of them," he urges. "For nothing is covered that will not be revealed, or hidden that will not be known. What I tell you in the dark, utter in the light; and what you hear whispered, proclaim upon the housetops. And do not fear those who kill the body but cannot kill the soul; rather fear him who can destroy both body and soul in hell." In short, Jesus tells them to get their fears in order.

Have you ever thought of that? Have you ever dared to take out your fears the way a coin collector looks over his collection? Maybe some of those fears are old and battered, no longer worth much, and ready for the discard pile. Maybe some cost you more than you should have paid for them. Maybe some are duplicates; no point in cluttering up your collection with those. Above all, which are the real ones, and which are counterfeit? Let's turn to that group of fears associated with sharing our faith and see what we find.

Jesus suggests that there are *two* kinds of fears involved. One is the fear of what might happen if we speak up. The other—and this is often overlooked—is the fear of what might happen if we don't. To bottle up the message of God's power, you see, has its own dire consequences. As the old saying goes, "Truth will out," and woe be to the timid soul who tries to stifle it.

The prophet Jeremiah described how it felt when he tried to hold back from speaking the message: "If I say, 'I will not mention him, or speak any more in his name,' there is in my heart as it were a burning fire shut up in my bones, and I am weary with holding it in, and I cannot." Amos echoes the same necessity when he writes, "The Lord God has spoken, but who can prophesy?" The message is clear. God's good news was meant to be shouted from the housetops. If we choke it back, or muffle it, or try to contain it, we will be the ones to suffer.

This powerful reaction shouldn't surprise us. Psychologists tell us that when we "repress" certain vital forces and refuse to let them come to expression, the power of those forces is turned inward, striking deep into our unconscious life. Somehow, somewhere, those forces will find release, in dreams, in peculiar behavior, or in slips of the tongue. Often the results are more embarrassing than the expression of these forces would have been in the first place.

Political life, too, knows the immense damage of a "cover-up." Once again, facts that would have caused some embarrassment are hidden, for fear of the consequences. But "truth will out," and the results of the "cover-up" prove far more devastating than any disclosure could have been. An accurate balancing of the dangers would encourage "speaking out" rather than "covering up."

Jesus asks his disciples to weigh the fear of man against the fear of God. What is really more dangerous, to cover up the truth of God, or to risk the displeasure of men? "Do not fear those who kill the body but cannot kill the soul," he warns, "rather fear him who can destroy both body and soul in hell." Put in that perspective, the choice is easier. As John Witherspoon wrote many years ago: "It is only the fear of God that can deliver us from the fear of men."

But now what a problem we have! We have discarded our former fear for a greater one. How can Jesus expect anyone to speak joyfully on behalf of a God who has the power to destroy "both body and soul in hell?" I know that I would tremble to say anything if I felt that my life hinged on whether or not I could repeat the message of such a monarch! Granted, I wouldn't be afraid of what other people might do to me any more; *now* my hesitation would come from what *God* might do to me if I made a mistake. Lloyd Douglas once said that "If a man harbors any sort of fear . . . it makes him landlord to a ghost." What kind of haunted house do I live in if I am scared of God?

Before pursuing that question further, let's pause a minute to clarify things. We must not shy away from this topic with any easy comment like, "Oh well, God is love." We must recognize what we are saying when we say "God," before we skip on to chattering about his love. To speak of God means to speak of him who has absolute power over life and death. To speak of God means to speak of one who is truly fearsome, "whose robe is the light, whose canopy space." To speak of God means to take seriously Isaac Watts' warning:

Before Jehovah's aweful throne
  Ye nations bow with sacred joy:
Know that the Lord is God alone,
  He can create, and he destroy.

But how do I, a mere mortal, dare to speak in the name of this awe-inspiring God? Listen to Jesus' further words in today's Gospel: "Are not two sparrows sold for a penny? And not one of them will fall to the ground without your Father's will. But the hairs of your head are all numbered. Fear not, therefore; you are of more value than many sparrows."

We Have Value to God

There's the answer! The one who has power to create and destroy is called "your Father." He who holds our fate in his hand knows us better than we know ourselves. (After all, which one of us knows the number of hairs on his own head?) The God of all power and might is on our side! His fatherly will extends to the smallest of birds—and we are of much greater value. No matter what the public may think of us, no matter what status we may lose in the eyes of our neighbors, we have value to him whose image and superscription we bear.

That knowledge changes the attitude with which we approach the question of speaking about our faith. God is not checking after us to learn how well we did. He is not standing by with a notebook, grading us on how effectively we argue his case. He is not seated before some cosmic television set, waiting to see how many votes we got him in our local precinct. He is beside us as we timidly speak in his name. "Fear not," Jesus says, because your words will be used to accomplish God's purpose. God is on *our* side of the interview, working through our feeble, fumbling, and faltering words.

The Gospel concludes with a surprising picture. Two courtrooms appear. One is here on earth, wherever Jesus Christ is on trial. The other is in God's presence, where the whole human race is on trial. Jesus tells his disciples that a simple connection exists between the two. "Every one who acknowledges me before men, I also will acknowledge before my Father who is in heaven; but whoever denies me before men, I also will deny before my Father who is in heaven."

At first these words seem harsh, legalistic, and even "un-Lutheran." Where is grace in this equation? Where is forgiveness? Aren't we being saved by works, then instead of by faith?

Perhaps we need to recall the total sweep of the lesson. Jesus tries to calm our fears about testifying before men by assuring us that we are not alone in the hour of trial. God stands with us. If we trust that promise, then we will not deny him. If we doubt his help, or if we fear men more than God, then it is likely that we will betray him. And that is the one thing that the all-powerful God cannot change. He cannot force us to love him or trust him. He must accept our own verdict on our lack of faith.

That is certainly a high risk. But the main message of today's gospel rings out in the thrice-repeated reassurances: "Fear not." It is when we risk our standing with men that we discover the power of God.

Today is June 22. In the ancient church, this day was set aside for the honor of a wealthy French poet named Paulinus, who gave up his wealth and became a bishop in Italy. During his later life, the barbarians swept into Italy, sacking Rome and occupying the territory which he administered. One day, the chronicles state, a widow came to him with the sad news that her son had been captured by the Gothic high command. Paulinus had no more money to ransom the lad, so he hit upon a desperate plan. He went incognito to the barbarian camp and offered to exchange places with the prisoner. His offer was accepted, and Paulinus went to work in the vegetable garden as a slave. One day he was called before the Gothic chieftain, Alaric. "You are no vegetable gardener," said the ruler, "Who are you?" Remembering Jesus' words, Paulinus confessed that he was a Christian bishop, and then he nervously awaited the verdict. "I had a dream," began Alaric, "in which someone who looked like you came and took the sword from my hand." He went on to say how impressed he was with the bishop's deed, and he concluded by releasing the bishop and all the citizens of his diocese.

"Fear not," said Jesus, and generations of Christians have learned to trust those words.

Hugh George Anderson
President, Lutheran Theological Seminary
Columbia, South Carolina

THE SOUND OF MUZAK

Sixth Sunday after Pentecost
Matthew 10:34-42

Our wonder world of technology has supplied us well with noise. I push my cart down the aisle of the supermarket and hear music coming from above. I get into my car and with hardly a thought lean forward and turn on the radio and listen mindlessly to whatever happens to be on. I sit in waiting rooms supplied with soft background music. I walk in the mall of shopping centers, and the ceiling loudspeakers follow me right out, playing this never-ending background music no matter where I go.

In America this perpetual background music that clutters our lives has a trade name. The name is a grotesque parody on the good word music—we call this noise *muzak!*

You will not find this word *muzak* in the dictionary, because it is still a trade name, but the dictionary is about the only place you do not find it. You are surrounded by it.

About a half a mile down the street from our church is a store front with the word *muzak* printed on the window, and behind the window you can see a monstrous reel of tape rolling away, the source of all this sound blanketing our city, piping this *muzak* to those shopping, those waiting, those walking, or those sitting. Next to the tape player is a desk from which the bills are sent to those who subscribe to this perpetual background music business.

If you are a business man, it is probably a good investment, because its effect is to lull people into a relaxed, pleasant mood, and that is a helpful mood to get your customers into!

What Is This Muzak?

Let me tell you a few things about this *muzak,* this product of our electronic age.

In the first place, it is supposed to be soothing, restful and comforting. If you own a store, the whole object is that you want background music which will make your customers feel good all over, because in that frame of mind they are more likely to buy something.

It is *mood music* you want, music to create an effect. One is not concerned about the music itself—its musical value, its harmonies, its melodies, its rhythms, and so on—as long as it produces the desired effect. As long as it relaxes, one does not care what kind of music it is.

This means, of course, that *muzak* avoids dramatic music. Stirring, exciting music is too risky. *Muzak* leans heavily on smooth harmonies, and shies away from jarring dissonances. You can always count on "nice music" when you listen to *muzak!*

In the second place, you and I are not really supposed to *listen* to *muzak*. It must not be distracting. How annoying it would be if suddenly the triumphant strains of Beethoven's "Ode to Joy" were to flood the supermarket, and everybody stopped shopping to thrill to the music, or worse yet, were so enthralled by the music that they would just walk on by all the rows of groceries and show up at the checkout counter still transfixed by the melodies?! That would not do at all. Or how would it be if a patient were summoned from the waiting room only to ask if he could wait awhile until Mozart's "Jupiter Symphony" was finished? No, it would not do at all!

You are not supposed to listen to it. It should soothe without being noticeable. A good mood is what we expect from *muzak*.

Naturally *muzak* shuns melodies that stand out. Neither the haunting beauty of an oboe solo nor a strident trumpet fanfare that sends chills down your spine will be heard from those ever-rotating reels of tape. That would distract!

The Gospel as Muzak

What has this to do with today's Gospel text? Perhaps you have already guessed . .

How often have we made muzak out of the Christian gospel?

How often have we shaped and molded the vigorous gospel of Jesus Christ into a comforting and soothing message, so that each Sunday morning we can rest our bone-weary souls? Of course there is a comforting side to Christ's gospel:

> Come unto me, all you who labor and are heavy laden,
> and I shall give you rest.
> Peace I leave with you; my peace I give to you. . . .
> Let not your hearts be troubled . . .

But Jesus makes it quite clear that the rest and peace he brings are not the kind of easy-chair variety cut off from the pathos of this world. In today's Gospel text from Matthew 10, he sends his disciples out on their own "mission trip," and he warns them that the message they are proclaiming will not be received with comforting good cheer! They will be announcing, "The kingdom of heaven is here," and the message will cut into the hearts of people, causing frictions and fractions wherever people hear it and take it seriously.

And they will take this message seriously, Jesus tells them. "I am sending you as sheep in the midst of wolves," he forewarns them, "and men will deliver you to be whipped, then dragged before rulers."

This gospel was no *muzak* when the disciples went on their way. Jesus had peeled back the crust of religious practices, cultic sham, and human pretension down to the bare inner core of the central questions of life and death, guilt and forgiveness, pride and shame. He speaks plainly, to us as well as to those of the first century: This world has turned its back on the Father in heaven, fashioning its religions and its pleasures as it pleases. I have come, he says, to launch the transformation in you from self-centered to God-centered lives of love, mercy, and forgiveness as disciples.

That stark honesty led Jesus to the cross, and he warns his disciples that they will likely follow that road to martyrdom as well.

The Gospel as Strong Music

The Gospel must be important. It will be heard. It will be accepted by some and rejected by others. It will divide families. It is strong medicine—not so much vague background *muzak* which people hardly notice!

In today's Old Testament Lesson the prophet Jeremiah confronts another prophet, Hananiah, a false prophet who appeals to the people by sugarcoating the harsh prophecy of Jeremiah and making it more soothing. The kingdom of Judah had crumbled before the mighty empire of Babylon, and Jeremiah foresees long years of exile and bondage. As a graphic portrayal of his message he takes a yoke as the oxen wore and walks the streets of Jerusalem with it around his neck. Hananiah meets him, wrenches the yoke away and dashes it to the ground, singing a more pleasant tune to the people: Babylon's power will hold only a couple more years. But God's call for repentance through Jeremiah was meant to be taken seriously. Hananiah died soon thereafter. Jeremiah lived, and the harsh exile stretched out over the years.

This is the message of this Gospel text: Jesus, the gospel of Jesus the Christ, is meant to be taken seriously! There is power there, not just to soothe and comfort, but to transform and recreate. There is strength in this music, strength in the life which Jesues himself lived and now passes on to us. When the music of that life is allowed to flood its melodies and rhythms into our lives, old patterns are shaken up and lives are remade. Prejudices, hard feelings and dislikes which we have nurtured in our hearts are discarded. We no longer react in the customary "eye-for-an-eye" manner. The horizons of our lives are flung open!

Yes, this new life might meet resistance, as Jesus cautioned his followers. Your closest loved ones may not accept the life you have adopted as your own. Your love for them might be even more intense than before, but in spurning the source of your life, they may well spurn you too.

This was no fictional illustration Jesus used. He meant it literally, and it happened that way. Families were torn apart when the gospel took root and spread. In mission areas today the same thing occurs daily. And in our own so-called "Christian country," it happens, when one person in a family takes the gospel seriously over the objections of others.

Die First to Live!

The apostle Paul uses a striking image to show us how much weight this gospel carries. In today's Epistle text, from the sixth chapter of his letter to Rome, he writes to us, "To be baptized is to die!" In that brief splash of water we drown! Our old self dies. We are lifted from that baptismal font reborn in Christ, just as he rose to life from his tomb ~~on Golgotha~~. The gospel does not just round off our rough edges and polish us up a bit. It kills us! That old self-centered self is meant to die. We are intended to live from then on full of the breath of life from God's Spirit. The gospel does not play soft *muzak* to accompany us as we go; it becomes the very music soaring out of our whole being!

This Gospel text so full of warning and foreboding ends as Jesus repeats that grand and glorious paradox of the New Testament: We die to live! To cling to the old way of life is never to breathe the fresh air of the gospel. To die to the world means to come alive in God.

The gospel of Jesus Christ is not the innocuous *sound of muzak*. No! Let us not make it so! It is the stirring symphony of the universe. To listen to it and to live by its melody is to let the New Life overflow our hearts and lives!

MICHAEL ROGNESS
First Lutheran Church
Duluth, Minnesota

TRUTH IN ADVERTISING

Seventh Sunday after Pentecost
Matthew 11:25-30

I Hurt Inside is the title of a recent book by Dr. Ralph C. Underwager, a clinical psychologist and Lutheran clergyman. Church libraries, which are often not all that well patronized, report that this is one little volume that is off the shelves almost constantly. Apparently a lot of people hurt inside and are looking for some sort of pain-relieving remedy.

In today's Gospel Jesus makes some outrageous claims about his person and his ability to get people right with God the Father, and goes on to make a fantastic offer to all who feel beat, bushed, and burdened. In fact, Christ's claims about himself are so extravagant and his offer so unbelievable that one wonders if perhaps we have here a case for the Truth in Advertising council.

All of us, no matter what our age, are consumers. All of us are constantly exposed to advertising—in our newspapers and magazines, on radio and TV, on billboards, in circulars and catalogs that come into our homes by mail. We are constantly being urged to buy goods and services, to invest some of our resources for a return in the future, to indulge ourselves in food, drink, or entertainment for the gratification of our desires of one kind or another. Almost all of us, I'm sure, have been stung in our purchases or payments more than a few times. The toy we bought began to fall apart almost as soon as the kids began to play with it. The appliance we purchased needed several service calls before it began to do its job properly. The car in which we put a sizeable portion of our savings turned out to be a lemon. The value of our savings and investments was eroded by inflation. The neighborhood in which we finally purchased a home began to change and go downhill. And frequently the patent medicine or health product we saw advertised, bought, and tried turned out not really to help all that much.

And in recent years especially we have learned that things are not always as represented by the government, by the news media, by the major institutions in the fields of education, medicine, science, or religion. The confidence of people in the institutions which have been considered the very foundation of our society has been declining steadily, and to a great extent we have become a nation of skeptics and cynics. We are willing to trust some of the people some of the time but nobody all of the time. Repeatedly, leaders to whom we at one time looked with some confidence have betrayed our trust, and if we're not yet ready to sign up as recruits for Nader's Raiders we at least are more willing and ready to concede that a great many things are not to be taken at face value and we do well to maintain a healthy skepticism toward claims and offers.

Now along comes Christ with his

Outrageous Claims

"All things have been delivered to me by my Father; and no one knows the Son except the Father, and no one knows the Father except the Son and any one to whom the Son chooses to reveal him."

Now really! It is not likely that even some of the outlandish gurus and religious prophets of recent years have dared to go that far. Christ says in effect, "I've got it all—the Father has delivered the whole business into my hands!" The business he's talking about is what the "Father, Lord of heaven and earth" chose to hide from the wise and understanding (NEB and TEV, learned) and reveal to babes (NEB, simple; TEV, unlearned). What is the quest of man that perpetually frustrates because the goal always seems to elude us or be just beyond our grasp? What is the supreme dream beyond the solution of our energy and ecology problems and the conquest of space? What is it that always seems to remain hidden from man's perception in spite of the sophistication of our scientific instruments? What is the secret that some persons seem to be in on that gives them a quiet confidence and the competence to cope with whatever life may throw at them? What knowledge and understanding is it that some people have that seems to be quite unrelated to intelligence tests or academic degrees?

It is the knowledge of God as Father! Oh, you may well be among the 90 percent or so of Americans that give an affirmative answer in a Harris or Roper poll to the question, "Do you believe in God?" You may approve of the fact that we now incorporate in our Pledge of Allegiance the words, "one nation under God." It may be reassuring to you to know that the words, "In God We Trust," appear on our currency. But it's quite another thing to know God as the Father that Jesus Christ revealed him to be. God as creator, preserver, provider, lawgiver, judge—that's awesome indeed. God as eternal, almighty, all-knowing, all-seeing, omnipresent—that's almost frightening. The God of the burning bush and the fiery furnace and the smoking mount—who really wants to get very close to such a God?

But a God who is Father is something else! And that was the

God that Jesus came into the world to reveal to men. He himself could address the "Lord of heaven and earth" as Father in a way that no one else who has ever lived on earth could do, and he tells us in today's Gospel that the knowledge that God the Father has of Christ his Son and the knowledge that Christ the Son has of God the Father is revealed to men through himself, Jesus Christ. The inadequacy of the words God had had his prophets use to communicate to men his nature and attitude toward his creation and creatures led him to choose to speak to the world in the person of his Son. As St. John puts it in the prologue to his Gospel: "The Word became a human being and lived among us. We saw his glory, full of grace and truth. This was the glory which he received as the Father's only Son" (John 1:14 TEV).

And it was in that flesh that Christ wore as our brother that he demonstrated repeatedly the validity of his claims. The manifestations attested to in the New Testament of his power over nature, over illnesses and afflictions of the body, and even over death itself—all back up his outrageous claims to unique oneness with the Father and ability to make him known to men, claims further substantiated by his own death, resurrection, and return to the Father. Retain the posture of a cynic and skeptic about these claims of Christ at your own peril. "Buy" them in faith, and then listen to the fantastic offer Christ makes.

Fantastic Offer

"Come to me, all who labor and are heavy-laden, and I will give you rest. Take my yoke upon you, and learn from me; for I am gentle and lowly in heart, and you will find rest for your souls. For my yoke is easy, and my burden is light."

This really sounds like one of those too-good-to-be-true offers! Nothing to send in, no limited time offer, no purchases required, no minimum order—just Christ, who has just made one of the most ecstatic utterances of his ministry extending a gracious in vitation to come to him to all who are badgered and burdened by life and conscience and find rest.

Have you ever felt cornered by a chain of events that appeared to back you deeper and deeper into a situation from which you could see no escape? Have you ever felt on the verge of sheer panic as you faced choices which seemed to offer you only varying degrees of disaster? Have you ever lain awake at night in a cold sweat burdened with anxious fears or a broken heart? Not one of us has to live many years beyond childhood without experiencing some of those feelings. And Christ knows that. He knows where we are in the world all the time, and he knows how desperately we need the comfort and hope that an offer like this brings. It is a universal offer. Don't think for a minute that it's for somebody else but not for you. If you find yourself laboring through life in travail trying to bring some sense out of the madness all about, this offer is for you. If you bend beneath time's load, longing for the relief you anticipate when the bundle of the years is lifted, this great, gracious invitation is for you. Come to Christ in faith. Believe in him as the Son God the Father sent into the world to live, suffer, die and rise again from death to reveal God's love and concern that not one of his creatures perish eternally, but that all who would believe in his Son and Lord might live as his sons and daughters in everlasting bliss. Don't miss out on this fantastic offer just because it sounds too good to be true. Act now! You'll be glad you did! Come.

An understanding of the setting in which Jesus originally spoke these words enriches their meaning even further. When Jesus addressed himself to those who were laboring and heavy-laden, he was also, and perhaps particularly, conscious of those who were laboring to do the works of the law, straining by their efforts to measure up to God's demands, working like mad to achieve a measure of rightness in God's eyes that would give them some assurance of consideration from a God thought of primarily as judge. And that, surely, is the ultimate burden—to be weighed down with the anxiety that in spite of all one's most earnest efforts one may still not be right with God. To have really tried to do pretty consistently the right things for the right reasons with and for the right people, and then to still have the nagging feeling that perhaps it has all not been enough—to carry around that kind of baggage in one's conscious self-awareness and in one's subconscious intimations—that's the load that cruelly crushes into utter despondency and total despair.

And then to have Christ come along and offer rest from that kind of laboring—that's a fantastic offer that's really hard to believe. Christ says, "Here, let me take that. Let me take all that burden of sin and shame and guilt and fear. Let me take it to the cross with me. I'm going there, you know, with the burden of all the inadequacies and transgressions of the whole human race to show the Father's love for all his children. I'm going to die there to show there are no limits to that love. And then I'm going to rise again from the dead to prove that the offer is genuine. You can really believe this one. It's for real. You're not being had again. My death and resurrection will be the guarantee that this offer is good—for even more than a lifetime. Here, you rest now."

And Christ offers still more. He offers us a yoke, a partnership, a relationship, fellowship with himself, the opportunity to learn from him the art of gentleness and lowliness of heart, the chance to find fulfillment and meaning in life, real rest and peace for our souls and loving service to him, the role of yoke-fellows with Christ himself. Your life has seemed to have no direction or purpose? You have made a half-dozen false starts in life already, and you seem to have gotten nowhere? Or you have gotten where you thought you wanted to go, and you find it's not really where you want to be at all? Or you really thought you'd make it by playing the game strictly according to the rules, but you still feel like a loser—or worse yet, that that's not the name of the game at all?

Christ says, "Come along with me. My yoke is easy and my burden is light. Learn that love frees. Learn what it means to experience genuine disciple-joy. Know what it means to be not a slave to the law but a child of the gospel, nothing less than a son or daughter of the heavenly Father through your faith in his Son. Find out how much fun it can be, how hilariously exciting it can be, what a merry time you can have when you let me carry not only your load, but you yourself. Then you are free to give of yourself in gleeful abandon, knowing that yes, you do have it made. I have made you right with the Father. I have made you able by the Holy Spirit to be a little Christ in the world. I have made it possible for you to forget your obsession with yourself. I have made it possible for you to be victorious over death and live with me and your Father in heaven eternally."

A fantastic offer? Indeed. But you'd better believe it!

NORMAN D. KRETZMANN
Christ Lutheran Church
Minneapolis, Minnesota

SPIRITUAL AGRICULTURE

Eighth Sunday after Pentecost
Matthew 13:1-9, (18-23)

The parable that our Lord tells about the sower and the seed is one of the best known of all the parables in the New Testament. He gives the interpretation that the seed is the Word of God and that the different kinds of ground or soil that it falls on are the different kinds of human hearts. Some joyfully accept the Word, others accept it part-way and others turn it down entirely.

But I think there is another legitimate interpretation of this parable, one that would fit the members of the average Christian congregation, and it is this: *there is a little bit of all these different kinds of soil in each one of our hearts.* From time to time, the Word of God gets a different reception in the same heart. My heart may one day accept a part of the Word of God, and another day reject another part of the Word of God; and it changes just like the soil in a garden or field might change from season to season. I'd like to go through this parable and show you how this applies.

Hard Ground

Jesus begins by saying concerning the sower and the seed, "And as he sowed, some seeds fell along the path, and the birds came and devoured them." Then in the explanation to the parable, Jesus says: "When anyone hears the word of the kingdom and does not understand it, the evil one comes and snatches away what is sown in his heart; this is what was sown along the path." I believe that from time to time in almost every heart there's an area that's just as hard as this soil on the path that's been beaten down through this field, and the words of God hit it and almost bounce off; they have no opportunity to take root. Before anything can be done about them the birds of the air steal them away.

Forgiveness is one of those seeds or words of God that very often gets this kind of reception. Someone may hurt us in such a way that, with all our Christian faith, we find it impossible to forgive that person. We may come to church on Sunday and pray the Lord's Prayer, "Forgive us our trespasses as we forgive those who trespass against us," but we still can't get ourselves in our heart of hearts to forgive that particular person his wrong to us. And so to that degree, you see, Jesus' parable comes true for our hearts: that the Word of God has hit hard ground, and it simply can't take root. The devil takes it away, and the desire for revenge and to hold a grudge and be unforgiving takes over. During an evangelism program, one of the workers reported a very humorous but tragic experience. A man on whom he called said he would join our church, but he had something to do first. He said, "I've got to lick a Norwegian neighbor of mine, and then I'll join your church!" So, as far as he was concerned, there was an area in his heart that was absolutely impregnable to God's Word of forgiveness. We're told by God to forgive our enemies. It's easy to talk about that, but if you've had a son or husband in the war who has been killed or injured for life, or perhaps even if your husband has been away because of the war for a long period of time and it has destroyed your happiness for those years, you might find it impossible to allow God's word of forgiveness to take root in the soil of your own heart.

Rocky Ground

Jesus goes on to say, "Other seeds fell on rocky ground, where they had not much soil, and immediately they sprang up, since they had no depth of soil, but when the sun rose they were scorched; and since they had no root they withered away." Then he explains it by saying, "As for what was sown on rocky ground, this is he who hears the word and immediately receives it with joy; yet he has no root in himself, but endures for a while and when tribulation or persecution arises on account of the word, immediately he falls away." It's good for every one of us as a believing Christian to examine himself from time to time to see whether or not the Word of God really has taken any deep root in his heart and mind and soul. We ought to ask ourselves periodically, "Have I got the kind of faith that can stand me in good stead when temptation comes? Or am I going to fall away?"

Now in these days there's a lot of what I call "pink pill religion." It's easy stuff to sell, and it claims that you and I can pull ourselves up by our own bootstraps, so to speak, out of any predicament or discouragement in which we find ourselves, simply by adopting certain techniques like repeating, "This is going to be a wonderful day! This is going to be a wonderful day! This is going to be a wonderful day!" And so we make ourselves a path to happiness and peace. The other part of this religion that's so easily saleable is that God is simply a means of getting what we want out of life. If you want happiness, if you want success, if you want influence over other people, if you want money, we'll show you how to use God to get these things. But that's only rocky soil! In a heart like that the Word of God has only shallow, superficial roots; and in the time of temptation and hardship and fear a religion like that is washed away in the flood, and the person who has depended on it hasn't anything left.

There's another kind of rocky soil we call *emotionalism*. I'm talking about something that people quite frequently say: "I get a good feeling out of going to church," or, "I get a wonderful feeling when I receive the Lord's Supper, or when I hear a sermon." That's fine. You should get a good feeling out of going to church and receiving the Lord's Supper and hearing the sermon and reading the Bible, but—it had better be more than just a good feeling! That's only the outward sign of something deeper down inside; and you and I ought to know *why* we have this good feeling, and what it is about our faith and the promises of Christ that give us this assurance and peace of mind. Because, if all we have is just a good feeling about Jesus and about the church, then once again when we really come up against it and the going gets tough, and we should hang on, we're going to be swept away with the tide. You might be faced with the prospect of a long illness. And when it goes on month, after month, after month, do you have the kind of a faith that can still turn such suffering into a victory? Or will you go down in defeat because God's Word has sent out only shallow roots in your heart and in your mind? You may suddenly be faced with death, as thousands of people are every day. What's it going to do to you? Are you then going to feel sure about all these promises concerning eternal life, the fact that whether we live or die we belong to Christ? My dear Christian friends, whenever you and I fall to any temptation, large or small, it's an indication that just to that extent the Word of God has not taken as deep root in our hearts as it should, and in that certain area it has hit rocky, shallow ground and withered away.

Weedy Ground

Jesus continues: "Other seeds fell upon thorns, and the thorns grew up and choked them. . . . And as for what was sown among thorns, this is he who hears the word but the cares of the world and the delight in riches choke the word, and it proves unfruitful." Most of us have had some kind of experience with a garden or a farm, and we know that one of the big problems in getting a good yield is to keep our tract of ground weeded. Because if you don't, the grain, or the flowers, or the fruit you expect is either not going to be there at all or it will be stunted. We had that experience with some carrots of ours in the parsonage garden—we let too many of them grow and didn't weed them out. The result was little, unedible things about an inch long and about as tough as rocks! And the garden of our heart is the same way. If we don't keep it weeded of the pleasures and cares and concerns of this life, the first thing we know this word of God that has started to grow in it is going to be smothered out. I experience many examples of this parable of Jesus when I go calling in homes. I talk to people who were baptized and confirmed, and were active in church as young people; then for some reason or other they got away from it. They tell me, "Well, I got a new snowmobile and I spend the weekends up north at the cabin." Or, "I moved so often that I couldn't put my roots down in any one place, and I just got out of the habit of going to church." Or, "My work takes so much out of me that when Sunday morning comes I'm no good in church anyway, because I'm simply fagged out." Or, "I married someone of another faith, and the only thing we could do was to compromise so that neither of us goes to church at all anymore." Or, "We've got so many children at home, and it's such a rat race to get ready for church on Sunday morning, that we're going to wait until the children grow up." You see, illustrations of Jesus' parable! The weeds of the world have choked out what once was planted and had started to grow. It's a constant conflict for every one of us to keep down these weeds in the gardens of our hearts: our business concerns, our social obligations, our recreation, so that they don't choke out and stifle this word of God, this plant that is supposed to bear fruit in our lives if it's to be any good at all.

Good Ground

Finally, Jesus says, "Other seeds fell on good soil and brought forth grain, some a hundredfold, some sixty, some thirty. . . . As for what was sown on good soil, this is he who hears the word and understands it; he indeed bears fruit. . . ." We've been doing a lot of talking about the fruits of the Word of God that are supposed to be born in our lives. What do we mean? St. Paul gives us a list of them in the New Testament: "The fruits of the Spirit (which comes to us through the Word of God) are love, joy, peace, patience, kindness, goodness, faithfulness, gentleness, self control." These are the things that are supposed to become realities in our lives if we hold fast to the Word of God and keep it in good and honest hearts and give it some good soil to take root in and grow. Just one illustration of what happens when you do that. If you allow the Word of God that says "Remember the Sabbath Day to keep it holy" to take root in your heart, a lot of very practical and important things happen in your life. In the first place, you give your mind and your body the rest that God your Creator intended it to have one day out of the week. One reason for the mental and physical breakdowns among people today is that they are openly violating this Word of God en masse. You are also going to find that your home life goes better if there's one day a week that you're with your family. That's why the American home is breaking down. The family is never together any more. You'll find that you'll be able to face your work week with an entirely new outlook and attitude because you're rested in body and mind and spirit, having had at least one hour in church that you can count on, apart from the world, and in communion with your Heavenly Father. You then become one with those St. Paul is writing about in today's Epistle "Who have the first fruits of the Spirit."

The Word that we read this morning, and that you are hearing preached now, like a seed, has miraculous power within it—the power of the Spirit of God. And if you give it the right soil in your heart, then it begins as if by magic to send out roots and it begins to leaf and to flower and to bear fruit. And this will mean a very practical and noticeable change in your life: It will change your relation to yourself, your fellow man, and to God. As God himself promises in the Old Testament Lesson for today, "So shall my word be that goes forth from my mouth; it shall not return to me empty, but it shall accomplish that which I purpose, and prosper in the thing for which I sent it."

LOUIS E. ULRICH JR.
Bethesda Lutheran Church
South St. Paul, Minnesota

GOD'S ENEMY LIST

Ninth Sunday after Pentecost

Matthew 13:24-30 (36-43)

Jesus Christ told 36 parables and 7 of them occur in one of the chapters of Matthew, chapter 13. Nearly every one of the parables uses nature as the key framework of the story. Each parable deals with an ultimate truth and teaching of Jesus. "The Tares and the Wheat" is no exception.

In this parable the field represents the world. The good seed is the person in whose heart the Word accomplishes its primary purpose. The tares are they who are within the periphery of the Christian church and thus in the purest sense are true members of the kingdom of God.

But the enemy of God introduces foreign elements namely tares, and these are sown by the enemy of God, the devil. God has enemies and they are actively engaged in overcoming his kingdom and spoiling God's rightful harvest. But God permits this action only so he might be able to save his own at the final harvest. The parable teaches that the kingdom of heaven in its earthly estate is a blend or mixture of good and evil, true and false, wheat and tares.

The thrust of the story is that there is no church or body of believers on this "great, green footstool" that is made up of only the righteous. The church militant, operating in this world, has enemies within as well as without. The enemies within and amongst us, can oftentimes be worse than those that are outside and beyond our community of faith. The subtleties of Satan can equally if not more devastatingly immobilize than the monstrosities of larger and more obvious enmity.

Over a hundred years ago, Macaulay said to the British Empire, "Your Republic will be as fearfully plundered and laid waste by barbarians in the 20th century as the Roman Empire was in the fifth, with this difference: the Huns and Vandals who ravaged the Roman Empire came from without, and your Huns and Vandals will have been engendered within your own country by your own institutions."

Wheat and tares will grow together within one's own country and yet the good citizens will on occasion "fall asleep" and not seemingly be aware that hypocrites and subversives will be working within the system to cause its downfall. Secularism, moral laxness, faithlessness—can be the rotten core deteriorating the innards of a nation, a person or even a church.

There will always be those who are camp followers of the Christian army who live like parasites off the good and healthy and disciplined soldiers of Jesus Christ. Sometimes just a difference in sophistication can make for lesser aggressiveness in the Christian vineyard. A friend of mine gave me this couplet indicating various depths in soul winning. Someone has said these lines indicate the difference between doing "church work," or doing "the work of the church."

Some want a church with an imported bell,
Some want a mission within a yard of hell.

The time will come when the church shall be purified and purged but until that time comes, tares and wheat, good and bad, true and hypocritical shall grow together in our Father's world. That time when the church on this world's real estate shall be transfigured into the City of God is at the Chief Harvester's discretion. Not even the angels in heaven know the time for that harvest.

While we are in this growing estate where tares and wheat grow together, the tares have been sown "while we slept," and that is when the "enemy has done this," as Jesus said. We must constantly remain alert and aware to the dynamic and enthusiastic activity of our adversary so we can distinguish the tares from the nutritious and healthy wheat.

Preaching the Word

Jesus repeatedly compares preaching the Word to seed being sown in the ground. In fact, the seed is never referred to in any other way by Jesus than that which is preached from human vehicles of grace. "Preach the Word, in season and out of season," he says. He might have said, "Sow the seed, in season and out. Why this comparison? I think he uses the comparison so continuously because there is a secret and mysterious power of growth in a farmer's seed and this mystery carries over into the preaching of the Word day in and day out. The farmer does not know how it grows. "The earth bears fruit of itself."

Although the sowing of the seed is a constant mystery, little understood, yet it must be done or there will be neither crop nor consequently any harvest. Although he doesn't know the total process, nevertheless, he knows and must pursue his responsibility for the sowing. "Man sows, and God gives the increase."

So the responsible church is called "God's field." In this field the preachers of the Word of God work as "fellow workmen for God," as St. Paul says in 1 Corinthians. They plant and water but it is God who gives the increase. Let God be the judge as wheat and tares, believer and unbeliever, grow together in this planetary world of ours and even in our churches.

There are at least three common enemies in this world that somehow and sometimes face all of us:

— Death

— Those who can kill the body, but not the soul.

— Enemies who prevent little children from learning of Jesus Christ.

The Last Enemy

Let us look at each of these briefly and pointedly.

St. Paul in 1 Corinthians 15:26 declares, "The last enemy to be destroyed is death." In this same vein the identical writer says, "O death, where is thy victory? O death, where is thy sting?" There is no victory for death because Christ will come again and enliven all who have preceded us in death.

The brilliant author, John Gunther, greatly bereaved the loss of his brilliant and beloved teen-aged son, John, Jr. many years ago. He was heartbroken with grief but was sustained in the depths of bereavement by the medieval poet introducing his book, *Death Be Not Proud,* with this phrase indicating the affirmation of his belief in the ultimate victory of resurrection. He said,

> Death, be not proud, for thou too
> Shalt surely die.

Yes, death is but a temporary bereavement for a permanent joy. A physical bereavement because of the physical loss of a loved one is understandable and a necessary catharsis for the bereaved. But underneath is the victory premise for the Christian that we shall be raised as the good wheat in the final harvest and resurrection when Christ comes. The resurrection separates the wheat from the tares.

Body and Soul

The second group on God's enemy list are those who can kill the body, but cannot harm the soul.

By so stating, Jesus Christ indicated strongly that not only do we possess a soul dear to God, but that it can be seduced away from the presence of him who in the name of the Holy Spirit, "calls, gathers, enlightens and sanctifies the whole Christian church."

Bishop Fulton J. Sheen, speaking on this idea that the soul that is "non seeable, non weighable, non filterable" and is our most priceless possession can be eroded and corroded by the seven pall-bearers of the soul. He said these are they: lust, greed, hate, envy, pride, avarice and unbelief. These are universal, "air-born" diseases that not only can kill the body but what is infinitely worse can also kill the soul so that it no longer even cares, craves and consults with things that are precious, pleasing and priceless to the God-Creator who integrated them into one unit called a "living soul"!

"Fear those who can deteriorate the soul"

3 John 2, claims a pre-eminence of the soul over anything else. In writing a letter of thanks to his hospitable friend Gaius he says, showing his pre-eminence for the value of the soul, "Beloved, I pray that all may go well with you and that you may be in health; I know that it is well with your soul." An unknown author reminds us in poetic rhythm that nothing is more important than God and the soul.

But were the universe
Back into darkness rolled,
Two lights death cannot dim—
God and the soul.

High on God's enemy list is anyone who can harm the soul.

To Discourage Learning

The third group on God's enemy list are those who do not encourage the little children to come unto Jesus.

The Bible tells us that it would be better for that one that a millstone be hung around his neck and he be cast into the sea. The point here is that anyone who discourages or prevents a little one from learning about the love of Jesus is like tares among wheat. That one whether parent, guardian or neighbor although living a life of community interest and concern, looking like a good friend, will not be gathered up and harvested in the great ingathering when the Savior comes to separate the wheat from the chaff or tares.

The great Swiss theologian, Karl Barth, once told newspaper reporters that the most important single truth he had learned in all his many decades of Bible study and learned dialogue was the simple little truism we learn in rhythm as Sunday school students:

Jesus loves me, this I know;
For the Bible tells me so.

High on the enemy list of God is that person or that group who withholds this living truism and life uplifting fact, from little children. This is the Bible's open secret.

In the novel, *The Secret of Santa Vittoria,* the people of that town discover that the tower bell, which had cost them plenty, rings so loud and clear that the city across the valley benefits from its sound. Horrified that another community is awaking, going to work, breaking for lunch, gathering for worship by their bell, the elders of Santa Vittoria meet in a lengthy emergency session until at last they unveil the solution to their problem "a cork clapper for the bell." Now, the muffled ringing can be heard no further than their own city wall.

Could it be possible that Almighty God permits the tares to grow with the wheat until the judgmental harvest with the hope that perhaps by listening to us, our speech, our concerns, our loves, they too might experience a miracle by the Holy Spirit and become bundled with the others for the heavenly harvest? God grant that our lives, our churches, our witnessing have no "cork clapper" muffling the true ring of our best witness. Amen.

NORMAN G. ANDERSON
St. Stephen's Lutheran Church
West St. Paul, Minnesota

THE PRICELESS POSSESSION

Tenth Sunday after Pentecost
Matthew 13:44-52

If we are to discern any unity in today's Gospel, it will be necessary to begin at its end. In the concluding paragraph our Lord talks about a theologian who was fortunate enough to be alive at that hinge of time which was the commencement of the New Testament era. This theologian, he says, has been a teacher of the law, an expert in that compendium of revelation which we call the Old Testament. It has been for him a veritable gold mine of wisdom concerning God and God's will for man. But now recently he has discovered something new and still more wonderful. He doesn't know a great deal about it yet; he is still a learner in the kingdom of heaven. He knows enough, however, to be able to talk about it. He is, after all, a professional teacher, and, though he may not have earned his doctorate in New Testament studies, he is a theologian whom the Spirit of God has brought to faith in Jesus Christ. Therefore, he has a foot in two worlds: in the law, of which he has been a student for many years, and in the Gospel, which he has come to believe with joy and thanksgiving. He resembles a householder, says our Lord, "who can produce from his store both the new and the old."

Ideally this is a description of any teacher in the Christian church. He ought to be a person who has a pretty thorough knowledge of both parts of the Bible. He ought to recognize on the one hand that Christianity has strong Hebraic roots, which means that many prominent Christian teachings can be fully appreciated only if their Old Testament background is understood. For example, the whole thrust of the sacrifice of our Savior is surely illuminated by the Hebrew ceremonies of the Day of the Atonement, and the Holy Eucharist is powerfully adumbrated by the Old Testament Passover. So it goes: the history of the chosen people, particularly the story of the Exodus, the giving of the law, the utterances of the prophets, the sacrificial system—all were "shadows of things to come," and a Christian teacher can make good use of them in this presentation.

But his major emphasis inevitably will be on that which is new, on the Gospel, on the person and work of Christ. This is what is distinctive, this is what is salvific, this is what is supremely wonderful. The early apostles exclaimed that they could not help speaking of the things they had seen and heard; the Gospel was an explosive power demanding expression. It still is. This is the very reason for our existence; this is the preacher's assignment. Woe to him if he preaches not the Gospel!

The Hidden Treasure

This brings us to the parables in today's Gospel, or at least to the first two of them, which are both concerned with the priceless value of the kingdom of heaven. The first of these, we might say, seems to approve some dubious behavior. It has to do with a man who discovers a treasure lying buried in a field. He buries it again, and then, by selling all his property, he gets together enough money to buy that field, and so becomes owner of the treasure. Now if I were the original owner of the field, I wouldn't be too happy about the whole thing when it came to light that the purchaser had become a rich man. I couldn't protest any illegality, but I could say—and probably would—that morally I was entitled to some share of the treasure, since I had deliberately been kept in the dark about the value of the field in which the treasure lay.

But all this is the kind of thing one must not do with the parables: one must stick to the point the parable is intended to make, and not raise all sorts of objectionable side issues. The point of this particular parable is that the kingdom of heaven is something of tremendous value—only that, and nothing more. One must therefore establish as the supreme desideratum of life the possession of this kingdom. Nothing else is even comparable to it. Everything one has must be sacrificed to the acquisition of this priceless treasure. In actual experience, of course, it is not necessary to cheat anyone else out of his share of the treasure; there's enough for everyone. That, however, is not central to the teaching of the parable. The point is solely to inculcate a proper sense of values.

The Pearl of Great Value

This becomes clear in the second parable, which has none of the dubious morality of the first. Here is an entirely above-board business transaction, that of a merchant selling everything he owns in order to purchase a fine pearl of exceptional value. He must have wanted it very much. And that's the point of the story: the great desirability of the kingdom of God. To possess this jewel one must be prepared to sacrifice a great deal. The implication is that no one who has ever done so regrets it in the least.

The Fishing Net

These two parables then portray people who evaluate the kingdom properly and take appropriate action in order to possess that which is offered. Unfortunately not everyone has the same appreciation for God's gift. Some have only a dim knowledge of its value; others are indifferent to it, and still others despise it. There are all kinds of attitudes, and, as experience abundantly demonstrates, there are all kinds of people in the company of the baptized. There are undoubted Christians, and there are those who behave as though they had never heard of Jesus Christ. The former are "the good fish" of the third parable in today's Gospel, and the latter are characterized as "worthless." A lot of people no doubt are somewhere in between these two extremes, so that it is often difficult to tell whether they are good or worthless fish. This is why our Lord earlier in this chapter warned his disciples against making judgments of this kind. "Wait," he said, "until the end of time, and let the angels do the separating." He teaches the same thing here: "The angels will go forth, and they will separate the wicked from the good, and throw them into the blazing furnace, the place of wailing and grinding of teeth." In the meantime, it seems, we shall continue to be engaged in that strange fishing expedition which will finally result in that very heterogeneous assembly of human beings. We have a strong intimation of that in the church here and now. We keep on wishing that all church members were people of uncontroverted Christian character, but it's not like that and never will be until the angels have done their job. We, meanwhile, do ours as best we can.

It is somewhat unsettling to notice how often in our Lord's teaching the note of judgment is sounded. We like to think of him as being the embodiment of the gentle virtues: kindness, forgiveness, love, etc. And when we hear him talk about people being thrown into the blazing furnace to the accompaniment of wailing and grinding of teeth, we sometimes wonder if this is the same man. Well, it is. Sometimes he was not gentle at all; he could get pretty rough. His pictures of the judgment are very grim. And sometimes they are the more so because the judgments do not come on hardened criminals or vicious characters, but on people who simply did not respond to the Gospel with faith and joy. Perhaps one might describe them as spiritual clods. They were certainly not the kind of people portrayed in the first two parables, who were ready to go to any lengths in order to be the possessors of the priceless thing God was offering to them.

A Double Teaching

This I think comes close to the central teaching of today's Gospel, which is on the one hand a warning against leading dull, uncomprehending lives, and on the other a sharpening of our awareness of the preciousness of God's kingdom. It may be helpful, as we reflect on this pericope, to consider carefully this double teaching. First, then, it is a fact of life that the great mass of humanity live out their days in drabness and dullness, settling for the lower when they could have the higher, finding limited pleasure in the imitation when they could experience the joy of what is genuine, never coming out into the exalted dignity of being true children of God. The obverse of this is really saying the same thing: that all the while these people are stumbling through their unbeautiful days there is that treasure, that pearl, which awaits their discovery. Now in both these illustrations the valued thing does not lie around exposed to the view of the casual passer-by. The treasure is hidden in a field, and the pearl, let us say, is carefully locked away in some jeweler's safe. This is to say that some searching is called for, some expenditure of effort. A man must operate on the assumption that this precious thing is to found and must be willing to persist in his search. It's as the prophet says, "If with all your hearts we truly seek him, ye shall ever surely find him." Or, as the Epistle to the Hebrews puts it, "Anyone who comes to God must believe that he exists and that he rewards those who search for him."

Here no doubt is a major difficulty with those who lead a more or less animal-like existence: they cannot bring themselves to believe that God, if he exists at all, can possibly be as good as the Christians say he is and that, furthermore, the joy of discovering him could not conceivably be as great as is sometimes described. Their sin is basically unbelief. It is for that reason that they never make the great discovery, never become possessors of the treasure. There is nothing more tragic than this. The whole thing is so unnecessary. God in Christ has done everything he could, and his Spirit is certainly very serious about bringing men to the knowledge of the truth, but if they will not have it, what is left? Nothing ultimately except that wailing and gnashing of teeth that our Lord talks about. This is a terrible business. All that treasure, and all that rejection of it! Can anything be more tragic than that?

What can be done about it? Nothing really new or different. It's just a matter of trying to carry out the same assignment which the church has had from the beginning, and to do it in ever more effective ways. This assignment, in terms of the first two parables, is to keep shouting, like Archimedes of old, "I have found it!" I have come upon the priceless treasure, and I want to share it with you.

There's enough there for everybody, and it's absolutely the most wonderful thing you could possibly imagine. Believe me when I say this, because I know what I'm talking about. I have had this great experience, and I want you to have it too. So put your hand in mine, and let me lead you to the place where the treasure is to be found. Or should I rather say, to the person who is himself the treasure. His name is Jesus Christ, in whom is to be discovered all mercy, peace, joy and love. It was he who told us these stories about the treasure and the pearl, and he also warned us of the coming judgment in the parable of the fishing net. If you don't believe me, at least listen to him. It's of the utmost importance that you do. If you treat him as one of little or no value, so much the worse for you. If on the other hand you learn to esteem him as the supreme good, you will be rich beyond all computation. For in him is salvation, life, and resurrection from the dead, and by him we are redeemed and set at liberty.

HERBERT F. LINDEMANN
Redeemer Lutheran Church
Fort Wayne, Indiana

TO BE A MIRACLE

Eleventh Sunday after Pentecost
Matthew 14:13-21

Many people today do not have a place for the word "miracle" in their vocabularies. Words like "competence," "confidence," "achievement" and "certainty" are much more attractive as they describe some things one can count on. Miracle suggests the unreal, the uncertain, the irregular, the change, the freak of nature—but certainly not that which one can count on. It is in this context that one must look at the miracles of Jesus for our day. They seem unbelievable both in what they tell us about God and man. To the eyes and ears of faith, however, the miracles of Jesus open up new dimensions of the presence and the action of God in Christ.

These new dimensions are not so much a "doing for" someone as they are a "participating in" the all sufficient power of God. In the miracle of the feeding of the five thousand the disciples participate in the action of Jesus. It was Christ who performed the miracle; it was the crowd who was fed; it was the disciples who were the agents and mediators, of the action and who experienced the sufficiency of their Lord.

Miracles Occur When the Negative Intrudes

The beginning of a miracle is always a negative situation. The people were tired and hungry. In other miracles of Jesus one can note the negative—the person was blind or lame or deaf. On one occasion at Cana, they ran out of wine. Participation in miracles always has a negative context. It is the person healed from cancer (a negative) who calls it a miracle. Given the context of the negative, each of us has plenty of occasions for participating in a miracle. Guilt, failure, a sense of inadequacy, a feeling of uselessness, death and inevitable disappointments are just a few of the negative intrusions in our lives. We don't always see negative intrusions as occasions for our participation in God's action. Often we feel he has abandoned us. On other occasions negative intrusions solicit only an attitude of despair and doom and for others they are countered only by "thinking positively." The dialog of the disciples with Jesus suggests that they did not see much possibility or resolution to the negative situation of thousands of people, little food and hungry mouths. "We have *only* five loaves and two fishes." It is not difficult to identify with their feelings. The hopelessness of negative intrusions is a common experience. While not all negative intrusions are sinful, sin, itself, is the master negative intrusion as it destroys life, produces endless despair and inevitable death. The message of the cross is, of course, that sin was the occasion for the miracle of Christ's victory over it.

How Could God Be for Us?

The reason that we are so easily overwhelmed by the negative intrusions in our lives is that we have difficulty seeing how God could be for us and yet permit them to occur. This problem is as old as man. It stems from our forgetting God's creative goodness in the Genesis story and remembering only man's rebellion and the subsequent despair in life. The perspective of God's presence in the negative situation is the biblical message. That presence is a creative, redeeming, life-giving presence. That presence is the one which Paul in the Epistle for today says,

> If God is for us, who can be against us? He did not even keep back his own Son, but offered him for us all! He gave us his Son—will he not also freely give us all things? Who will accuse God's chosen people? God himself declares them not guilty! Can anyone, then, condemn them? Christ Jesus is the one who died, or rather, who was raised to life and is at the right side of God. He pleads with God for us! Who, then can separate us from the love of Christ? Can trouble do it, or hardship, or persecution, or hunger, or poverty, or danger, or death? As the scripture says, 'For your sake we are in danger of death the whole day long, we are treated like sheep that are going to be slaughtered.' No, in all these things we have complete victory through him who loved us! For I am certain that nothing can separate us from his love: neither death nor life; neither angels nor other heavenly rulers or powers; neither the present nor the future; neither the world above nor the world below—there is nothing in all creation that will ever be able to separate us from the love of God which is ours through Christ Jesus our Lord (Romans 8:31-39 from *Good News for Modern Man).*

The testimony of the biblical message is that God is the giver of life's situations and there is no escape from him. The psalmist says,

> Where could I go to escape from your Spirit? Where could I get away from your presence? If I went up to heaven, you would be there; if I lay down in the world of the dead, you would be there. If I flew away beyond the east, or lived in the farthest place in the west, you would be there to lead me, you would be there to help me. I could ask the darkness to hide me, or the light around me to turn into night, but even the darkness is not dark for you, and the night is as bright as the day. Darkness and light are the same to you (Psalm 139:7-12 from *The Psalms for Modern Man*).

The negative intrusion is not an occasion for wondering "where are you, God?" but rather given His presence, "what are you saying, God?" When one looks at the lives of the great heroes of faith: Abraham; Moses; Amos; Peter; Paul; Luther; Martin Luther King, the negative intrusions in their lives opened the way for them to participate in God's Good News. God *is* for us, the question is "are we available to hear what He is saying?"

The Ingredients for the Miracle Are Always Present

It was not necessary to go to the store to buy bread to feed the people. The answer was there all the time. That answer was Jesus—not bread! Jesus is the Word of promise and possibility to the negative intrusions. The fact that bread and fish were needed only affirms the way in which God always responds with what's needed! Christ said on another occasion,

> Or what man of you, if his son asks him for bread, will give him a stone? Or if he asks for a fish, will give him a serpent? If you then, who are evil, know how to give good gifts to your children, how much more will your Father who is in heaven give good things to those who ask him! (Matthew 7:9-11).

God's Word of promise and hope to life's situation is always Jesus Christ. It takes the form of what is needed! That was his mission.

> The Spirit of the Lord is upon me. He has anointed me to preach the Good News to the poor, He has sent me to proclaim liberty to the captives, and recovery of sight to the blind, to set free the oppressed, to announce the year when the Lord will save his people (Luke 4:18-19 from *Good News for Modern Man*).

The Word of Jesus always speaks to what's happening to free us from despair, emptiness and hopelessness and makes it possible for us to live, to love, to rejoice in our situation. When the intrusion is guilt, the Word is forgiveness. When the intrusion is hunger, the Word is food. When the intrusion is loneliness, the Word is caring. When the intrusion is death, the Word is life! To the alienated, the oppressed, the "loser," the disenfranchised, he is the beginning again.

Jesus Christ is an affirming, renewing, redeeming, restoring

Word. He is always present! He is life accepted, the future opened, the present celebrated!

Called to Be a Miracle

The point of the miracles of Jesus is not that he be "Bread-king," "Health-king" or "wine-king" but that those who experience the miracle, strengthened in faith, might give witness to the power of God in Christ. That, indeed, is Good News.

It must have meant much to the young lad in Mark and Luke's account of the feeding of the five thousand. It must have meant much to Andrew who brought the lad to Jesus. It must have meant much to the other disciples as they reflected on Jesus' response to the negative intrusions of life they shared with him —the most dramatic of which was the week that ended with Christ's death on the cross and the resounding reassurance of God's power in the resurrection.

The story is told of Lord Tennyson in Lincolnshire when two people met him at a church. Tennyson asked, "Well, what is the news today?" One person replied, "Why, sir, there is only one piece of news that I know; the news that Christ died for all men and he is Lord of life." The poet replied, "Yes, that's old news, good news and new news too!" That is the recurring miracle of life.

This is the message the Christian church has to proclaim to the world. The church does its best when she herself participates, as did the disciples, in the miracle. Sensitive to the human situation, the church must, through Word and Sacrament, affirm again and again God's presence at life's negative intrusions with a Word that "makes all things new." To live in this confidence is not only to have a future; it is also to be a miracle.

Donovan J. Palmquist
The Village Church
Milwaukee, Wisconsin

WALKING ON WATER?

Twelfth Sunday after Pentecost
Matthew 14:22-33

"In addition to being able to *walk on water* he should. . . ." That is the way a letter began which described the characteristics necessary to be the president of a theological seminary. To be able to walk on water would be handy not only for seminary presidents but for most people. Haven't you secretly wanted to miraculously surmount the problems that seek to overcome you by strutting gingerly off on top of the waters? "O, wouldn't it be loverly" if I could only walk on water!

The main concern, however, for most people is not to be able to walk on water, but simply to keep the head above water. Many people do not consider that "making progress" or "getting ahead" or "being better off next year than you are now" is important, but their concern is more immediate, simple *survival!* "Will I make it through this day? Can I survive the next hour?" Those are the questions of concern.

Trapped

Many people have difficulty facing a single day. They are terribly depressed with themselves, paralyzed by fear of little things, caught by drugs or alcohol, or enslaved to a way of life that is degrading, but can't be shaken.

Several years ago a play was produced on the New York Stage entitled *A Place Without Doors.* It was the story of a woman who ultimately triumphed over the tragedy of a wasted life. She had made so many mistakes and done so many wrong things that life seemed to close in on her, leaving no point of escape. She felt imprisoned; as though she dwelt in "a place without doors."

Caught

Some people live lives that are that hideous; they are *trapped* by their frustrations. Unrealized dreams, dashed hopes, impairment of health, domestic difficulties, tensions with jobs, insecurity of position, inadequate finances or conflict with family may entrap us. Add to those personal worries the panic about our environment, the energy crisis and disillusionment over intrique in high government positions and you feel *caught.* Despair over the plight of Indians and Blacks and terror in far-off places all contribute to the sensation of living in a place without doors.

False Hope

Recently I read a sermon directed to people who were trapped in their frustrations. The preacher had the audacity to suggest that trapped individuals should consider six practical steps in their plight. One, remember who you are; two, think on the positive; three, try to think of the entrapment as an external condition; four, do what can be done; five, develop a sense of humor; and six, keep a victorious image.

With all due respects to the well-meaning preacher, such advice is a very depressing message for a person who is going under in personal calamity. To one who is really trapped and has that impossible hopeless and helpless feeling, such words of advice are no assistance at all.

Imagine Jesus giving such advice to Peter, the apostle, as he was sinking in the raging waters of the sea of Galilee. "Think positive, Peter! Keep a sense of humor! Remember who you are! Keep a victorious image!" That's not much help, I'd say, for Peter, or anyone sinking in life's abyss.

True Help

The story of Jesus coming to the disciples on the water in the midst of a 3:00 A.M. storm offers something else by contrast. Jesus had sent his disciples by boat across the lake after he had fed the five thousand. At prayer Jesus realized the storm was distressing his men so he went to them in their trouble. They were frightened, their strength was exhausted in trying to control the boat. They were pushed to the shore with a fury. Would they wreck on the rocks? In the tiny boat the disciples were out of control, helpless, and hopelessly driven to potential distruction. Jesus came to them in the midst of that storm, not with advice or six easy steps, but with his personal assistance.

Jesus Meets Our Need

Scholars argue about whether or not Jesus actually walked over the water or towards the water, but that discussion is of little concern to us. The interpretation of the Greek does not matter. The meaning of the story is clear. *In the hour of the disciples' need Jesus came to them.* That message is clear. Jesus came to give help and to save His disciples. There are many times in life when the direction of the wind is contrary, and we are up against it. Situations turn with such devastating force on us that we can't make it alone. We may struggle with ourselves and the circumstances, but that is not enough. Our temptations and sorrows and the fury of life overcome us. We need not struggle alone. When we are most down and being destroyed, Jesus comes across the storms of life with hands outstretched to save. His clear voice bids us not to be afraid and he calms the storms of life. Here is a manifestation of the power of Jesus the Son of God who is able to defy the powers of nature and assist his people who are in trouble.

Christ Is Real

I do not want to suggest that in some general way Jesus comes to all people who are in trouble to provide a miraculous escape and a stilling of the waters. I do mean to suggest that Jesus Christ is a very concrete person with whom we can have a relationship in faith. He meets us in baptism. We know him in the Scriptures. We experience him in the church. We confront him through the lives of others. We are touched by him in Holy Communion. We speak to him in prayer. Christ is not a figment of our imagination, nor some mysterious power to calm a storm by magic. He is real and meets us in the concrete place of our need through faith.

The first requirement for anyone to get help is to admit that something is wrong. The disciples recognized their need. The storm was about to swamp them. Christ comes to us when we acknowledge our concrete need for him, when we admit things are wrong with us.

What Happened to Sin?

Karl Menninger the famous American psychiatrist recently published a book entitled, *Whatever Became of Sin?* Menninger agrees with Paul Tillich that, "There is no substitute for words like sin and grace." Sin is something that can't be expressed adequately in words like crime, disease, delinquency, or deviancy. From a human psychological viewpoint it is important to deal with sin as sin, in both word and concept. There is such a thing as simple immorality and wrongness which is rooted in a willful, defiant act against another person and God. To speak of sin is to deal with the responsibility for evil. We are not excused on the basis of our genes, environment or an over-protective mother. We must deal with personal responsibility for evil behavior. The wrongness of sin is not merely in an act of non-conformity or inappropriate behavior, but in its aggressive and ruthless quality. Sin hurts another person, breaks away from God and the rest of humanity, creating alienation, rebellion, and a refusal to love others or to love God. I suggest that Sin, our own basic evil, is at the eye of the storms of our life. We are sinners and that is at the heart of our troubles.

Sin Is the Trouble

If we let God deal with our sin, then, we have faced the basic element in the storms of life that confront us. When we let Christ the Forgiver, and savior stop the contrary winds that undo us, through his forgiveness, we are dealing with the core of our problems. To accept the forgiveness of God is the fundamental matter in our staying afloat in stormy waters.

Impulsive Peter stood up in the boat and said "Lord, if it is you, bid me come to you on the water." He got out of the boat and began to walk to Jesus. "Lord, others will deny you, but I will never forsake you!" Peter, like us all, was often ruled by his heart. We want so much to walk on the water *with* Jesus and *to* Jesus, but we are not willing to count the cost. We fail because our faith gives way in the raging seas of life. Time after time our fickle faith causes us to fall down, to mess up and to break our word and promise to God. The picture story of Peter sinking in the water is the story of our faith.

But Peter, bless his heart, wasn't too proud to weep bitterly, to ask for forgiveness, or to reach out clutching for Jesus in the black waters of the Galilean Sea. "Lord, save me!" he said. Jesus stretched out his hand and rescued him. "O man of little faith, why did you doubt?" Jesus asked. Then he stopped the winds and all was calm. Those in the boat bowed down reverently and confessed, "Truly, you are the Son of God."

God's Grace

Peter recognized his sin, his faithlessness, and reached out to Jesus to receive his forgiveness and grace. Actually, none of us needs to be able to walk on the water. We *do* need to admit when we are in trouble and being swamped and sinking. We need to recognize our problems and our sins. We need to take responsibility for them as our own willful acts. Then Jesus Christ comes to us with his grace. He reaches us with his strength and forgiveness so that we are not overcome. He offers his companionship as our Savior in the midst of life's difficulties. It is his amazing grace that keeps us afloat. God will come to his people on the waters, even uninvited, to calm the storms. That is grace.

We have a firm footing because we are attached to the Lord himself in faith. He gives strength. We are not helpless bits of debris driven by the whims of the storm. God has claimed us as his own through Jesus Christ.

At Holy Communion we come to the table as sinners, admitting our trouble, confessing our sin and recognizing that the storms of life overwhelm us. Faith in God is our distress signal calling for his forgiveness. Here at the altar is a meeting, a moment of receiving and tasting his forgiveness. In the quiet of the sacrament, may we receive his peace and calm—the manifestation of his grace.

We need not be able to walk upon the waters. It is enough that Christ walks upon the water to us.

WARREN A. SORTEBERG
Our Saviour's Lutheran Church
Minneapolis, Minnesota

PRACTICING THE PRESENCE OF GOD

Thirteenth Sunday after Pentecost
Matthew 15:21-28

If someone were to ask you, "what is prayer?" what would you say? Prayer is not some kind of white magic. It is not an attempt to control God by praying for the right things in the right way to obtain the desired results. It is neither a self-induced pep session, nor is it a demand note. Prayer is need finding a voice. It is embarrassment seeking relief. It is a friend in search of a Friend. Prayer is a relationship. Prayer is a way of practicing the presence of God.

In a very real way human beings are alive to what is in their awareness. To live in the awareness of God is to be alive to Him. It is to live in the cathedral of His presence and blessing. Those of you who saw "Fiddler on the Roof" may remember the way in which Tevye, the Jewish milkman, talked to God like a man talks to his friend. He even asked God, "Why couldn't You have made me rich?" When his horse became lame, bringing him home later than usual; he asked, "Why did You have to make the horse lame?" You and I may smile at the thought of a man blaming God for not making him rich or for making a horse go lame, but we dare not smile at the beauty of a relationship in which people can talk to God both openly and boldly. Each of us is to practice the presence of God in prayer. Prayer is not merely something that one does in the morning, at meal time, in the evening, or at church. Prayer is a reflection of the attitude we have toward God.

Varieties of Prayer

We reflect this attitude in prayers of different kinds. There are prayers in which we *praise* God by acknowledging His blessings upon us. With the Psalmist we pray, "Bless the Lord, O my soul; and all that is within me, bless his holy name! Bless the Lord, O my soul, and forget not all his benefits." Especially do we thank God for salvation as we pray with St. Peter, "Blessed be the God and Father of our Lord Jesus Christ! By his great mercy we have been born anew to a living hope through the resurrection of Jesus Christ from the dead." (I Peter 1:3)

We engage in prayers of *confession.* In pain and shame we acknowledge that we have sinned against God's will, violated his commands, delayed the fulfillment of his plans, disappointed him, and worked against our own true welfare. To confess is to acknowledge our sins and to express our craving for forgiveness. We are eager to return to God and to accept his help in returning. Then in Jesus Christ we come to know the joy of having been forgiven, accepted again, and loved by the one whose forgiveness, acceptance, and love are most crucial to our lives.

The prayer before us is a prayer of *supplication* or *request.* This is the kind of prayer that is most associated with the word "prayer." Such prayers flow spontaneously from the heart, at least from the heart that is overcome with its troubles. Luther's fellow reformer, Philip Melanchthon, said with regard to such prayers, "Trouble and perplexity drive us to prayer, and prayer drives away trouble and perplexity."

The Woman's Request

This was the experience of the Canaanite woman who came to Jesus with a problem. Her daughter was possessed by demons, and she was hurting and confused. How could she bear the sorrow of having her daughter tormented by a demon? She did not know, and she cried to the Lord for help. By so doing she revealed both her needs and her faith. She loved her daughter very much. She needed help, and she believed that Jesus could provide that help. She cried out, "Have mercy on me, O Lord, Son of David; my daughter is severely possessed by a demon. But he did not answer her a word." She cried for help, but at first our Lord ignored her. He treated her as though she did not even exist. To be ignored by one whose recognition we desire is one of the hardest treatments on earth to bear, and she felt this. From the depth of her being she may well have asked, "Why is he so silent to me? Is it, because I am a Gentile and he is a Jew? What is the reason?"

She did not know why Jesus was so silent, but she became even more insistent. She became so insistent that our Lord's disciples urged him, "Send her away. She cries after us." Did they mean he should heal her daughter and send her away, or did they mean he should "get rid of her?" It's impossible to tell, but their concern seemed to be more for themselves than for this poor woman. If their conduct disturbs us, what about our Lord? At first he ignored her. When he did speak, he rebuffed her. He said, "I was sent only to the lost sheep of the house of Israel." He seems to be telling her that his ministry was confined to the Jews at that time. Choosing to brush aside his objections, this poor mother knelt down before him, saying, "Lord, help me." She had a problem. She believed that he could help. She would not allow herself to be put down or cast off. "And he answered, 'It is not fair to take the children's bread and throw it to the dogs.' " He seems to be saying that he can help only Jews, while assigning to her the role of a non-Jew, whom the Jews called "dogs."

The word Jesus used for dog refers to a household pet, and she dared to take the Lord at his word. In effect she now says, "You call me a dog, Lord. That's all right. Only afford me a dog's privilege. Permit me to have the scraps that the children do not want and let fall to the floor. It will be enough for me. You are so great that even the crumbs that fall from your table are enough." Here was a woman who exercised one of the really great freedoms of being a human being, the freedom to take a stand toward one's conditions. Jesus treated her with silence. She kept pleading, making a spectacle of herself, the Lord, and his disciples. He rebuffed her. She pleaded for help. He called her a dog. She accepted it. She accepted her position as a dog and asked for a dog's privilege. "Just let me have the crumbs that fall from the master's table."

The Response of Jesus

Now at last Jesus answered by granting her request. "Then Jesus answered her, 'O woman, great is your faith! Be it done for you as you desire.' And her daughter was healed instantly." At long last we learn the reason for our Lord's long delay in responding to her requests. Through his seeming inattention, silence, and rebuff Jesus was testing her faith in order to strengthen her. Now by a word, spoken from a distance, he healed her daughter instantly. At long last the strange remarks of Jesus begin to make sense. Through their relationship he was teaching her and all of us to be persistent in prayer.

We are not to lose heart, if we do not get an immediate response to our prayers. Prayer is not a demand note. It is a relationship, a relationship in which we make our requests known to God. We make our requests known and leave it to him to decide what to do. Often, I fear, when God responds to our needs immediately, there is a tendency to say, "My, what a coincidence! I prayed about this matter, and now my situation has changed."

When, however, we are left to agonize in prayer, we learn our total dependence on God. We are more apt to believe and understand that the change in our lives has come from God in response to our prayers. When the Lord has answered our prayers, let us not question his delay in answering. Let us rather be grateful. Let's remember what God has done in our lives and joyfully share the fact that he had mercy on us.

What the Miracle Means

By healing the daughter of this Canaanite woman Jesus revealed himself as the Messiah, the Son of David. That's what she had believed about him. That's why she came to him. She would not easily come to doubt it. Jesus is the long-awaited Messiah. He is the Son of God and the Savior of both Jews and Gentiles alike. That was prophesied already in the Old Testament in many different ways. In the Old Testament lesson for today Isaiah foretold that "foreigners," Gentiles would join themselves to the Lord. They would minister to him, come to love his name, and become his servants. In the conversion of the Gentiles to Christian faith these promises were kept.

The Epistle for the day underscores the universality of salvation by describing St. Paul's ministry as the apostle to the Gentiles. In the hope of making his fellow Jews jealous enough to investigate the claims of Christ and be saved St. Paul made much of his ministry to non-Jews. For him the matter was very simple. God had found all people disobedient in order to have mercy on all of them. For us and for all people the Son of God endured the Father's silent wrath on the cross. He suffered. He bled. He died. He was buried, but on the third day he arose in order that we might be forgiven all our sins and become God's children. In him our greatest needs have been met, and we are equipped to live in the cathedral of God's presence and blessing.

By faith in Jesus Christ you and I live beneath a heaven that

God opened by sending his Son to be born a man. We are equipped to bring our prayers of blessing, confession, and petition to him in the full confidence that he will both hear and answer us. Prayer is our way of practicing the presence of God. It is talking in a loving, intimate manner to the God who became our Father at the cost of his own Son's life, suffering, and death. There is only one thing more to be said, "Let's pray! Let's *really* pray. Let's pray for each other, for our congregation, for the nation, and the world." The goal of considering prayer cannot be fulfilled apart from the regular and persistent prayers of God's people.

ALLEN A. GARTNER
Lutheran Church of the Messiah
Princeton, New Jersey

IS GOD A MYSTERY?

Fourteenth Sunday after Pentecost
Matthew 16:13-20

Karl Marx, as the founder of modern communism, called religion the opiate of the people. Dwight Eisenhower, with his enthusiastic defense of the "American way of life," insisted that religion is at the base of any healthy society. For Marx religion was a mischief maker and the good future society he envisioned would be possible only if religion was destroyed. Eisenhower was optimistic about America, partly just because he believed Americans had so much religion. For Marx religion was a bad thing while for Eisenhower it was a good thing, but both agreed there was a lot of it around. Only a few years ago it was being predicted by the so-called "God is dead" theologians that modern, technological society was outgrowing traditional religion. Now we know that was a false prediction. Whatever else one might say, the emergence of the "Jesus people," or the new pentecostalism or the strong interest in religious mysticism are all of them signs that the religious quest is still going on and, you can be sure, will keep going on.

Religion is the attempt to come to grips with and find some answers to the mystery of human life and the mystery of that creation in which we live and move and have our being. I hardly have to tell you that life is a mystery. We look at ourselves and at the world itself and ask, sometimes only half consciously but at other times with a genuine urgency, what sense does it all make? What can we make out of this strange, unpredictable and baffling mixture of things that we call life? What kind of a world is it? Is it good or bad? For what do we dare hope?

To be sure, there is goodness in the world. There is also indescribable badness. Both are real. The same ambiguity is true of my own life. I love and I hate. I hope and I despair. I believe and I doubt. I can be kind and generous but also dreadfully cruel. I build and I destroy. I can be trusted but I also can betray. So also in creation itself there is goodness and there are signs of light and hope. But the deep mystery of evil is also present. Creation, just as my personal life, is in no event any sure sign that goodness will triumph. Ancient people knew very well that there is evil in the world. There are dread powers over which people have no control. To say that God is in his heaven and all is right with the world is certainly no self evident truth. Neither is there any sign that the world is getting better every day or drawing any closer to goodness. Things continue to happen *to* a person—frightening things, cruel, damnable things. Such things also happen within a person. To be sure, amazingly wonderful things happen also, but both the good and the bad frequently happen as sheer, unexplainable accident. When ancient people came face to face with the mystery of evil they spoke about such things as devils and demons and demon possession. The New Testament speaks in these terms and even refers, for instance, to our adversary the devil who walks about as a hungry, roaring lion seeking whom he may to devour.

Nowadays we regard the language of devils and demons as old fashioned. Yet, for all our sophistication, we wrestle with the same issues. It's just that we use different words like heredity, environment, alienation, brokenness or accident. The reality is the same. I am not master of my own fate. I am caught, for better or for worse, by all kinds of things. I did not choose that which made me what I am. Within me too there are powerful drives at work. When the bad drives get a hold of me I am afraid of what I may do or say or become. That, if you please, is our form of demon possession.

We could go on and on with the puzzle and in the end remain as baffled as when we began. Think for a moment of death. It is the final puzzle and the final sign of our insignificance. "Ashes to ashes and dust to dust" our burial liturgies say. That is just about right. For what, after all, is a person's life but a series of events that lie between two lines of nothingness? A baby is born (even that birth the baby did not ask for) and a new life begins. There is a progression from infancy, through childhood, through adolescence to adult life. One gets a job, probably gets married and has a family and may be successful or unsuccessful. In any event every life moves step by step toward death. One day there is a burial. For a while one may be missed but eventually is forgotten. A hundred and fifty years from now neither you nor I will be anything but a name on a cemetery marker or a name in a family record book. The psalmist is matter of fact in his description of life:

> In the morning it flourishes and is renewed;
> In the evening it fades and withers. . . .
> Our years come to an end with a sigh.

And so, you see, our perpetual religious quest is exactly a quest to make some sense out of just this perpetual mystery, to make sense out of what appears to be nonsense. Traditionally, this has meant to speak of God, and to speak of man as having something of the image of God and hopefully then capable of achieving some kind of relationship with God—so as to make possible a knowledge and a fellowship that will assure a hopeful future. But how?

There is a hymn that most congregations enjoy because of its vivid poetry and the magnificent Welsh melody to which it has been set.

> Immortal, invisible, God only wise,
> In light inaccessible hid from our eyes,
> Most blessed, most glorious, the Ancient of Days,
> Almighty, victorious, thy great Name we praise,

The hymn ends on a similar note:

> Great Father of glory, pure Father of light,
> Thine angels adore thee, all veiling their sight;
> All laud we would render: O help us to see
> 'Tis only the splendor of light hideth thee.

The hymn is vivid in its description of a high, distant, totally holy God who knows all, sees all and can do what he wills when, where and how he wills. It is a God who is so righteous that no one could see him and live. Yet, the hymn offers little comfort. The real rub is in the last line—" 'Tis only the splendor of light hideth Thee." If that is so, that God really is a mystery. The best you and I could hope for would be some hints into God's reality and some hints as to how we might attain to his presence. Life, then, if we are even half serious, would *have* to be *our* eternal search for God. If God's splendor hides him from man that God cannot be known except to himself. Either we would have to forget about discovering God at all *or* strive as best we could to lift ourselves up to heaven. Neither would be an encouraging prospect. If we chose to try anyway to get to God how could we know we were on the right road and how be certain that when we finally did meet him we would be carrying enough in our hands that God would say, "Well done, earnest searcher. With you I am well pleased."?

The passages you heard from scripture this morning speak a radically hopeful message. You heard the story of Peter's confession and Christ's reply, with its assurance that in that confession he would build a fellowship against which even the gates of hell shall not prevail. You heard too the perhaps puzzling words about "keys of the kingdom" and about binding or loosing so firmly that heaven itself would honor the decision. All that you heard introduced as "the holy gospel." Gospel means "good news"—an announcement of a fact that is to cheer up and encourage its hearers. You also heard a reading that tells us how God one day appeared to Moses with the promise that he would deliver the people of Israel from Egypt and that he would be their God and they would be his people. That story was also read as good news for us.

My brothers and sisters, these are two sides of a single coin. That coin is a gift that comes as totally good news to tell us that the God of Abraham, Isaac and Jacob and the God of Jesus Christ in whose name we were gathered has determined that he refuses to be a mystery. There is more to be said than that God is immortal, invisible and hidden from sight. There is more to be said than that life is a puzzle with its only sure future in death. The beautiful story of the promise to Israel already prefigured and set in motion a decision that culminates in Jesus Christ.

> I will be your God and you will be my people.

Or this good word,

> The Word became flesh and dwelt among us, full of grace and truth; we beheld his glory.

Notice that Israel will not only be known by God but will also know him. The New Testament assures us that in seeing Christ's glory we see the heart of God himself. That means that God is here among us and that he is radically, intimately and completely involved in man's history in all its diversity and mystery and its beauty and ugliness. God refuses to be by himself or hidden by such a splendor of light that he is for all practical purposes inaccessible. All this is an announcement to be spoken to and heard by just such ordinary people as us. It's purpose is to make the mysterious unmysterious or, put another way, to let us know who God is and what we are called to be so that we no longer have to rely on our pious guesses or our sentimental hopes. Neither need we resign ourselves to accepting the universe as a mystery with no answers.

Peter is allowed to see Christ as the manifestation of the Father and in seeing that he sees into the very heart of God. Even that is a gift of the Spirit and not something Peter managed to figure out. The same gift comes to us, as to Peter, not as a message which we might or might not believe but as a message which is also an effective good deed. The Spirit calls, gathers, enlightens and sanctifies the whole Christian church on earth and preserves it in union with Jesus Christ. Christ promises to Peter that he would build a fellowship on earth. Within that fellowship, as also the Lord's promise to Israel, God will be known so that as his good and gracious will rules heaven and earth so also it can be recognized and participated in by men. That is what it means that to the church will be given the keys of the kingdom of heaven, so that what is bound on earth will be bound in heaven and what is loosed on earth will be loosed in heaven. That certainly does not mean that some extraordinary power has been given to the church so as to manipulate God or allow the church to unlock heaven in the face of God's "No." Neither is this word a word to terrify people and tell them that if the church so chooses it can or will refuse to forgive the misdeeds of repentent sinners. Nor does it mean that the church has such power that it could call good what God calls bad or vice versa.

No, quite the opposite. It means that God and the church can agree because in this church built upon Christ as its Lord, God's will is proclaimed, affirmed and, however feebly, followed. The church has the awesome responsibility and the joyful privilege of speaking and living the Word of God. The church already now can speak the word which God himself will speak in the last day. With no "ifs" or "buts," but as though God himself were saying it, the church can tell us that our sins are forgiven. And then add, "Where there is forgiveness of sins there is also life and salvation." Therefore too it can say that you as my people are a chosen generation, a royal priesthood, a peculiar people, that you may henceforth demonstrate the goodness of him who has called you out of darkness into his glorious life.

The keys of the kingdom of heaven open those doors that let us see light instead of darkness, give us clarity instead of unsoluble puzzles and point us, as the end of our journey, to him who is Alpha and Omega, the beginning and the end, but who wants to be what he already is only in order to share with us the fulness of his own life.

We are weak. We stumble and we fall. We go from dust to dust. Yet, our God endures forever. He invites us, together with Peter, to deal with every word and promise of his with faithful hearts and obedient lives. And by the witness and joy of our own lives he invites us also to let our light so shine that in a world which scarcely dares to believe, others too may believe and join us in our confession that "Christ is Lord to the glory of God the Father." Therefore too our future is not the future of sin and death but the future of life and fellowship with one another and with him who assures us that "I will be your God, and you will be my people."

LEIGH D. JORDAHL
Lutheran Theological Seminary
Gettysburg, Pennsylvania

THE WAY OF THE CROSS

Fifteenth Sunday after Pentecost
Matthew 16:21-26

It is "not unlikely that this work of God's Spirit . . . is the dawning of that glorious work of God which . . . shall renew the world of mankind . . . and there are many things that make it probable that this work will begin in America." This was the opinion of Jonathan Edwards, the theologian of the first revival in America, as he pondered the Great Awakening in New England in 1740. What strikes me is Edwards' view of America's role in God's plan. The Puritans had come to build the kingdom of God on the rocky shores of New England and now Edwards thought he saw the first light of that dawn on the not-so-distant horizon.

> Columbia, Columbia, to glory arise.
> The queen of the world and the child of the skies,
> The genius commands thee; with rapture behold,
> While ages on ages thy splendors unfold.
> As the day-spring unbounded, thy splendor shall flow
> And earth's little kingdoms before thee shall bow;
> While the ensigns of union, in triumph unfurl'd
> Hush the tumult of war, and give peace to the world.

The notes of America's glory and power are sounded like a strident trumpet in this hymn to America by Timothy Dwight, the president of Yale. A few years later, in 1783, Ezra Stiles preached a famous sermon on "The United States Elevated to Glory and Honor." From these words celebrating the *creation* of the Republic we move to *salvation* of the Union and the *redemption* of the slaves in "The Battle Hymn of the Republic." The *sanctification* of the land "from sea to shining sea" is sought in "America the Beautiful"—a product of the "Gay 90's" of the Gilded Age. But as the "patriot's dream" of brotherhood and the "American dream" faded for so many, we heard "Bye, Bye, Miss America Pie." Is it Miss Liberty—Columbia, America—who laments, "This'll be the day that I die"?

Something has died! Is it the "dream" of Martin Luther King for America or of Kent Knutson for American Lutheranism? Has Christian hope also faded? Or is it civil religion that is passing away? Is this a patriotic perversion of Christianity whose demise should be celebrated rather than mourned? Is our flag-waving religion significantly different from that of Nazism or Shintoism in World War II? This much, at least, we must say: the American religion we have been talking about is very much like the popular civil religion Jesus encountered in his day. The way Jesus' countrymen regarded him is the way we tend to regard him today in America. The questions they asked, we ask:

> Jesus Christ, Superstar
> Who are you? What have you sacrificed?
> Jesus Christ, Superstar,
> Do you think you're what they say you are?

But Jesus always has the disturbing habit of turning our questions around. Just as he did with his questioners, he does with us. Soon our questions are countered by his questions. He asked his disciples about the popular religious beliefs concerning himself and got almost as great a variety of answers as he would have received today: John the Baptist—a fire-and-brimstone preacher of judgment; Elijah—man of prayer who prevailed over the pagan priests and even death; Jeremiah—unlikely and unwilling spokesman of an unpopular and unpatriotic prophecy; or one of the other prophets. A prophet indeed! But the disciples knew better. That is, they knew more! Peter said it for them: "You are the Christ"—the long-awaited Messiah, the Son of David, the King who comes in the name of the Lord! Indeed Matthew records the deeper insight: "You are . . . the Son of the living God." But even this revelation could be misunderstood.

And they did—just as we do! God's ways are not our ways and Peter's insight was once again overshadowed by the misconceptions of Jewish civil religion. The people were looking for a popular hero—a king who would drive out the Romans and re-establish Israel's power and glory. Then Jesus announced to his disciples that he was going to Jerusalem to die. That's when it all started.

No Way!

"No Way!" said Peter the Rock to Jesus the Christ. It is the same kind of reaction to his impending death that Tim Rice portrays in the characters of Judas and Pilate in *Jesus Christ Superstar.* Before the betrayal, Judas says to Jesus: "You want me to do it! . . . You sad pathetic man—see what you've brought us to do. Our ideals die around us all because of you. And now the saddest cut of all—someone has to turn you in like a common criminal." Pilate too after vainly trying to get Jesus' cooperation in his effort to release him cries in frustrated anger:

> Don't let me stop your great self-destruction
> Die if you want to you misguided martyr
> I wash my hands of your demolition
> Die if you want to you innocent puppet!

These are not, of course, the actual reactions of the historical figures. They are rather the reaction of modern man—our reactions! We try to psychoanalyze everyone—even Jesus. And when we can't "psych" out his inner being or figure out his actions, we decide he must be crazy. That's apparently the conclusion arrived at by Jesus' friends and perhaps even his family: they thought he was "beside himself" (See Mark 3:19-35). Peter's reaction seems to indicate he was worrying about the same thing. He took Jesus aside and started to chew him out. He said in effect: Heaven help you, Lord! After all, you're God's Messiah! You're God's anointed King! You can't be killed. You can conquer the world. You're God's Son! You can feed the hungry, clothe the naked, compel men's confidence and win their worship! Use your power! Use your head, Jesus!

That's not just Peter's cry! It's the position of popular religion in every time and every place. Like our civil religion that seeks a kingdom, power, and glory for America, Jesus' disciples sought the same for him and for themselves. The only glory Jesus seemed to want was the glory of the cross. The only power that the cross projected was the weakness of defeat and death.

The only kingdom established by such a "misguided martyr" belonged to a different world. Paul had the same kind of reaction: the message of "Christ crucified" is a "stumbling block to Jews and a folly to Gentiles" (1 Cor. 1:23). Popular piety wants the crown without the cross. Civil religion wants the kingdom, the power, and the glory without the gory death. Such religion operates with a theology of glory, not a theology of the cross!

One Way!

"One Way!" Peter learns. There's only one way for Christ to save the world: the way of the cross. Peter's objection to the cross became a stumbling-block and a temptation to Jesus. Thus Jesus directed his strongest rebuke at Peter: Go away, Satan! Get out of here, you enemy of God! You follow man's way and oppose God's way.

Peter, the leader, becomes the representative of Satan, the tempter. Peter, the disciple becomes the agent of hell's attempt to destroy the church. The church's rock is cracking and crumbling. There is a human roadblock on the way to the cross. Peter is that obstacle. How could you, Peter? How dare you, Peter?

How indeed? Is that really such a puzzle? What would we do? What *do* we do? What are we but crumbling rocks? What are we but obstacles and stumbling-blocks to God's work of salvation? Like Peter we are tempters and deniers of Christ. We are "poor miserable sinners"—sinners upon whom God has had mercy, sinners from whom Christ has died. We are the enemies whom God has rescued. We are the estranged whom God has reconciled. We are the enslaved whom God has redeemed. We are sinners and we are saints, both at the same time. Like Peter, we are brittle and broken humpty dumpties whom the king himself puts back together again. We want to avoid the way of the cross not only for ourselves but also for Christ. But he chooses to walk the path of suffering alone for our sakes. Like Peter, we are bothered—scandalized—by the thought of God being pushed around in his world. But that's the kind of God we have; as Bonhoeffer said, "God lets himself be pushed out of the world and on to the cross."

His Way!

His way is our way; our way is his way. The way of the cross is the only way we can go. For "if any man would come after me, let him deny himself and take up his cross and follow me." This call to discipleship is repeated elsewhere; but here its meaning is clearest. Christ demands not only that we deny ourselves but that we ourselves die. The disciples could have no illusions, as we sometimes have, about what cross-bearing means. In the first century, one who carried his cross was normally carrying it to the place of his own execution. We speak about physical affliction, family problems, financial burdens, as the crosses we have to bear." The suffering these can cause is very real, but it is not the cross Jesus is talking about. The cross he speaks about is the cross of death.

Jesus makes this clear when he says that whoever tries to save his life will lose it. Yet when we go the way of the cross, even though we lose our lives for his sake we find them through him and in him. It seems like a crazy mixed-up kingdom out of *Alice in Wonderland* where gain is loss; saving your life means losing your life; and winning the world means forfeiting your life. On the other hand, losing is winning; debit is credit; defeat is victory; and death is life. Like the topsy-turvy world of Alice, even childhood proverbs are turned upside down and inside out: in God's kingdom finders are weepers and losers are keepers! And it all comes about by carrying our cross and following Christ to death.

But this does not mean some kind of imitation of Christ. We can't die as he died! Peter came pretty close. Tradition tells us he was crucified, by his own request, upside down. Perhaps by that time he had learned better than to try to imitate Christ perfectly—even in death. Remember how Jesus warned the disciples that they would die with him before he deserted him. Jesus reacts: Die? Not quite! Not yet, Peter! You'll deny me before you die for me! You want to die for me, Peter, but first I have to die for you. You can't protect me. My death protects you and all mankind from the desertions and denials, from the destruction and death you bring upon me. Someday, Peter, when you are far less willing and far, far less proud, you will be compelled and carried to your death for me. But now, it is I who must die.

Then what does it mean to take up our crosses and follow Christ to death? Whose death? First of all, *his* death! Paul explains that our baptism links us to Christ's death so that his death is our death. He died for sin; we die to sin. That's what our self-denial and death by crucifixion means: our relationship to sin is severed and broken by his death (See Rom. 6). Thus Paul can say: "I have been crucified with Christ. . . ." (Gal. 2:19 f.). Because he died for our sins, we are dead with respect to sin's claims on us. We are free from its dominion to live under God's rule. Because Christ lives, we too shall live. Death too has lost its power over us. And though death threatens us, by his cross and resurrection, Christ has conquered death and rescued us. When we follow him to death we find life in his cross—life given to us in his body broken for us and his blood shed for us. And having found that, we find that we can lose our life for his sake.

Ralph W. Quere
Wartburg Theological Seminary
Dubuque, Iowa

ORGANIZING THE ORGANISM

Sixteenth Sunday after Pentecost
Matthew 18:15-20

In this text Jesus is talking to his disciples. Is he talking to us too? We have to hear him doing so if we are going to get anything out of this sermon. He is indeed. He is talking about a gathering of people of which he is the chief member and the head. Down through the ages since his ascension to heaven we have called that gathering the church, that is, a group of people in the succession of the first disciples, people who acknowledge God as their Father and who have been baptized into Christ as their Lord and Savior. I have to make this clear at the start, for here Jesus is making quite a demand on us. He is asking us not merely to belong to the gathering we call the church, but to accept responsibility for one another in it. Christ's church is his body, it is an organism; and here Christ is showing us how we can be about the task of

Organizing the Organism

But he says that to each of us individually, too. The whole organism of the church begins to function as each one of us responds to Jesus' words.

Jesus wants to help us help fellow-Christians in need.

It's as simple as that. He starts out by recruiting us to help children, God's little ones. We are so apt to belittle them, because as adults we fancy ourselves to be more important than the children. No, says Jesus, to assume responsibility for the organism you have to be humble, get yourself down where the child is, make no claims of rank or age, apply yourself simply to the business of helping.

Another illustration that Jesus uses is that of a shepherd. The good one is concerned particularly for the sheep that strays. He finds it more fun to find the stray than to take care of all the ones safely in the fold.

St. Paul likens the partnership of the members of the church to the fabric of limbs and organs of the human body. Each has a task to perform for the sake of the others (1 Cor. 12). When we see the damage that goes on between people, sometimes right in the church and in Christian families, it is apt to be due to the apathy or laziness or pride that causes some to go their own way instead of being concerned for the needs of the rest. That isn't the way that our Good Shepherd, Jesus Christ our Lord, led the way; he gave himself up for us all.

Jesus wants us to help but not for selfish motives.

A damage that lurks in the wings of this business of helping our fellow-Christians, one that we thought we overcame in the very act of helping, is the pride that we did a job of helping. When Jesus welcomes his body the church to his right side at the day of judgment and speaks his joy that they are there and helped one another to get there while they were on earth, far from being proud about it they will say, "When in the world did we do that?" Our helping must be as natural and regular a thing for us as Christian people as it was for the Lord Jesus to go all the way, to get in there and die for the sins of the world; "it's my food," he said, "to do the will of my Father."

Especially when we remedy weaknesses and wrong in other people we are tempted to imagine ourselves superior. This becomes especially evil when we gossip about their weaknesses and magnify their failures in order to strut our own competence and correctness. Therefore our Lord sets up simple rules for reproving wrong in a person. Talk to him privately about it. It doesn't make any difference how public you think his wrong may have been; you are in the business of helping him improve if he was wrong, or of correcting the report if it was wrong. If the process didn't work out, take a helper or two so that you don't fancy yourself as the one great purifier and so that the importance of improvement is made clear. A stalled automobile is not helped by shouting "it stopped." It needs fuel or a new part. In God's business it is God who has to give the power to move and to repair, and he isn't helped by helpers who are simply strutting their own excellence.

Jesus wants to help us help people do the will of God.

It's important not to be misled by homely analogies for organizing the organism of the church. It's wonderful to be neighborly to friends and strangers alike when they are in distress. But in this business of the church, the chief help for which Jesus recruits us is to help people who sin, whether against us or against other people. That means that Jesus is enlisting us to work for God, to sustain God's people, to be his agents in sustaining the body of Christ, the church. He counts on us to help our brothers and sisters as they fail in carrying out the will of God and doing what God has placed them in the world to do.

This is difficult, for we are apt to feel that the thoughts and actions that people imagine involve God are their own and private business. Or, as happens in our permissive age, people find it possible to exclude God from acts of sexual or business morality or from their ordinary selfishness because everybody is doing it. That is why Jesus stresses "between you and him alone." If we think a person we know has sinned, the information is either false or true. If it's false, it is important that we help the individual get on the track of correcting the rumor. If it's true, it is even more important that we help the individual face up to the damage that he is doing not just to himself or other people, but to God and his commission to serve him. As we talk to a person who has committed a wrong against the will of God, we are really beginning to function as agents of God, as organs of the body of Christ. *Jesus wants to help us to be workers for God.*

As we talk about the whole church helping the individual, let's not get away from being the target, each one of us, of Jesus' counsel. We can practice this most regularly in what St. Paul calls the church in the house, the Christian family. There the crunch of help develops most frequently not just on the family council, but on one member, parent or child, spouse or friend, that says the good word in season because they stand in special closeness to the person in need.

Here we come to an element that our Lord makes central: this is an operation that we pray about. That means that we are taking human need of sin and weakness to God and pleading that God preserve his own, and help us in the process. We do this because we are gathered in his name, literally "into his name." In our own baptism we have been plunged into his death, and torn up into the refreshment of his resurrection. We remember his redeeming work in sermons like this or in the sacrament in which we consume the very body and blood which he gave on the cross for us, in order to share in the outcome of his redemption.

That is why this story from nineteen and a half centuries ago means us today. As then, we are disciples gathered into his name and into the exercising of his redeeming work upon one another.

He has to give us the concern of love that causes us to pray; he has to give us the skill, humble though it may be, to speak to one another.

Jesus wants us to help people be released from bondage and freed for life.

When a person sins, Jesus once said, he is a slave to sin. The Christian is in the business of freeing people from sin. It's a churchly custom to confess sin in the group and receive absolution. Or we engage in a bit of private counseling and confession and receive private absolution. That is a great experience. We have the habit of imagining that this is uniquely the pastor's business to do this. In Matthew 16 Jesus gave the authority to St. Peter. But by this chapter it becomes the business of all of the disciples. The Lutheran Confessions stress that the business of forgiving the sins of people belongs to every Christian. This is wonderful. We can bring the forgiveness of sins right from God to every fellow-Christian who confesses and looks in faith for forgiveness.

But this is more than just speaking forgiveness. This is setting men free. This is bringing that liberation to every man who sees his need and joins in the prayer for help and healing. How wonderful to be a person who "receives" one of God's little ones, takes him back into the functioning company and body of Christ's people.

Maybe we can catch the importance of this when we realize what happens if we fail. It may be that we did what we could and others helped, and when the whole church tried and failed, that we have to say that the person is behaving like an unbeliever, like somebody who sold out to the enemy like the tax-gatherers in Jesus' time. Then we have to take a deep breath and start over again, just as we send missionaries to unbelieving nations or struggle to bring Christ to people who have not known him or have conceived a prejudice against him. So frequently Christians heave a big sigh of relief when they can eject a useless or troublemaking member from their midst. But how earnestly are they taking the word that Christ died for the ungodly? How can they congratulate themselves when a person chooses death instead of life?

Jesus is tremendously serious about the task of salvaging sinners.

Our Lord puts possible failure in very personal terms. "Whoever causes one of these little ones who believe in me to sin, it would be better for him to have a millstone fastened round his neck and to be drowned in the depth of the sea." "Whatsoever you bind on earth will be bound in heaven." How do we bind people? How do we tie them up in the bonds of sin? Simply by formal words of excommunication from pulpits or in church magazines? Let them go until they "excommunicate themselves" as the saying goes? Much worse: Being so listless in our association with Christians, so careless about their lives under the gospel, that they find it easy to wander; so remiss in our own demonstration of the life of discipleship that they find it more pleasant to be a non-disciple.

These can be disconcerting thoughts. Our business today is not just to feel conscience-stricken and fearful about our remissness. But it is to become more closely knit into the fabric of the body. "When each separate part works as it should, the whole body grows and builds itself up through love," says St. Paul (Eph. 4:16 TEV). That we can do today as we behold the pain through which Jesus Christ went to shape us, each one, into the body; as we remember our pledge of unity with one another as we receive the body and blood of our Lord and at the same time discern the body we are together; as we look each other in the eye and say "Peace of the Lord" with the handclasp of fellowship; as we realize that Jesus Christ himself is with us at this moment, anxious to answer our prayers and speed us on our missions of mutual renewal. In his name we resolve to be organs of the organism of his church!

RICHARD R. CAEMMERER SR.
St. Louis, Missouri

FORGIVEN AND FORGIVING

Seventeenth Sunday after Pentecost
Matthew 18:21-35

It isn't easy to forgive. Oh, you can mumble your forgiveness, but really to mean it from your heart when a particularly nasty trick has been played on you, that isn't so simple. Downright meanness doesn't normally trigger mercy as a response. Vicious gossip about you in the beauty shop, a brazen lie to you by your teen-age child, violation of your property repeatedly by your next door neighbor, a mean and unjust accusation against you by your marriage partner in a heated exchange, someone running a red light and then blaming you for the accident at the intersection—all these are hard to take, to say nothing of returning mercy for meanness. Forgiveness isn't easy. Sometimes it's the most difficult thing in the world.

At the same time, the forgiveness that leads to reconciliation is the most needed thing in the world. The greatest lack in society is precisely at this point. Reconciliation is the missing element in so many relationships. Personal relationships are often frazzled because the swiftness of the modern pace finds us colliding with each other, but we don't take time to heal the damage. Blacks and whites are pitted against each other in many areas without the forgiveness that can bring conciliation. Organized labor and management feel misused by each other, and neither party wants to do the magnanimous thing lest it be interpreted as weakness. The larger the grouping of persons, the harder it is to initiate reconciliation. East and West both feel done in by the other side, but how can forgiveness be managed in a global context? Peace can only come through reconciliation, and reconciliation can only come through forgiveness, but forgiveness doesn't come naturally. What to do?

God gave us the answer in his forgiveness of us. Jesus spelled it out in a parable. A king in auditing his books discovered an official who owed him millions. The official was hopelessly over his head in the matter of clearing himself with his king. One who reads this parable could treat it as a theoretical possibility in a rare instance. Jesus meant it to be understood as the actual standing of every person in the presence of a holy God. As sinners, we are under the judgment of the throne, and there is no way by which we ourselves can satisfy the debt. The official broke out into a cold sweat. He saw his whole world going down. This finally was it. Since he couldn't pay, the king ordered the official's complete assets liquidated and his whole family sold into slavery. At that the official found his voice. Falling to his knees, he begged, "My lord, be patient with me and I will pay you back in full." The last words were a ridiculous claim, but the king responded to the first words. Just as the official felt that the sky was falling down on him, compassion welled up in the king's heart. "Moved with pity," the record reads, "the master let the official go and wrote off the debt." What a deliverance! Within an inch of doom he was saved. At the edge of the precipice he was pulled back to safety. The sense of relief in his heart was indescribable. It was the greatest experience of his life.

Even at the human level to receive forgiveness at the hand of another can be an exalting experience. Have you ever gone to somone's house to ask forgiveness for a very bad thing you did? You approach the house at turtle speed, suffocated with guilt. You can hardly bring yourself to ring the doorbell. Once inside, somehow you confess, express your shame and sorrow, and ask forgiveness. What response will come forth? Suppose the other party refuses to accept your apology. But no, with beautiful Christian grace that person forgives you completely, even apologizes that you were tortured about it, and assures you that he never even took it to heart. Coffee is served, and a friendship grows deeper than it ever was before. You walk down that person's sidewalk on your way home with your feet not even touching the ground. You are so grateful and comforted that you feel ten feet tall.

A Million Times More

Multiply this joy by a million when it comes to experiencing the forgiveness of God. We have wronged him more than we have wronged all other human beings combined, for the hurt we have caused others was even a deeper hurt for him. The one we love most we have hurt worst. After all that he has done for us, we have caused him indescribable pain. But wait! As we lie prostrate in repentance before him, doom doesn't fall. Sweet pardon descends instead. God has swept our whole mess behind him. Nothing at all stands against us. There's a rainbow around that throne of judgment. The rainbow of his mercy encircles the throne of his justice. It's like being snatched from before the firing squad at the last moment. The joy and relief we experience have no parallel on earth.

Our gratitude deepens when we discern behind the rainbow a cross. The price God paid to be able to express that mercy is incredibly high, for it cost him his beloved Son. Jesus paid that price, "not with silver and gold," as Luther's Small Catechism reminds us, "but with his holy and precious blood and with his innocent sufferings and death." As recipients of pardon at so high a price, we thrill with gratitude and joy which overflow our heart. Indeed, this is the costliest possession we own.

Elton Trueblood tells of an elderly refugee woman who fled half way around the world to Trueblood's home in America with a ball of yarn and her knitting. Every day she would knit, and every night she would unravel what she had knit and roll it on the ball of yarn again. She showed him the huge pearl she had hid in the center of the ball of yarn. It was the only thing she had salvaged out of her tragedy to take with her. Our pearl of great price is the incomparable experience of God's forgiveness. Tucked deep in our heart, it motivates us to go out and do likewise toward those who wrong us.

At this very point Jesus' parable takes a strange turn. The forgiven official went out on the street and happened to meet a fellow who owed him a few dollars. Without even being civil, he grabbed him by the throat and growled, "Pay back what you owe." What followed looks like an instant replay of what the official himself did before the king. This fellow dropped to his knees and begged, "Just give me time and I will pay you back in full." It's hard to believe what happened. The official turned a deaf ear and had him thrown in jail. The official didn't need the money. His king had written off his whole debt. Besides, the amount of money involved was only a mere fraction of what he had owed the king.

Handcuff the Two Together

The official made one bad mistake. He looked upon the forgiveness he had received from the king as one situation over there. He looked upon the forgiveness another man begged of him as another situation over here, and he didn't make any connection between the two. They were two entirely different worlds miles apart. But you can't do that. When the angry king got the official back in his presence again, he explained, "I canceled your entire debt when you pleaded with me. Should you not have dealt mercifully with your fellow servant, as I dealt with you?" The two situations are both part of a single whole. Never let them get separated. Handcuff them together. Each bears a direct relationship with the other. Jesus locked them together for all time when he taught us to pray, "Forgive us our trespasses, as we forgive those who trespass against us." The beatitudes promise, "Blessed are the merciful, for they shall obtain mercy." Five words in Jesus' parable set the direction for the Christian in every relationship with others. God speaks them: "As I dealt with you." Because we have received his mercy, we also are merciful.

It is a fair question as to whether the official really received the king's forgiveness. He was offered it. The parable says that the king "let the official go and wrote off the debt." But the parable also says at the end that the king in anger "handed him over to the torturers until he paid back all that he owed." Did he still owe it or didn't he? Was he forgiven or wasn't he? It appears that he had not really accepted the forgiveness in his heart. It hadn't registered. Otherwise how could he have treated the way he did the man who owed him a few dollars. Pardon had been offered by the king but not truly received; therefore, the debt still remained. The implication is that those who refuse to forgive another who has wronged them have not really themselves accepted the forgiveness which God has offered them.

Adding Machine Not Needed

Now examine the situation out of which this parable arose. Peter asked, "Lord, when my brother wrongs me, how often must I forgive him? Seven times?" Seven was a liberal number. Some Jews of that day held that three times was enough. Peter doubled that, and more. He was ready to keep score. Notice Peter's choice of words. "How often *must* I?" He seemed to be dragging his feet in this matter of forgiveness. Jesus answered, "No, not seven times; I say, seventy times seven times." By the old math or the new math that would be 490 times. But nobody is going to count that high. If you forgive that many times, you will be so much in the habit that you will keep on forgiving your brother as often as he needs it. That was exactly Jesus' point. Leave the adding machine out of it. Forgiveness is not a matter of arithmetic, but of attitude. As many times as God forgives us, we should forgive another. Suppose God started counting the number of times he forgave you. Just suppose that it ran over 500 times in a short while. Where would you go for forgiveness after that? God doesn't care to count. All he cares about is healing a broken relationship so that there can be joy and peace in the heart again. "As I dealt with you." God's way with us sets the pattern for our way with others.

Such an eager spirit to forgive is precisely what the world needs today when so many relationships are at the breaking point. This kind of forgiveness could save many a marriage, bridge many a generation gap in a family, heal many a disaffection between relatives, restore to happiness many an employer-employee fall-out, overcome many a racial alienation, unify many a polarized congregation, and bring peace to many an inflamed situation in the world. When Joseph was asked for pardon by his brothers who had sold him into slavery, he graciously forgave them this dastardly deed, saying, "You meant to do me harm; but God meant to bring good out of it." God can bring good out of every situation in which one person does another person harm, if there is repentance on the one side and forgiveness on the other.

Whenever anybody is wronged by another, the person who was wronged has the opportunity to make two persons supremely happy or utterly miserable. The initiative is his. A Christian, remembering God's amazing pardon toward him, also forgives for Christ's sake, thus bringing supreme happiness to the one who wronged him and also to himself in the pardoning. If he withholds forgiveness, he will make two persons miserable—the one who asks his pardon and himself. "As I dealt with you." That is the key in every fractured relationship. God's way with us shapes our way with others. The forgiven becomes the forgiving. "Moved with pity, the master let the official go and wrote off the debt." We only live once. Live it this way and really live!

ROBERT W. STACKEL, Executive Director
Division for World Mission and Ecumenism
LCA—New York

FREE TO ACT

Eighteenth Sunday after Pentecost
Matthew 20:1-16

The three lessons for this day point to radical differences existing between God and men. They are not described in categories of time or space, but rather in categories of character and quality. In the Old Testament lesson Isaiah, underscoring the nature of God, reminds us ". . . my thoughts are not your thoughts, neither are your ways my ways, says the Lord"—emphasizing the superior quality of the former. In the Epistle, St. Paul, speaking out of the fulness of a life in Christ, demonstrates the "freed" nature of his existence by asserting a certain casual dispassion toward the threat of death or the continuation of earthly life—"which I shall choose I cannot tell. . . . My desire is to depart. . . . But to remain in the flesh is more necessary on your account." However, the lesson that really bangs home the differences and dramatizes the free and superior nature of God is the Gospel.

Matthew's presentation of the parable of the householder is striking to say the least. Scholars generally agree it is in response to what has gone before—thus the importance of context. Our Lord has encountered the rich young ruler, a man eager to justify himself. Instead of endorsing his self achievement thesis, Jesus gives the invitation, "Sell what you possess and give to the poor . . . and come, follow me."

One senses the ruler's disconcert: "All I asked is what good deed must I do to have eternal life, and he ends up with this business of joining people on the beach and following him."

The quality of Peter's thought isn't much better. Seeing the young man leave, he asks Jesus the logical question. "We have left everything and followed you. What then shall we have?" Nothing like good old self sacrifice, is there?

Well, the Master does indicate some things disciples can expect, even to the point of reminding them that the first day may be last and the last first, but the basic challenge for him is to try to cut through this inherent human legalism, this action-reward motif—and say something about how it is in thy kingdom, that is, under the rule of God. Ergo the parable.

The Bane of the Merit Mentality

Being preoccupied with justice, and equal opportunity acts, and "commensurate reward for service given," and unions, and fair employment practices, we've stumbled and fumbled with the meaning of this text. It's an outrage, we murmur, an unholy outrage. Isn't God fair?

Emotionally our sentiments are with the rich young man. "There," we say, "was a man who knew how to run a railroad." His kind of creed breeds success. His philosophy builds department stores and guarantees noble eulogies. It also guarantees having buildings named after you on a college campus. We resonate with him because our ethics, like his, are ethics of self-justification and self interest.

Nothing is harder than the switch from self-justification to trusting God himself as the justifier. That is a true conversion. Must we always end up arguing about fairness or just rewards instead of letting grace take hold and making of us new creations?

What's Unique in This Parable?

Jesus' use of this parable strikes immediately at self-justification and obsession with rewards. The rich young ruler blew it—as did Simon Peter. Neither got beyond the merit routine and into thoughts that were higher and ways that were different.

The lesson, however, is more than an immediate indictment of human self-justification and a reaffirmation of justification by God. It's a profound lesson on grace with implications that just won't quit; take ownership for example. The assumption is that he is the gracious lord of this cosmic fief. It's his vineyard, his payroll, he can do what he wants with it. "Im I not allowed to do what I choose with what belongs to me?" Or consider a subsequent right "the householder's freedom to act," that is "God's freedom to act." He is not beguiled by a desire for greater popularity, coerced by value systems that say "this is fair and this isn't," or intimidated by threat of revolt. His freedom emerges from his selflessness, his concern for others. The New Testament words for that are grace and love.

Things are different in the kingdom of heaven, that is under God's direction. If we posit ourselves outside of that direction or say "this pertains to a time after death," we render this parable meaningless for the here and now

The Parable as Invitation

If, conversely, we take God's ownership seriously, we can begin to appreciate these words as an invitation to share the dynamics of the kingdom in the parameters of life, and the ethical clout is tremendous. Rather than being otherworldly, it invites us to work like slaves and be free as lords here in this one.

Governed by prudential self interests, the ruler and Peter weren't programmed to respond to that. Their questions: What good thing must I do? What then shall be receive? manifest their disorientation. They're hung with concerns of self-acclaim, reward, justification.

Can we ever experience freedom where ambition and the desires for security dominate? I think not. Those things inhere in the kingdoms of men. Yet how reluctant we are to face our passions for popularity, our confidence in value systems, our drives for reward and security. Are we programmed for a better response?

Implications of Relationship and Freedom

Here we come to some very critical issues. The first has to do with "native turf." We usually think about that in terms of geography and real estate—but the intriguing element in the parable is that our "native turf" is not a unique place but rather a unique relationship

Space-time categories betray us. They allow us to make location pre-eminent rather than relationship, and they do violence to a dynamic understanding of God in this world. If, e.g., we locate our Lord in heaven (a spatial heaven) we remove him both temporarily and spatially. (St. John reminds us, "He was in the world and the world was made by him, and the world knew him not.")

If we don't know the householder, everything, even his world, is alien. We look for compatible surroundings. When we know him that changes. The relationship assumes such significance that where we are or where we work is inconsequential. The important thing is who we work for.

Doesn't this have something terribly important to say to persons who think, "If only I could change locations, then life would have meaning"? I do like D. H. Lawrence's comments:

> Men are free when they are in a living homeland . . . not when they are escaping to some wild west. The most unfree souls go west and shout of freedom. Men are freest when they are most unconscious of freedom. The shout is the rattling of chains, always was.

Let Augustine's cry be heard—"My heart is restless 'til it rests in thee, O Lord." That's of first importance. Our living homeland, our native turf, is our relationship to him. Understanding that we gain some perspective on freedom and security.

While the question of commensurate pay is fundamental to the worker's complaint, see what Christ really points to—viz. the opportunity to work, i.e. freedom to work. "Where your treasure is there is your heart also." The workers located theirs in reward and security. Our Lord infers it might be in freedom and in the joy of living it out under the direction of and in relation to the householder.

Fydor Dostoevsky does a masterful job of describing the freedom-security tension in *The Brothers Karamazov.* (Cf. the section—"The Grand Inquisitor.") It is presented as a critique of the first temptation of Christ.

> Thou wouldst go into the world . . . with some promise of freedom which men in their simplicity and natural unruliness, cannot even understand; which they even dread . . . for nothing has ever been more insupportable for a man, and for a human society, than freedom. But seest thou these stones in this parched and barren wilderness? Turn them into bread and mankind will run after thee like a flock of sheep, grateful and obedient, though ever trembling lest thou withdraw thy hand and deny them bread. . . . Feed men and then ask of them virtue. . . . In the end they will lay down their freedom at our feet, and say to us, "make us your slaves . . . but feed us."

That he will not do. Freedom to be—in relation to him—is where ultimate security lies. This yammering for proper pay is only prolog to "feed us." The opportunity to live under a gracious lordship is ignored.

Summing It Up

What does all of this add up to? Candidly, everything hangs on grace. The merit bit is out, Kaput! It says, "Here's an invitation, and the avenue to new life." To accept it is to enter the kingdom of heaven! The world is now recognized as my householder's estate.

In this context, where the old becomes the new, I am not to be meanly occupied with what my compensation will be. Rather, having been bequeathed the freedom to be I am joyfully turned loose to do a job. Now I dare to embrace life and labor without being misdirected by passion for popularity, pressure of value systems, or the spurs of ambition.

If we really accept life in the kingdom we'll know, and grow in, grace. Like our Lord we'll also be free to act. We will trust the owner enough to believe "we shall not want"; we will trust him enough to believe that security is in the freedom he gives not in the "pay" we take.

The kingdom is at hand. Those who enter will find life mighty interesting—mighty interesting indeed.

WALTER R. WIETZKE, Director
Division for Theological Education and Ministry
ALC—Minneapolis, Minnesota

PROPER AND POLITE OR PENITENT AND PRODUCTIVE?

Nineteenth Sunday after Pentecost
Matthew 21:28-32

Promises, promises. This familiar expression aptly describes one of the two young men of the parable serving as today's text. The second son in the story was quick to make promises but zero on follow-through and fulfillment. He was polite and proper in his words to his father, but he didn't do anything. There was no action to match his nice words. He is a perfect illustration of the truth that promises are not enough.

Leaders Who Are Proper but Not Penitent

This fictional son of our text had a lot of real-life company among the leaders of Israel. That's why Jesus made up a story about him and his brother. The priests and the elders talked very politely and properly about religion and everything else.

They were long on promises but short on obedience, and for that reason Jesus repeatedly took them to task. In Matthew 23:3 he is quoted as saying of the scribes and Pharisees: "They say and do not."

It so happened that the priests and elders who were in Jesus' audience in the temple as he spoke the parable of our text were also men of political clout. At that point in history there was no stated separation between the government of Israel and its established religion. Some of the religious leaders were involved also in running the government and operating the courts—under the Roman aegis, of course. They had positions of power and influence in both the spiritual and political realm.

Offhand we might say it is different in our land in 1975. After all, we make quite a distinction between church and state; each has its own set of officers. Yet, this American separation between the religious and the political is not as sharp and complete as we once believed it to be. We like to think of our national leaders as those who give moral tone to our nation. Our culture claims to be religious. We put slogans about trusting in God on our coins and currency. We mention God in our pledge of allegiance. Politicians sprinkle their speeches with references to God (but seldom mention Jesus Christ!). Our civil religion in America is a mix of references to righteousness, the work ethic, cleanliness, thrift, and the heavenly Father. In 1973, the United States Secretary of the Treasury identified "that old-time religion" as "balance the budget." However, this hodgepodge of piety and morality is not yet the Christian religion, which calls for repentance and faith in Jesus Christ. Even so, we come awfully close to thinking of the United States as the chosen nation of God, and most of us would like to believe that our civic leaders are men and women of virtue on whom God must be smiling and whose example we can imitate.

However, through the years our confidence in our leaders has been shaken. We have found that a White House religion can proclaim a deity and a kind of piety and propriety without calling for repentance. If Israel in the first century had a problem with leaders who were not as pious as they appeared to be, we seem to have a similar problem in our day. In the 1970s, Watergate has come to be more than the name of an office building in Washington, D.C. Because of the shenanigans and skulduggery that went on in that building, Watergate, however overplayed, has come to be a term standing for hypocrisy and moral decadence in high places. It's a disease similar to the insincerity that afflicted men in high places in Jesus' day.

It really should not be disillusioning to us if we find a veneer of piety instead of penitence among leaders of both church and state. Satan seems to work the hardest on those who have been named to high office. Nevertheless, it does shake us when a respected preacher elopes with his organist or a government official is caught leading a double life. Unfortunately, things like that have always been going on, and, while the frequency and persistency of such scandals do not make them any more tolerable, the fact that in his time Jesus was dealing with disgraceful conditions and shameful situations not wholly different from those of 1975 should help us to get our spiritual sights in focus. We cannot control the moral fiber of those who sit in a city hall, a state house, a capitol, a church study, a synodical office, or a denominational headquarters, but we do have jurisdiction over our own lives—and that's why today's text has a message for us. It has relevance for all of us nearly 2000 years after it was spoken, because it is a pointed call to every individual to personal repentance.

Jesus Did Not Condone Impoliteness or Misspent Time

It is an abuse and misuse of our text to give the impression that it takes an easy attitude toward sin or smart-aleck behavior. It is wrong to say that, with its commendation of the young whippersnapper who at one point sassed his father, this story condones impoliteness and discourtesy. The Bible admonishes us to be not curt but "courteous at all times" (1 Peter 3:8). Jesus did not compliment the first son's brassy talk or brutal tongue, but his change of heart. The ideal child of God is not one who is brazen today but obedient tomorrow; a mature Christian is courteous and polite, obedient and productive, both today and tomorrow.

Furthermore, in using prostitutes and dishonest tax collectors as examples of people who will go into God's kingdom ahead of polite and proper priests and elders, Jesus did not mean to say: "Go ahead, sow your wild oats; that'll be okay as long as you repent sometime before you die." No. What he is simply stating is the fact that many people with a shoddy and shabby background do get into his kingdom because they come clean in their repentance. The Mary Magdalenes and the Matthews of yesterday and today don't try to justify their earlier conduct. They deplore their pasts. Once they come to faith in Jesus of Nazareth they are heartbroken over their misspent years. They cannot undo those days when they were saying "no" to God, but they can and do accept the invitation of a Savior who says: "Come unto me, all who labor and are heavy laden, and I will give you rest" (Matt. 11:28). They do that and they will find Jesus to be the One who took their place under the law to redeem them, that they might yet receive adoption as sons and daughters of God. Once that truth dawns on them, they cling to that Savior for dear life. They not only turn away from their sullied and sorry past; they turn to Jesus and walk with him. Thanks to the power of the Holy Spirit, they are new creatures who do "know how to love him" and who do know how to show and share their gratitude. They are both penitent and productive.

God's Incarnate Son: Obedient and Productive

Some Bible scholars have suggested that Jesus should have introduced a third son into the story of our text—one who would have both promised and performed, who would have said "yes" and acted accordingly. Apparently Jesus did not think it necessary; such a possibility and its desirability are perfectly obvious. But there is a third son involved in this story—and that is its teller. As you well know, he was more than a good storyteller. He was excellent at that as he preached judgment and forgiveness to the people of his day. Furthermore, he spoke as one having authority. It is no surprise to us that his contemporaries were sometimes amazed at his authenticity and the authority with which he spoke. We know that he was the incarnate Son of God, who came not only to preach and teach and speak parables but, above all, to reveal the true story of God's love for all his sons and daughters, including those who say "no." God so loved us, his wayward children, that he sent his child to be our brother, and, as we read in today's Epistle (Phil. 2:8), "being found in human form he humbled himself and became obedient unto death, even death on a cross."

God's Sons and Daughters Today: Penitent and Productive

That's how much God loved and loves his disobedient sons and daughters. Therefore, as we begin to appreciate the love that went all the way to Calvary, we shall pray for the Spirit's strength to show love and obedience to him—not only in proper words, but also in helpful works, and that's what repentance is all about. In repentance the man is turned from the deadness of his former works to live works of faith. Once we have been drawn to the cross, we say with the hymnist:

> And [now] for work to do for Thee,
> Which shall so sweet a service be
> That angels well might envy me,
> Christ Crucified, I come.

With the second son of our text we say to our Father: "I go, sir"; and with the first son we do go. We say and do what our Father asks, because we are grateful for all that his only-begotten Son has done for us.

True penitence will reach to every corner of our lives, including our duties as citizens in a country that is hurting and groaning because of corruption and corrosion in high places. As penitent sinners, we shall do more than groan, because we are aware of the fact that our heavenly Father expects us to do something about the situations we can improve. He is counting on us to be productive. "I chose you and appointed you that you would go and bear fruit," Jesus said in John 15:16. "By this my Father is glorified that you bear much fruit and so prove to be my disciples" (John 15:8).

If we are really hearing our Lord, we'll try hard to be responsible and trustworthy citizens even when sanctimony and irresponsibility are rampant as a way of life. We "shall not follow a multitude to do evil" (Exod. 23:2). More than that, in a land where we say that the government is not only for the people but also of and by the people, we must take seriously our Lord's words about our being a salt, a light, and a leaven. We dare not piously wash our hands of the "dirty business" of politics. Rather, we recognize the need for persons of integrity to assume and assert leadership. We need to do more than vote. Our choices are limited at the polls. The selection of candidates for public office begins far ahead of the voting booth, and not until more committed and consistent Christians are involved in those selections, not until more committed and consistent Christians are ready to offer themselves as candidates for public service can we expect an improvement in the public affairs of our nation.

To say polite things to and about our government, to be proper in our conduct in church is not enough. The need today is for obedient sons and daughters of God who know what it means to be both penitent and productive.

Promises, promises are not enough. What the Lord asks in addition to promises is performance, performance. So pray God in Jesus' name that our way of life will show us to be not just proper and polite, but penitent and productive.

Bertwin L. Frey
Messiah Lutheran Church
Fairview Park, Ohio

DREAM EXPLOSION

Twentieth Sunday after Pentecost
Matthew 21:33-43

Events and happenings or visions and imaginings portray an almost certain expectation, but then a new reality enters the scene and a dream explodes. Thus there was—an election landslide, then Watergate: *Dream Explosion.* The Lombardi era, then the Green Bay Packers, 1973: *Dream Explosion.* Church statistics upward and onward, then the 1960's and 1970's: *Dream Explosion.*

Dream explosions are not only found in world markings and events, but how true they ring within the personal drama of individuality.

> First there is man's vision of success, then the "Peter Principle": *Dream Explosion.*
> A family's portrayal of the ideal, then communication loss: *Dream Explosion.*
> A bright vocational concept, then day-by-day gut issues: *Dream Explosion.*

The Dream

The Lord had a vision. As in any act that is to follow, first a man must have in mind that which is before him—his goal—his dream. Then the Lord acted—he planted his vineyard. He hedged it round about—dug the wine press—built the tower. Not only was he preparing for that day, but as he so completely acted out his vision, he prepared for the future as well. These too are the finest dreams—those which deal not only with the moment but try to conceive and thus envision the future. Having completed the act, the Lord then gave it into the hands of the husbandman to care for, to gather one day the fruits of his vision now completed. This too speaks about humanity's actions having a greater dimension, as they are spawned further through the lives of others.

. . . and Explosion

The fruit of the Lord's dream was to be received, and so he sent servants to collect his portion—that one-fourth or one-half as it may be. His servants were beaten, killed and stoned—not only once, but twice. In his frustration he sent his son and thought surely this was one the husbandmen would receive. However, with greedy thoughts and plotting words the husbandmen killed his son and sought to gain all things for themselves. Here was the final disruption or explosion of the dream of the Lord. Here too was the explosion of the dream found in the husbandmen's sinful thought and action. Their opportunity had also passed by.

However, the Lord came again with a new dream and this one was not to be thwarted. He disposed of the unfaithful and evil husbandmen, appointed others to take their places, and then received the fruits of his dream.

. . . This Is Living

This vivid parable presents many thoughts for our dreams, actions and determinations. Let us look at but a few of them. First, are we not reminded of the very gracious garden of life in which our living takes place? All of the wonder and power of God's creative being is found in our midst. How we need to stand each day in thankfulness and gratitude for this amazing opportunity called *living today.*

And yet we forget, fail to acknowledge, make full use of this opportunity called living. Yes, we have the great freedom to accept or turn down that which is before us, and in our sinful ways the opportunity slides by and is not seized. How often we turn that which is meant to be shared, and direct it only to ourselves. In that living stance we then lose even that which we have claimed as our own. We need to remember that our life is ours but only insofar as it is dedicated to Almighty God.

The real living is what goes on inside as experiences are born out of dreams and those moments are received.

> *The man who lives by himself and for himself is apt to be corrupted by the company he keeps.*—Charles Parkhurst.

True it is—when life withdraws into itself, it becomes lonely, empty, unfulfilled—and frustration and anxiety breed and multiply unrelentlessly. Life only finds fulfillment when it flows through one life out into that span of people, things, places and events which touch upon it.

. . . in One Day's Passing

Another thought which is certainly displayed in this parable is the potentiality of greatness which is passing by our lives. This potential can become our dream fulfilled as we see it, or it is our life's hellish judgment when we let it go by unchallenged and unclaimed.

Of course we handle our failures quite easily. We rationalize them away—excuse them away—or do whatever is necessary in order to put them aside. The words of Eugene O'Neil in his *Long Day's Journey into Night* are to be remembered: *"None of us can help the things life has done to us. They are done . . . until at last everything comes between you and what you'd like to be, and you've lost yourself forever."*

Yes, opportunities continually go by and those not seized become for us our judgment and soon we have lost all vision of ourselves. However, through God's grace of forgiveness, a greatness once passed by can come another way again and our life is renewed. In sincere confession may we come—as we fail to rise to God's invitation, or pervert that which is given to us which is good, or even rebel against his loving direction in our lives. Yes, let us come in confession daily and be renewed by his grace to live again.

. . . and Then Our Ego Trips

How clearly this parable portrays the Lord's bitter grief over our turbulent and rebellious natures. He came to give us all good things and yet we turn him away. Repeatedly, this occurs as we are dreaming our own dreams and forgetting his dimension in our lives. We need to remind ourselves that each day we stand in the spectrum of Jesus Christ and not in the prism-like vanities of our constantly changing ego displays.

> *Courage, or ambition, or love of notoriety may take you to the Antarctic, or any other uncomfortable place in the world, but it won't take you far inside.*—Admiral Richard Byrd.

In this world of which we are a part, how easy it is for us to get caught up in the turbulent assaults of humanity's vain desires and leave undone those Christ-centered things which really speak of life.

A man once wrote, *"You can test all your sentiments about love for humanity by what you are doing for individuals."*

How necessary it is to siphon down many of our wild imaginations to the practicality of day-by-day living, and there live our glib words of profession.

Thy Kingdom Come

There is one divine absolute which we must sear into our consciousness: As we reject the kingdom and the Lord's presence so it will be gone from us—forever. Neither by Baptism nor faith's emotional explosion is the kingdom of God an absolute dimension of our lives. We can reject—we do reject; we can desert—we do desert. Certainly, the Lord is not restricted to us—when we turn him aside there is no unbreakable tie in his relationship with us. Maybe this is the dream that needs to explode most in our lives —this cantankerous, prideful, sin-swept conviction that often marks a man's life: his unfounded assertion of an inside track with the Lord of life. This dream must explode so that we can find what is the real dimension of our life. To experience life in its fullest the urgent exigency is to open up our lives—receive, respond and reach out. Thus, joy and hurt, sorrow and exultation are together diffused in each person's historical moment called *me.*

The words of Dietrich Bonhoeffer: *"To renounce a full life and all its joys in order to escape pain is neither Christian nor human."* We are called on in our lives today not to turn aside any moment, person, or place, but there mediate and know God's grace.

Dreams need to be dreams—visions need to be enacted—explosions need to take place—that you and I might know the fullness of God's grace and the assurance of his kingdom's mark on our lives.

C. L. JOHNSON
Fox Point Lutheran Church
Milwaukee, Wisconsin

CALLED TO CELEBRATION AND COMMITMENT

Twenty-first Sunday after Pentecost
Matthew 22:1-10 (11-14)

It was during that period between the Sunday of the Palms and the Friday of the Cross. Jesus had come to proclaim the good news of the kingdom of God and for three years had gone through the land preaching and healing, but the leadership challenged him at every opportunity and rejected both him and his message.

The opposition of the religious leaders toward Jesus had been growing more and more intense and open. This hostility reached its apex following Jesus' Palm Sunday entrance into Jerusalem. Jesus confronted them with their hostility toward him and his message. Through the use of parables he tried to open up this matter in the hope that they might see what they were doing. The parable of the "rejected invitation" is one of these parables.

The point of the parable was surely obvious. Throughout the years of Israel's history God again and again had sent his servants, the prophets, to his people. Again and again the people had rejected those prophets even as they were now rejecting Jesus. Therefore, the message of the kingdom would be taken beyond Israel, the chosen people. It would be taken to the gentiles. They would listen and believe. They, too, would be invited and received into the kingdom of God.

This parable was told some 2000 years ago, but as so many of Jesus' parables, it has that enduring quality that gives it a meaningfulness for all men and women of all times and places. It speaks to us too. We, too, are called to the kingdom, to the feast of God. Through the gospel of Jesus, the Holy Spirit calls us to faith in our day. He calls us into the Kingdom, the body of those who name Jesus as Christ and Lord of their life. That's you and me. That is what we were affirming to each other a few minutes ago when we said, "I believe in Jesus Christ his only son our *Lord.*" We affirm our call to the kingdom and the lordship of Jesus of Nazareth in many ways. In our Baptism, in our celebration of the Lord's Supper, in our worship, in our statements of faith and in our deeds of faith we proclaim that we belong to Christ and his kingdom. This parable opens up some of the dimensions of what it means to live in that kingdom. It is truly a parable for us who claim we are called to the kingdom.

Cause for Celebration

This parable tells me that to live in the kingdom means we ought to live a life of celebration. When the Scriptures describe the kingdom of God it most often uses the image of a feast or banquet. The mood that is conveyed is always that of joy and celebration. We are to consider our life in the kingdom. And well we should. To live in the kingdom is to acknowledge the presence and grace of God in this world, in our lives. That is surely cause to celebrate.

Some people ask: What do you possibly have to celebrate in a world that continually lurches from turmoil to catastrophe? All about us we see warfare, suffering, starvation, inhumanity of man to man, political crises, energy crises, personal crises, sickness, sorrow and death. One could go on and on with such a cataloguing of woes. What is there to celebrate? A hymn writer put it this way:

> That is my Father's world,
> O let me ne'er forget
> That though the wrong seems oft so strong,
> God is the Ruler yet.
> This is my Father's world;
> Why should my heart be sad?
> The Lord is King, let the heavens ring
> God reigns, let the earth be glad!

This is still God's world and he claims us as his own. There is cause to celebrate.

The parable indicates both the good and bad were invited. We are not claimed as his because we deserve it, but because God cares for us and wants us to be his. Through Jesus he calls us to be his own. He promises that all things work together for good for those who love him. Out of the worst of situations God can yet enable good to come. He promises that nothing can separate us from his love, no matter how terrible it is. He promises to forgive our sins. Though our "sins are like scarlet, they shall be white as snow." He promises us victory over death. As Christ has been raised from the dead, so shall we. He promises us his love which enables us to love one another. There is cause to celebrate.

To live in the kingdom is to be called to celebrate this presence and grace of God. That's why we gather here in worship. Let our gathering not be out of obligation or habit. Let it not be to seek the favor of God or man. Let our worship arise because we have received the good news of God's kingdom and we are compelled to celebrate it because our hearts are overflowing with joy, peace, and hope.

We ought to be a celebrating people every day of our lives. We must never allow disappointment with people or destructive events to turn us into cynics and pessimists. Then we will have lost one of the gifts the people of the kingdom have to share with the world—hope in God. Rather than lamenting over what the world has come to, we ought to celebrate the news that God has come to our world. He is with us. Each day can be begun, lived, and concluded in the faith that "the Lord of hosts is with us; the God of Jacob is our refuge." Let us daily celebrate the faith, hope, and love he pours into our lives which enables us to be a people of faith, hope and love, celebrating through our lives with the future we hold. "For not with swords loud clashing, nor roll of stirring drums, but deeds of love and mercy, the heavenly kingdom comes."

Conflicting Invitations

We are told in the parable that some who were invited wouldn't come to the marriage feast. They had other things to do. They had other concerns on their agenda which were in conflict to the invitation to the feast. In fact, they became very hostile about the matter, even mistreating and finally killing the messengers. We, too, are involved in the struggle over invitations which conflict with the invitation to the kingdom.

There are too many to enumerate, but they are represented in the following thoughts. There is the invitation to self-service, which is expressed in the idea that we ought to take care of ourselves first and use other people for our gain—but the kingdom of God is a kingdom of serving others. There is the invitation to garner wealth and possessions—but the kingdom of God is a kingdom of giving away what we have for others. There is the invitation to sell our souls, our principles, for popularity or gain—but the kingdom of God is a kingdom of justice and integrity. Each day these and other invitations which compete with the invitation of the kingdom of God are laid at our door. Each of us has those particular areas where we are most vulnerable, where we have to struggle with our self, our own pride, and our prejudices. This means that there is a daily struggle as we work out in practical reality what it means to take Jesus seriously when he said "seek ye first the kingdom of heaven." That task runs the full gamut of all my relationships and activities, from relationships with my family and neighbors, to what causes I can or ought to support (or oppose) with my energy and resources. We are called to enter into the fray with boldness and the conviction that what we say and do in the very commonness of our daily life needs to affirm our acceptance of the invitation to the kingdom and the importance that invitation lays upon us in our decision making. The daily struggle is captured in the verse of the familiar hymn:

> Jesus calls us from the worship
> Of the vain world's golden store;
> From each idol that would keep us,
> Saying, "Christian, love me more."

Who? — Me?

But perhaps some of us are saying: wait a minute. We don't identify with those who in the parable rejected the invitation. We haven't rejected it. We do claim Christ as Lord. We are here to celebrate his presence with us. This parable can't really be addressed to us who are here.

Jesus concluded the parable with this little note about those who accepted the invitation (22:11-14). Those who went to the kind of banquet described in this parable were expected to wear suitable clean attire. It was to be a garment fit for a wedding and not some soiled street clothes used in making the trip. The parable depicts one who had accepted the invitation but who was not willing to accept the obligations of a wedding guest that went with acceptance of the invitation. Such a guest forfeited his invitation. Jesus concluded the parable with those haunting words: "Many are called, but few are chosen." Many are invited, but few respond in the manner consistent with the invitation. We are always more willing to celebrate than to serve!

Cheap Grace or Commitment?

This parable calls us to examine our claim of discipleship. That we live by the grace of God is, for us as Christians, a fundamental understanding of our relationship with God. We love to sing "Amazing Grace." At the same time we must take care that we do not fall into that spiritual trap which says that to live by grace means there need not be a response of commitment to Christ. To have that idea of grace is to live under what Dietrich Bonhoeffer called "cheap grace." He said "cheap grace is grace without discipleship." Cheap grace is to accept the invitation to the kingdom, but not commit oneself fully to living as a son or daughter of the kingdom.

Is it clear by what we say that we are followers of Jesus? Is it clear in our concern and care for those in any need? Do we follow our words with deeds? Is our commitment evidenced by our personal witness to the faith? Is it seen in our participation in the life and program of the church, in our community service, in addressing the social, political and economic issues in our community and nation and in our every day dealings with each other? What are those specific needs that cry out for my attention as a Christian? And what about those nooks and crannies in my life where I don't want Jesus to be Lord because then I would have to change my attitude and actions? Helmut Thielicke reminds us that it is at the points where I least want God involved that God most wants to get into my life. Are we willing to open ourselves up and follow through even there? Are we committed to keep the faith no matter what the cost in terms of power, prestige, pride, or possessions?

Acceptance of the invitation to the kingdom means commitment. The invitation is by grace, freely given. There is nothing I can do to deserve it, but again we need to recall the words of Bonhoeffer: "grace is *costly* because it calls us to follow, and it is *grace* because it calls us to follow Jesus Christ. It is *costly* because it cost a man his life, and it is *grace* because it gives a man the only true life."

We are called and invited to receive the new life of the kingdom of God. Let us respond with celebration and commitment. Let us celebrate the presence and grace of Christ and commit ourselves to follow him with lives of faithful service.

THOMAS F. LOFTUS
St. John's Lutheran Church
Madison, Wisconsin

THINGS FOR CAESAR — THINGS FOR GOD

Twenty-second Sunday after Pentecost
Matthew 22:15-21

One of the major events in 1973, was the Senate of the United States selecting a special committee to investigate what we have come to know as Watergate. The discoveries of that committe left many people in this nation fearful of the survival of the nation.

Select committees have a long history. According to the Gospel for today, they can be traced back to the time when our Lord Jesus Christ lived on this earth. We find there, a select committee of church people, disciples of the Pharisees and Herodians. Unlike the Senate's select committee on Watergate, this committee had as its purpose the entanglement of Christ in wrong speech and wrong doing—sins against Caesar or God. The achievement of this purpose would make the death of Christ Jesus possible.

The U.S. Senate's select committee went about its investigation with the oath, with written statements, and with interrogating the witnesses. This select church committee goes about its investigation with great subtlety. The truth is used to produce evil. Look how the Lord is described, teacher, true, just and fair, courageous enough to speak his mind on any issue of the day.

The select committee of the U.S. Senate did not fail in its tasks. This select church committee failed to achieve its goal. They did discover, however, that there are *things for Caesar and things for God!* That is our theme for today.

Things for Caesar

The text gives us a list of things which belong to Caesar. The Imperial tax belonged to him. This select committee of church people seems trouble that this should be so. The whole text is built around this one thing. But from looking around in the city of Charlotte, one thinks that Caesar owned land, buildings, equipment of all descriptions. In Charlotte, the police department belongs to him, the fire department belongs to him, the jail belongs to him. In Charlotte, there are a great many factories, wherein the things Caesar owns are produced. Caesar made the things he owned. The coin was his, because he made it.

When Caesar made the things he owned, he stamped his image and inscription upon them. Notice how our Lord responds to their question. Whose image is on it? Whose inscription is upon it? Caesar's is the answer. They could see the image and read the inscription on it. I have noticed some tihngs the city of Charlotte owns. The picture of the city is there. The name of the city is there. One imagines it to be that way with Caesar and his things. That is why our Lord says things rather than just money, just a coin.

Caesar's ways are much with us. You own things, I own things. I own some credit cards, some clothes, a car, a house with a big debt, and some appliances. Most of the things I own are purchased from one place. This one place is to me a factory where the things one owns are made. Therefore, what I own, I own as if made by me. Caesar's ways are my ways too. Isn't that true with you?

Christ Commands Us to Give Caesar His Things

Listen to the text: Then he said to them, "Render therefore to Caesar the things that are Caesar's."

Give Caesar all his things is the command of Christ to this select committee. That is his command to those who sent the committee to him. In the text the tax is due him, that should be. paid. The money for the tax belongs to Caesar, that should be given him. It is interesting to me to note that our Lord did not have one of Caesar's coins in his pocket.

Allow me to stretch the point of this text a little. A certain amount of obedience belongs to Caesar, he should have it. A certain amount of respect and goodwill belong to Caesar, people should give that to him. When the people of Israel were in captivity, our Lord through his prophet counseled them: "But seek the welfare of the city where I have sent you into exile, and pray to the Lord on its behalf, for in its welfare you will find your welfare" (Jer. 29:7). St. Paul was echoing the words of that prophet when he proclaimed: "Let every person be subject to the governing authorities. For there is no authority except from God, and those that exist have been instituted by God" (Romans 13:1).

Caesar has his things now. He continues to make them. As soon as he makes them, he stamps his image and his inscription on them. We know his things. We use his things. We should be ready to give them to him. We are under the command of Christ to give him his things.

Caesar's sin is that he places things above people. He places himself above things, people and God. He would consider people as made by him. He would stamp his image and likeness upon people just as he does things. He would use people the way he does his things. When President Nixon was making his appointments of U.S. Justices, there was a cartoon of all the Justices sitting in their places on the court. They all looked like the President. They had faces like him, noses like him, and words like him. That is the way Caesar comes across to me in this text. If the text did not point to the cunningness of this committee, so clearly, I would believe he came across this way to the people who sent this committee to Christ. If the text did not call the actions of this committee malicious and hypocritical, I would believe our Lord got this impression from them because he added this phrase in the text; and (render) to God the things that are God's. Now let us consider the things that are God's.

Things That Are God's

We could define the things of God with one word: *everything!* God does it that way. Hear it from his word. "The earth is the Lord's and the fulness thereof, the world and those who dwell therein" (Psalm 24:1). "For every beast of the forest is mine, the cattle on a thousand hills. I know all the birds of the air and all that moves in the field is mine" (Psalm 50:10-11). Psalm 8:3

hints that the heavens and the stars belong to him. In one of the Lutheran Hymns we sing:

We give Thee but Thine own,
Whate'er the gift may be;
All that we have is Thine alone,
A trust, O Lord, from Thee.

The image of God is not written on his things. If he did not tell us so plainly in his word that everything that is made is made by him, we would never fully know it. Caesar goes around stamping his name on everything he makes, but not God. God, in the person of Jesus Christ, could be in our world, living, eating, sleeping, teaching and preaching the kingdom of God and neither the select committee nor those who sent them could recognize him, because the image of God is so unknown to them.

The one place where we find the image and inscription of God is among people. In the opening chapter of Genesis we read: "Then God said, 'Let us make man in our image, after our likeness'; . . . So God created man in his own image, in the image of God he created him; male and female he created them." This image of God made man special. He knew God. He walked and talked with God. He found delight in doing the will of God. He loved God with all his heart, all his soul. So blessed was man in the image of God that Luther wrote: "The naked man, without arms and walls, yea, without any garments, ruled in his bare body over all birds, beasts and fishes. . . ."

The devil went to Adam like the committee went to Christ. He asked him questions like this committee asked Christ. His purpose was to entangle Adam in his speech, in his thinking, and action and so destroy the image of God in him. Adam, the man who was stamped with the image and likeness of God, was overcome with the flattery of Satan. He was persuaded to snatch the image and likeness stamp from the hands of God to use it as if it belonged to him. Through this subtle device, man was entangled in his talk, deceived in his action and left to stand before God with enmity of God, hatred for God and rebellion against God. He sinned against God. The image and likeness of God was almost lost to him.

That image and likeness which was almost lost to Adam was almost lost to people, to you and to me. We are left with a veil of spiritual darkness over us. We are described as being "separated from Christ, alienated from the commonwealth of Israel, and strangers to the covenants of promise, having no hope and without God in the world" (Eph. 2:12). St. Paul gives the implications of not having the image and likeness of God in these words: "Therefore as sin came into the world through one man and death through sin, and so death spread to all men because all men sinned" (Rom. 5:12).

In the text, our Lord Jesus uses two words which identify the members of this committee with mankind in our spiritual condition after the fall. They are "malice" and "hypocrites." He is putting his finger on those evil purposes and desires we have toward God. He is lifting up those wicked ways in which we try to keep God out of our lives.

What man has lost, God makes available to him by grace through faith in our Lord Jesus Christ. Christ was incarnate in human flesh to make possible the restoration of the image of God in us. We, who believe in Jesus Christ as our Savior, we, who look to him for forgiveness of sins; know that God has duly punished him for us, that he has died for our sins, and that with his almighty power God has raised him from the dead and received him as his right hand. Knowing Christ as we do, believing in him as we do, we call ourselves his people.

Time was when God created man in his image and likeness. Now he goes to the baptismal font. He claims his people there. He washes away their sins there. He becomes their God there. He gives them his image and likeness there. He met me there. He blessed me there. I hope he has met you there. I know he waits for you there. Now let us consider in the fourth place that our Lord commands us to give God his things.

Render to God the Things That Are God's

I can fancy, in my mind, standing before my Lord like the committee of "church people." He looks me in my eyes in his way of seeing through people. Then he asks me his questions: "What do you own?" In my answer, I offer the list given here. Then he asks me again whose things they are? I pray that my response will be: "All the things I own belong to Caesar, but my heart, my soul, my body, all that I am belong to you, my Lord. Your image, your inscription is upon me." Then I pray that I will be bold to say to him, Lord, let me speak to you in some ancient words by one of your servant: "I am no longer my own, but yours. Put me to what you will, rank me with whom you will; put me to doing; put me to suffering; let me be employed for you, or laid aside for you; exalted for you, or brought low for you; let me be full, let me be empty; let me have all things, let me have nothing; I freely and heartily yield all things to your pleasure and disposal.

And now, O glorious and blessed God, Father, Son and Holy Spirit, you are mine, and I am yours. So be it. And the covenant which I have made on earth, let it be ratified in heaven.

I fancy, when I am finished with this statement of faith and that as I wait in silence, in hope, in anticipation, he will speak those glorious words of grace to me: You, my friend, have faith. You understand rendering unto God the things that are God's. God, your Father, is pleased when you render unto him the things that are his in that spirit and devotion. He commands it. You give it to him.

Lord, this response is what one desires, but it is not fully so. The glitter of things lingers on in my eyes. My sinful nature, keeps me hanging on to things. Set me free to render to Caesar that which is his and to you that which is yours, through Jesus Christ, our Lord.

May the grace of our Lord Jesus Christ, and the love of God keep your hearts and mind through Jesus Christ, our Lord. Amen.

BRYANT E. CLANCY JR.
Prince of Peace Lutheran Church
Charlotte, North Carolina

THE TRAP THAT BACKFIRED

Twenty-third Sunday after Pentecost
Matthew 22:34-40 (41-46)

"And one of them, a lawyer, asked him a question, to test him" (Matt. 22:35).

The Trap

It had turned into a real struggle. The Pharisees and the Sadducees knew they had to get rid of this young prophet from Nazareth named Jesus. Everything seemed to be going wrong.

The Pharisees had the first turn at bat. They waited until they had him out in the public eye and then they tried their plot from which he could not escape.

They asked him, "Is it lawful to pay taxes to Caesar—a false deity—or not?" But he did the impossible and escaped. "Show me a coin," he said. "Whose likeness and inscription does it bear?" They said, "Caesar's." Then he said to them, "Render to

Caesar the things that are Caesar's, and to God the things that are God's."

They marveled at that. It was a brilliant reply. However, they weren't finished as yet. Now the Sadducees, who didn't believe in the resurrection, had their turn at bat. They presented him with a problem that would surely discredit him before the people.

Moses had instructed that if a brother died having no children, then his brother must marry the widow and raise children for the departed brother.

Then they got into an involved problem of one woman married to seven brothers. "In the resurrection, to which of the seven will she be wife?"

"You don't understand Scripture or the resurrection," said Jesus. "They don't marry in heaven but are like the angels." "Besides," said Jesus, "haven't you read [in Exodus] where God says, 'I am the God of Abraham, Isaac, and Jacob? God is God of the living and not the dead!" And the Sadducees knew they had struck out—they had been permanently "silenced."

"Fools rush in where angels fear to tread." The Pharisees would make one more run at him and so they cleverly set their trap.

"Teacher, which is the great commandment in the law?" With hundreds of laws to choose from, that question would have to start an argument. They were lawyers and they could argue any point of the law. It was a trap he couldn't escape!

Except—he turned the law right back on those attorneys. He quoted some Scripture from Deuteronomy that every one of them repeated every day. A statement that completely satisfied that question:

> You shall love the Lord your God with all your heart, and with all your soul, and with all your mind. This is the great and first commandment. And a second is like it, you shall love your neighbor as yourself. On these two commandments depend all the law and the prophets.

He was truly amazing, for that was the perfect answer. *Strike three! They were out.* The trap had backfired!

We, Too, Are Trapped

The answer of Jesus to the Pharisees' trap was more than just a clever escape from a difficult plot. It was a statement of eternal truth that applied to all of us.

I have always maintained that the great difficulty of the Christian life does not lie in our inability to know God's will for our lives. Rather, it is the courage and commitment needed to do what God has so clearly shown.

"Love God above all things and love your brother as yourself." That is a man-sized assignment that none of us can escape.

A few years back, a sensitive young man came to my office to tell me that the Holy Spirit had been working in his life and he had committed himself to Christ. We rejoiced in that new relationship and spent time talking about ways he could serve Christ on his job, in our community, and at our church.

A few days later he was back to see me again. This time he was in tears. "What has happened?" I inquired. "I have discovered that Christ doesn't want just my time," he answered, "he wants all of me. I think he wants me to enter the ministry, and I don't want any part of that."

Obviously, he was snared. He resisted going to the seminary. He tried job after job and finally church after church, and he became a very unsettled man. He escaped Christ's demand on his life and it truly backfired on him.

In that same congregation is another young man who felt God's demand on his life. I was certain that he was heading for the seminary and a pulpit. Yet God led him in another direction. As a high school student he organized other youths to go into Appalachia and spend their summers constructing roads, building community centers and helping the disadvantaged in numerous ways. When he graduated from college he went to work for the Jaycees to help bring lunch programs to the children of America. This past fall he became the youngest elected mayor in the state of Minnesota. Those of us who know him realize that in his way he has responded to Christ's command to love God and his brother. It hasn't backfired on him, but it has brought fulfillment to his life.

How Do You "Love God?"

Luther says in explaining the First Commandment, "You shall fear, love and trust in God above everything else." That says it very well!

I watched a young musical group clapping their hands and singing "Put Your Hand in the Hand of the Man from Galilee." It was exciting and inspiring. However, I couldn't help wondering if they would put their hand in Christ's hand if he led them to witness to their faith at work, or go into a ghetto and help children with crafts, reading, and projects. What would happen if he led them to financially sacrifice as he did the Rich Young Man?

"Love, Love, Love, that's what it's all about!" is a song our children sing. But that love is not some sentimental, romanticized dream that causes us to leave the pain and suffering of this world. It is the type of force and direction that led Jesus to his cross and numerous martyrs to shed their blood for their faith in him.

Carlyle, in his book, *Sortor Resortus,* shows a lofty philosopher sitting in his high attic at midnight looking at all of the pain, suffering, and sorrow of a half million people struggling with their lives in the city below.

"But I," said the philosopher, "I sit above it all; I am alone with the stars."

Anyone who hears Christ's command to love God can never afford that lofty luxury. Jesus has made it clear. If a man is to follow him, he must take up his cross daily, denying himself, and then come and follow him.

For me, to love God changes my priorities in my life. I don't go to church on Sunday as a duty; it is my opportunity to worship and express my love to him. Daily prayer and Bible reading are not some meaningless habit but it is the life line in growth and development of my relationship to God. I no longer give him the loose change in my pocket as an offering but, like the Wisemen of old, I give him an offering suitable for a king—and that costs something.

In a medieval cathedral, an old priest was to have a Vesper service and his message was entitled "The Love of God."

It was dark when the parishioners huddled in the nave. They were very surprised when the old priest came into the chancel with a stepladder and a lantern. He placed his ladder beside the large crucifix on the altar and climbed to the place where he could shine his lantern on the nail print on Jesus' right hand. Then he went to the left hand. Next he went to the crown of thorns that pierced his brow. He climbed down to the spear wound on his side, and finally to the spikes in his feet. At each place he allowed the lantern to shine on the wounds of the Lord.

The old priest climbed down to the chancel floor and finally broke the silence with these words: "Can we do any less?"

Love Our Neighbor

Every time we speak about loving God, he always lays upon us a horizontal dimension. If you are going to love me, then you must express it to your brother in need.

In Matthew 25, Jesus shows that his judgment will be based on how we have or have not met our neighbors' needs. "Inasmuch as you did it to the least of these my brothers, you did it unto me."

"He who does not love his brother whom he has seen, cannot love God whom he has not seen," says St. John.

Dostoevski tells about a woman evangelist who traveled Russia talking about the love of God. Yet that same woman couldn't stand to be in the same room with another person. One man slurped his soup; a woman cackled when she laughed; another man snored when he slept. And so the great author said, "Although she loved God in general, she couldn't stand man in particular."

And that will never do! We can never love God if we do not love our neighbor.

In Johan Bojer's story, *The Great Hunger,* an illustration is given to show how to love our neighbor.

An anti-social newcomer moved into a rural community. He put up a fence around his property and "No Trespassing" signs to warn all intruders. To insure his privacy, he put a fierce dog behind that fence.

One day his next-door neighbor's little girl crawled under the fence to pet the dog, and that fierce beast grasped her by the throat and killed her.

The community was enraged. They ostracized that unfriendly neighbor. No one spoke to him. Clerks refused to wait on him. In the spring no one would sell him grain for his fields. He was destitute.

One day he looked out to see another man sowing seed in his field. He rushed to that man only to discover it was the father of the little girl. "Why are you doing this, you of all people?"

"I am doing it," said the father, "to keep God alive in me."

That father was trapped by Jesus' answer and in that forgiving deed he found healing and life. And so shall all of us who love God above all and express it to our brother. For we, too, are trapped by his love. Amen.

Paul M. Werger
St. Luke's Lutheran Church
Bloomington, Minnesota

AN OIL SHORTAGE— TO HAVE OR NOT TO HAVE

Twenty-fourth Sunday after Pentecost
Matthew 25:1-13

As I sat quietly in my study preparing this sermon, I kept getting colder. We had been keeping our house at sixty-eight degrees to conserve heating oil during a fuel shortage. Without such precautions, we were told, we might have long, cold winters, without enough fuel for everyone.

So I faced a decision as I began to shiver. My skeptical nature may have said that there is no real fuel shortage, and I would simply turn up the furnace. A sweater or blanket was easily available for wrapping around my shoulders and legs. I could jog around my study, or even take a hot shower. But, with my wife and children away for the day, I lowered the thermostats upstairs, and raised the one downstairs, where I was sitting. It was a neat decision, so I thought.

When I returned to the study of this text, Jesus' story really came to life! No one could help but make the connection. Our whole nation faces a fuel shortage, really an energy crisis, and apparently very few people really believed it would ever happen. Some are still skeptical about its reality. Ecologists and environmentalists have been telling us for years that this nation can't go on living with its fantastically high standard of living and not run out of energy. We use up too much energy in proportion to our population. So now we have to tighten our belts, grit our teeth, lower our thermostats, and slow down our golden god of progress in order to meet the crisis.

We've been warned. We've been told. We've heard impassioned pleas to limit our creature comforts, and we simply haven't listened. We weren't prepared for this situation. We now wonder how we will get along with things our grandparents never dreamed of, but which we call necessities. Warnings to be prepared haven't availed.

Jesus' parable is about this very thing. Five of those maidens were ready for the coming of the bridegroom, and five were not ready. Fifty per cent had not made adequate preparation, which is better than we can say in our crisis. So it comes through loud and clear, that the whole point of the story is the same as the Boy Scout motto: "Be Prepared." This is one of the few parables that Jesus interprets himself: "Watch therefore, for you know neither the day nor the hour." Be ready!

Wisdom in Readiness

Be ready for whatever God will for you. Be ready for whatever happens in this sin-sick world, full of hatred and evil. Be ready for tomorrow, and be ready for death. And the church's message at the end of its liturgical year is to be ready for the second coming of Christ. The message is plain and simple.

Our problem is how to convince you of that. No one will be convinced to be prepared if we just try to frighten you. Oh yes, if there were a ball of fire in the sky, and it seemed that Christ were returning today, you would certainly be trembling in fear trying to get ready. If you know your disease is terminal, you would do serious praying about it to be ready for death. If you are trapped in a terrible accident, and the end seemed near, your first cry, almost by instinct, would be, "O God!"

But how to convince comfortable, even slightly cooler people, to be prepared—there's a good question.

God Doesn't Scare You

Look at the other side of the picture. See what the opportunities are. Find out what is promised. Think about what being ready can mean. And for that we need to look at the bridegroom in the story. Consider the invitation he offered to the maidens, and to you. You will be a guest at the feast, a part of the celebration. You will be in on the fun, a part of the fellowship of the invited.

If you are like me, that's the ideal to hold in rearing children. We try to show where one alternative is better than another. We don't try to control behavior simply by threats of spankings. And the same holds true in a classroom. My wife who is a very good teacher lives by the creed that a bit of praise goes ten times further than a threat of punishment.

Jesus' story tells nothing about the feast itself. But in First Thessalonians St. Paul presents this picture: "But we would not have you ignorant, brethren, concerning those who are asleep, that you may not grieve as others do who have no hope. For since we believe that Jesus died and rose again, even so, through Jesus, God will bring with him those who have fallen asleep" (1 Thess. 4:13-14). And the promise goes on: "We who are alive, who are left, shall be caught up together with them in the clouds to meet the Lord in the air; and so we shall always be with the Lord" (v. 17). The same picture is amplified in the book of Revelation. It will be just wonderful. That's why you ought to be ready, so you won't miss God's wonderful promises as they are fulfilled.

St. Paul, in that wonderful fifteenth chapter of First Corinthians, also shows the wonders of that heavenly feast with the Lamb. Wow! What glory, what joy! That's the best reason I can give for being prepared. You have a marvelous future ahead of you. The benevolent bridegroom brings blessings unheard of by human standards. You can't be scared into anything. Just look at what is promised. Wouldn't you want to be ready for that?

The Bridegroom Is in Charge

Remember the story, no one knew when to expect the wedding party. The bridegroom comes when he wants to, whenever he is ready. Again, that's not to frighten anyone. It's simply to say that he is in charge.

You have been a passenger in a car and fallen asleep, I'm sure. You trust the driver, he is capable, he is in control of the vehicle, you are in his hands. You surely know some drivers with whom you couldn't sleep while they were at the wheel. You're sitting there about to drive your foot through the floorboard, attempting to put on the brakes.

Some of those young ladies went to sleep because they had no control over the coming of the bridegroom, and they weren't concerned about it. Maybe they had heard Jesus say: "Take no thought for tomorrow. Don't be anxious about anything. I've cared for the birds, and even the flowers, so why should you be concerned?"

When my children travel with us on vacation, they aren't concerned about the schedule, or where they sleep, or the people we visit. They are with dad and mom, and because they trust us, they are ready for whatever the next day will bring.

You don't know what the rest of today may bring. How will your normal business be next week? What kind of crisis or difficulty will you face before the year is out? When may illness radically change your life, or even end it? Isn't it a joy to be ready for whatever comes?

The obvious connection in the parable is between the bridegroom and Christ. He's the one who is coming, we don't know when. But he is in charge of the situation. He is the host at the banquet. And with your hopes and dreams set on him, through your faith in him, isn't that the incentive for preparedness? When you know that he will come when he is ready to come, because only he knows the best time, then you will never face an oil shortage. You will be listed among the "haves," those who have their lamps trimmed.

But we can't ignore the "have nots," those who weren't ready, those five foolish females who faced a fuel failure. Our immediate concern is not with those who never had oil for their lamps, or maybe didn't even have lamps. In other words, we are not talking about people who have never heard the gospel, people whose ears have never been touched with God's grace in Jesus Christ. They may exist right under our noses, or they may be half-way around the world. But other things are said about them elsewhere in Scripture.

What about those who have had oil, and ran out? What about the once active church member, who simply drops out of the congregation? What about the confirmand who lets Confirmation be his graduation from religion? What about people who worship every week, but still don't know what it's all about? What about people who are on church rolls, but never bother with questions about faith and purpose and meaning and mission? These maidens had oil, but they ran out. Why?

Organizational Activity

Maybe they simply burned up the oil in frenzied activity in a congregation, saw little or no purpose in what they were doing, and just threw in the towel. It sometimes happens in small mission congregations. There is the excitement of being a part of something new, there is a spirit of motion as people spend long hours building a church. But when a moral question comes along, or a religious crisis grabs their lives, they find their oil has been burned up on the wrong things. It happens in large, established congregations also. People are concerned with buildings, with organizational structure, with the social life of a congregation, and they run out of energy. Too much concern with activity and not enough with meditation, and they fall away.

Worship Forms

Sometimes people are caught up in worship forms, and fall away when those forms are changed. It could be a very structured, "high church," type of worship, or foot-stomping, emotional "gospel preaching." It doesn't matter. People can be caught up in the formalism of religion without catching the faith of the church. Then, when anything is changed—when the gospel songs become Bach chorales, or the beautiful vestments become a suit and tie, or the liturgy is chanted—they think the faith has changed, and their oil runs out. They are more interested in the formalism of faith than in the greatness of grace, in any form.

People in the Church

A major reason people leave the church is that they are disillusioned by the other people of the church. They follow that old line that "there are too many hypocrites in the church," and they decide to divorce themselves from their company. They find out that the man singing in the choir for thirty years has quietly become an alcoholic. The biggest contributor in the congregation is indicted on income tax evasion. They hear of a pastor who committed suicide. And their lamps run low. They face a fuel shortage. They go to sleep.

There is a common thread running through every reason listed why people leave the church, why their oil runs out and their lamps grow dim. They are concentrating on the other maidens, not on the Bridegroom. They are looking at structure, organization, and form. They are looking at their fellow sinners of the household of faith, and not at the Lord of the household. They aren't ready because they haven't heard the promises offered, or felt the security the Bridegroom brings. And so they drop out. Five maidens asked for oil from those who waited with them. And that isn't the place to get oil in the first place.

Yes, we Christians ought to be examples to others, we ought to be sharing our goods with others. We ought not be stumbling blocks on others' paths. But our primary concern is to point to Christ, to show Christ as having forgiven us, with our sins, our errors of judgment, our secret hatreds, our pettiness, and give God the glory for inviting this lousy beggar to his marriage feast.

Put yourself in the picture. *Are you ready?*

The Wise Wait Without Worry

We ought to point to the other main characters in the story. There were five maidens, lamps trimmed, ready to go in and enjoy the marriage feast. They were using up oil all along, but they had enough in reserve. Helmut Thielicke makes this analogy: "The oil obviously points to the fact that there is something in our Christian life that is constantly being used up and therefore needs to be replenished" *(The Waiting Father,* Harper and Row, New York, 1959, p. 178).

Hopefully there is where you stand. You can't live without continuous intake of food. The Christian life needs the continuous intake of God's grace. That comes through steady and faithful worship, continuous and thoughtful study, ongoing and concerned prayer. Sometimes these things are seemingly boring and fruitless. But every meal isn't a gourmet's delight. It is now and then when the cook keeps trying. Every concert the musician gives doesn't bring a moment of history, but it does now and then because of hours of practice with his instrument each day. Every kiss between husband and wife doesn't cause bells to ring, but it does now and then because the relationship is sustained by love.

We don't just sit and wait for things to happen. We plan, we think, we work, we attempt, and we fail. It takes work to remain prepared. If you want to identify with those five wise women willingly waiting without worry, then you must stay prepared. We are prepared by living in the forgiving grace of God.

At Christmas time in New Mexico, people practice an old Spanish custom of lighting little fires around their homes, called *firolitos,* to indicate they are ready to receive the Christ. Those little fires go out by morning. We need constant supply of oil to keep our fires burning in order to be ready. In God's grace there is never such an oil shortage.

God doesn't frighten you, or threaten you, to get you into his kingdom. He promises you a wonderful future with him, he gives you assurance that he is in control of every situation. He only asks that when he comes with his offer of grace, you be ready to receive it.

R. E. McClelland
St. Peter Lutheran Church
Fennimore, Wisconsin

TALENTS TO USE

Twenty-fifth Sunday after Pentecost
Matthew 25:14-30

Equal rights are very much in the news and will be for some time to come. The history of the equal rights movement is the story of a long development and a steady struggle for fairness and justice in the society. One set of rights gained by one group only deepens the appetite for other segments of the society to get their day in court. The struggle for rights is not unique to this country. The longing for freedom and human rights is universal.

In our nation, however, we have the fluidity and the built-in opportunities to dramatize the development of human rights. Perhaps in all of history there never has been nor ever will be, another political experience that has been so hospitable to the achievement of human rights as in our nation. At the same time we may also note that the strong emphasis on human rights may extend so far as to be cheapened or threatened when people no longer take them seriously. However, that is not so likely as the false interpretation of rights, the demand of rights with no sense of obligation, the abuse of rights through the failure to exercise them.

In the kingdom of our Lord, however, it is not so with rights. The world does not understand and at times we have trouble understanding how differently his kingdom does operate. In a parable our Lord tells us how it is in his kingdom. He talks about an unequal distribution of rights and talents, as he tells us how the talents are to be used.

Heavenly Talents

The parable Jesus tells is a familiar one. It is also similar to one we find in Luke. Yet the differences between the parables are significant enough for us to recognize that, undoubtedly, the evangelist wants us to note them. The Lukan parable is spoken to the multitude, and the parable before us is spoken to the intimates of Jesus, his disciples. The Lukan parable speaks of a larger number of servants and the equal distribution of the pound, about twenty dollars. This parable speaks of three servants and the distribution of talents, each worth about a thousand dollars on an uninflated market. These factors alone are enough to insure us that our Lord is here addressing himself to those who understand themselves to be his entrusted disciples or followers. The parable begins on that note, "A man going on a journey called his servants and entrusted to them his property." The man going on the journey is our Lord himself, and he trusts his servants as the dearest of friends and shares with them the blessings he possesses. He give to them of his kingdom. For us this means that our Lord permits us to be stewards of the very things of God. When he takes us into his employment he treats us as members of the household of heaven to share all that heaven possesses.

Unequal Distribution

However, he does not distribute the talents equally. "To one he gave five talents, to another two, to another one, to each according to his ability." The emphasis here is not at all on equality, but on ability. To one is entrusted more because he has more ability. Thus the original disciples are eclipsed by the apostle Paul, who can claim that he has become the chief of the apostles. Or we recognize that most of the names of the Twelve pass into oblivion except for some scanty traditions about them. Other giants come on the scene to stand out in the history of the church like Augustine and Luther. Every generation has its own figures who loom large on the scene and outdistance their brothers in performance. Our parable does not wrestle with the question of why one has greater gifts than another. Nor is that posed as any kind of a problem. Rather, the differences in the servants enable the Lord to entrust more to one than to another. We are not here speaking of the gift of the gospel itself for our own salvation which God does distribute equally to all his children. Rather, here the parable is making clear to us that the Lord has need of servants to whom he can entrust the work of his kingdom. He wisely distributes what must be done that it might be done for the blessing of many.

Distribution to Everyone

Yet in the kingdom of the Lord there is equality. If each is entrusted with the property of the Lord according to his ability, that is equality. One is not given beyond his ability. More is not expected of a man than he is able to handle. Nor is one not given anything, and his ability completely underrated. One is not left out or not trusted because he has less ability. What binds these servants to their lord is the fact that he is willing to share with them of the substance of his kingdom. That is the way it is with the kingdom of our Lord Jesus Christ. What Christ is willing to share with all men, of course, is the blessing of his righteousness. He has won for all men the right to be called the children of God. By his death he destroyed death for all men. By his resurrection from the dead he opened the fountain of eternal life for all men. But the assignments to carry on the work of his kingdom are distributed as men are able to handle them. The apostle Paul has indicated this in several ways as he talks about the variety of gifts that are spread about in the kingdom or the way in which different functions are obvious in the different members of the body of Christ. We cannot expect the same kind of performance from all Christians, because they do not all have the same kind of gifts. Christians are not look-alikes, because God has made them different and has given them different things to do in the kingdom.

No Contracts

Another great leveling factor in this story our Lord relates as an illustration of how the work goes on in the kingdom, is the kind of pay the servants get. There is no contract made at the start. There is no promise of reward or pay. There are no contract arbitrators. No deadlines are set. No production quotas. No insurance agreements. No hospital and welfare plans. No fine print of any kind. There simply are no benefits mentioned at all. But two of the servants put the money to work. They got the message. The master had given them a trust and they were supposed to do something with it.

They went out into the market place and they put the trust to work. They invested in the world they knew. They took what their Lord gave them and they risked it in the world where there was a good chance they could have lost it. Only the Lord knows how they invested it. He does not tell us how they did it. But they had to rub elbows with the world to make do with what they had. And they did it. The one who had five talents invested in such a way that he doubled what he had. He had a hundred percent return on the money. Not bad. The one who had two talents did as well. He ended up with four talents. They were pleased with what they had done, and so was their master. They apparently had no intention of collecting anything for their effort except to make the talents work for the boss. But they both received equal pay for their work. The master had trusted them as though they were co-owners with him, and now he rewards them in the same way. "Well done, good and faithful servant; you have been faithful over little, I will set you over much; enter into the joy of your master."

A Trust Fund

The point of all that is fairly obvious. There had been need of no kind of contract, because our relationship with our Lord is one of trust. There is no pay scale, because really there is no pay as such. What Christ does for us exceeds completely anything we could receive in proportion to what we do for him. However enormous our talents may be, or however much we accomplish for him we have to confess that we have been "faithful over a little." Even when we do that little bit the Savior is willing to share the fullness of his joy, the completeness of heaven. How different that all sounds from the kinds of popular blurbs that come in your mail and promise you how to use your Bible to extract from God all the promises that will make you rich, keep you healthy, and solve all your daily problems. That kind of manipulation of God is completely out of character with this story of faithful servants who know only that they are called to serve in the world with the sacred trust that their Lord has given them.

Faulty Conservatism

However, the central point of the parable is made with the description of that third servant who made no return on his master's investment. Given one talent, he takes it and buries it in the ground. His reasoning is that what he has received from the master is precious indeed. It is more than he ever had before, so he does not want to lose it. But his real motivation he expresses himself, "Master I knew you to be a hard man, reaping where you did not sow, and gathering where you do not winnow, so I was afraid, and I went and hid your talent in the ground. Here you have what is yours." That is conservatism of the worst kind. This man did not accept the trust given him, and he did not trust the one who had given him the opportunity of his lifetime. This man thinks he understands his master, and he is afraid of him, so he does what fear dictates. The applications are not difficult to make.

In the church we have all kinds of people who believe they are to do nothing but sit on the gospel God has entrusted to them. They are not in mission, because they believe that one cannot contaminate the gospel in the world. They are not sharing anything of the gospel because they are afraid they will lose it. But worst of all, they are immobilized because they are afraid of what God will say. They see God as an angry judge who will punish them severely if they make a false move. Their religion is not based on faith in a gracious master who has done everything for them, but they have a religion of fear based completely on God's judgment of them.

A Big Return

We all know Christians that are of this conservative stripe, but we are shocked by the way they thwart and frustrate the mission of the church by their gloomy picture of what God will do to us when he comes to hold us accountable. However, all of us have to admit that we are guilty of the same thing. We hold back in sharing the gospel, because we are afraid that we will contaminate it or lose it. We are not sure that one can take the risk of sharing. We have to fight against that kind of attitude. And that is the point of the parable. Our Lord meant it for us, his followers and servants. We are to see that if we harbor that kind of attitude we are not acting in faith, and God will take the words right out of our mouth and judge us on the basis of them. If we confess that he is a harsh God who will judge us, then he will do just that and judge us for not sharing the gospel of Jesus Christ. The parable is meant to warn us against doing nothing with the gospel. Christ encourages us to see that we have him as a gracious Master who shares everything with us and asks very little of us in return. No one is asked to do more than he is able. All he needs is a little faith for sharing the gospel. We can all be faithful in that. Then we will hear the Savior himself say, "Well done, good and faithful servant; you have been faithful over little, I will set you over much; enter into the joy of your master."

HARRY N. HUXHOLD
Our Redeemer Lutheran Church
Indianapolis, Indiana

THERE'S SOMETHING MISSING IN RELIGION

Twenty-sixth Sunday after Pentecost
Matthew 23:1-12

Some time ago I read the story of a hold-up man who put his gun into the back of a clergyman and demanded his money. When the minister turned around to hand over his billfold, the gunman, seeing his clerical collar, quickly withdrew his gun and said apologetically, "I'm sorry. I never take money from preachers." Hearing this, the minister relaxed and said, "Fine. Here, have a cigar." The gunman replied, "No thanks. You see, I don't smoke during Lent." He must have been very religious. Indeed, that was his trouble. In fact, the church is in great trouble because people are too religious—religious but not Christian.

In the twenty-third chapter of St. Matthew's gospel, our Lord, with powerful and sweeping strokes of judgment, paints pictures of barren religion featuring forms of godliness without power. Here we see religion so false and repugnant that it brings from Jesus seven frightening "woes," and his pronouncement of judgment.

A major maceration in the church today comes from the clash of religion versus the gospel. One is man-made; the other is God-given. One features the lash of duty; the other the law of love. In the text for this day we find pictures of religion indicating that something is missing.

Proselytism Without Conversion

Going beyond our text to verse 15, we find a devastating indictment of this kind of religion, "Woe to you, scribes and Pharisees, hypocrites! For you traverse sea and land to make a single proselyte, and when he becomes a proselyte, you make him twice as much a child of hell as yourselves."

The late Dr. E. Stanley Jones, in his book entitled *Conversion*, writes, "Proselytism is a change from one group to another without any necessary change in character and life. It is a change of label, but not of life. . . . Are the people inside the churches being converted? Or are they, having come into the church, settling down to half-conversions, living in half-lights, or worse, are they in complete emptiness under the respectable umbrella of the church? The acid test of the validity of a Christian church is whether it can only convert people from outside to membership but also produce conversion within its own membership."

It is well to recall that Jesus spoke to an "insider," Nicodemus, long ago and said to this respectable and very religious leader, "You must be born again." We need not wonder that the church is filled with sinful people. I'm glad it is a hospital for sinners. This means that I can get in. What should give us concern, as one pastor put it, "is not that so few come to church but that so little happens to those who come."

Infant baptism and adult conversion belong together. An inner change does take place in baptism. This comes by the regenerating power of the Holy Spirit through God's Word. I believe this deeply. It's the gospel in purest form. God's love is poured into a helpless sinner who cannot lift a finger toward his or her salvation. But infant baptism must emerge into a conscious acknowledgment of Jesus Christ as Savior and Lord—into a willingness to be born of water and the Spirit, thus, to be changed in character and inner life by the transforming power of the indwelling Spirit.

Alexander Pope was once quoted as saying, "O Lord, make me a better man." His spiritually enlightened servant replied, "It would be easier to make you a new man."

In our text we see the tragedy of being religious without being Christian, of placing primary emphasis on outer conduct rather than on inner character. Those of whom Jesus speaks did not recognize their need to be changed. They are like the man who said, "I pray that I might always be right because I never change." Jesus said, "Do not imitate their actions, because they do not practice what they preach." There's something missing in religion.

Piety Without Charity

Someone has said, "It is as difficult to get charity out of piety as it is to get reasonableness out of rationalism." In our text religious leaders used piety as a front for their hypocrisy. Their pretended charity was a lie. Here are Jesus' words, "They fix up heavy loads and tie them on men's backs, yet they aren't willing even to lift a finger to help them carry those loads."

Such religion specializes in exploitation. Striving for self-exaltation, many in the church have climbed on the broken hopes and hearts of other persons. Because of delusions of grandeur, some persons appear to them as inferior. Do we bind burdens of judgment and demands for conformity on others, telling them how they ought to live without helping them to really live? Religious America has robbed its Indian citizens of land, dignity and equal opportunity. If you and I treat persons with contempt as inferior, our religious exercises become sounding brass and clanging cymbals.

In the drama entitled *Rescue,* one scene depicts two women on their way to a prayer meeting at their church. They pass a deep pit and hear a man at the bottom crying out, "Help me. I'm sinking. Please save me." One woman says, "We cannot stop now. That would make us late for our prayer meeting. But when we get there we will pray for you." There's something missing in religion.

Authority Without Integrity

Religious leaders in Jesus' day loved the prestige and power of sitting in Moses' seat as interpreters of the law. But they used their power for personal gain. Echoes of Watergate corruption! Moreover, as a nation we have made military power our number one priority. Not first do we ask for wisdom or integrity or truth or for the capacity to repent or for the courage to lose face. We ask for and strive for military might and superiority. And we get it, losing moral strength and character in the process.

Proselytism without conversion. Piety without charity. Authority without integrity. There's something missing here. Such religion specializes in self-made men. It is Joseph Parker who said to someone who was boasting of being a self-made man, "Well, sir, that relieves the Lord of a great responsibility."

Self-made religionists lack love and character. Jesus said, "They love the best places at feasts and the reserved seats in the meeting houses; they love to be greeted with respect in the market places and have people call them 'Teacher.' " They love places but not persons. They love seats but not the Savior. They love greetings but not God. There's something missing. Do any readers find themselves in the story thus far? But something more is missing according to our text.

Display Without Devotion

Someone has said, "Painting the pump cannot purify polluted water." Jesus said in verse 5, "They do everything just so people will see them. See how big are the containers with scripture verses on their foreheads and arms, and notice how long are the hems of their cloaks!" In pronouncing one of the seven "woes," Jesus said, "Imposters! You clean the outside of your cup and plate, while the inside is full of things you have gotten by violence and selfishness. Blind Pharisee! Clean what is inside the cup first, and then the outside will be clean too" (Matt. 23:25-26).

Futile and tragic outward display is often substituted for devotion to God. Minimize the gospel and embellish the liturgy instead! If things aren't going well, add a new wheel (committee) to the machinery. There's something missing here!

A little girl was troubled about her father who was a bishop. She noticed his pride of office and his pomp and display. She said, "Daddy, did anyone ever tell you that you're wonderful?" He replied, "No, I think not." "Then, Daddy," she said, "whatever gave you the idea?"

Our text tells us the one way to be a person of distinction, a somebody, someone who is wonderful. We get a clue from one of the most impressive inscriptions that could be written on a tombstone, "Ole had a great God!" So with joy, relief and expectation we turn from things missing in religion to the great discovery of everything we need in the gospel.

Something Missing—Where to Find It

Conversion, charity, integrity, devotion to the highest and best —where are these to be found? Jesus tells us, "You must not be called 'Teacher,' for you are all brothers of one another and have only one Teacher. And you must not call anyone here on earth 'Father,' for you have only the one Father in heaven. Nor should you be called 'Leader,' because your one and only leader is the Messiah."

Where shall we find mercy and forgiveness for indulging in the corrupting religion of proselytism, false piety, harsh authority and superficial display? Where shall we find the fruits of love, kindness, goodness, patience, faithfulness, joy, peace, gentleness and self-control?

The answer is in the coming of the Holy Spirit to control our lives from within. He centers us in God our Father, in Jesus, the only true Leader and Teacher and Messiah. "There is one Lord, one faith, one baptism; there is one God and Father of all men, who is Lord of all, works through all, and is in all" (Eph. 4:5-6).

St. Paul writes in Romans 8:32, "He did not even keep back his own Son, but offered him for us all! He gave us his Son—will he not also freely give us all things?" In Jesus we become new creatures, converted persons. In him our piety reveals agape love. Under his authority we have the integrity of his truth. Jesus Christ will be on display in the life devoted to him.

True humility is rooted in reverence for God and for persons. To be truly great is to be humble enough to be a servant. "The greatest one among you must be your servant." An American college student visited the home of Beethoven in Bonn, Germany. Thinking that she was an accomplished pianist, she asked permission to play on the great musician's piano. After playing a few bars of *Moonlight Sonata,* she said to the guide, "I suppose all of the great pianists have played during their visits here." "No, miss," he said, "Paderewski was here two years ago but said he was not worthy to touch it."

An old adage reads, "A mountain shames a molehill until they both are humbled by the stars." To be humble means to be reverent in the presence of greatness.

To be humble and reverent means to be obedient. To be obedient means to know the truth about our Messiah and Leader. Jesus said in John 7:17, "Whoever is willing to do what God wants will know whether what I teach comes from God or whether I speak on my own authority."

We can learn a lesson in obedience from the little girl who saw some traps in a garden to catch birds. She was distressed. She said, "I have prayed that none of the birds would go near the traps." Then she added, "And I have prayed that if any did, the traps would not work." After a long pause and with a smile she concluded, "And just a few minutes ago I went out in the garden and kicked the traps to pieces."

If Jesus is Lord we will get rid of the traps of hypocrisy and false religions. We'll also get rid of the trappings of religion! We will surrender our pride and pretense for him to destroy. He will lift us out of our lowliness and lostness. He will make us great in his greatness. Belonging to Christ we all belong to each other in God's family and servant church.

All this "not by might nor by power, but by my Spirit, says the Lord." And for this discovery of what is missing we say, "Bless the Lord, O my soul."

William E. Berg
Augustana Lutheran Church
Minneapolis, Minnesota

THE KING AND HIS BROTHERS AND SISTERS

Last Sunday after Pentecost — Christ the King
Matthew 25:31-46

The Feast Today

The feast today celebrates our Lord Jesus Christ as king. It stands at the end of the church year, confessing now that all of the other feasts and celebrations we have kept in the year were signs in our midst that Jesus Christ rules, that he is born, manifested, killed, risen, ascended to be king of all, that he reigns. The feast sums up the church year with the proclamation that the hope for the kingdom of God is fulfilled in Jesus.

How Does He Reign?

But how is it that he reigns? While we keep the feast and confess the faith in his reign, that question nonetheless rises in our hearts, for we also know that we stand in the midst of a vast world, fully aware of all the crowd of people throughout the world and all of their innumerable needs. How can we assert that he reigns? You and I stand in a long line at the airport, and all those people, so foreign to us, so busy about their own concerns, so outside of our own understanding, so diverse in their needs, encounter our senses. And we are brought to asking, "How does he reign over all of these lives?" You and I sit before the television set and hear the evening news; the world seems to fall apart again and we ask, "In what does his reign consist? How does he rule over wars and fears of wars?"

We hear of a new book coming from the Soviet Union, telling once again of a world of oppression, which has existed since before the 1917 revolution. And we ask again, "Wherein does he rule? How is he king in the midst of that *Gulag Archipelago?*" And we face our own confusion, our inability to see the world put together. Sometimes in the depths of honesty we are able to face the fact that we ourselves are the oppressors of others, that we ourselves put our brothers and sisters in prison, prisons we construct. Wherein does the king rule?

A Picture of the King at the Last Judgment

The text for this feast is a picture of the last judgment, with Christ himself pictured as the Son of man ruling as a king on that final day. And all the people, in fact all those people about whom we have just been thinking, whom we encounter in the crowd-situations of our daily lives, who fall upon our ears in the daily news, about whom we think when we remember the worlds of oppressions in which we also participate, *all those people* are gathered before him on that last day. And he is reigning in their midst with all of the authority and all the angelic messengers which, according to the Old Testament, belong to *God* in *his* rule.

It is a *picture,* of course, not an accurate account of what will happen, but a picture which celebrates Jesus as both Ezekiel's God and who will gather the sheep and the very shepherd prince whom the prophet says God will install to justly reign in the midst of his people. It is a picture which celebrates in almost tangible ways something of what Paul means when he says, "he must reign," and at the end he will deliver the kingdom to God the Father after destroying every enemy of that reign of God.

A Picture Which Shows How He Reigns

But it is a *picture,* a picture which says that this one, this Jesus, the one who is at the heart of the proclamation of the church, this Jesus who here tells the story, is himself (to use the words that Simeon used at his birth) "set for the fall and rising of many," in fact of all people in all the nations. And what is pictured in this story as the criterion on which it is to be decided whether one stands or flalls, is sheep or goat? The criterion is what this same one, this Jesus, has said about love to the littlest and the humblest of all the people. And perhaps it is in *that* way he rules all things, in that he has borne eternal witness to the one criterion which really matters for life: love shown to the littlest of all the people in the world.

But He Is No King

But what can support that? It is really not evident that that is the criterion which rules in the universe, that the one criterion that decides between life and death, between success and failure, between making it or not making it, is the criterion of love to the littlest of human beings. All of human history seems to contradict that. And certainly the history of our twentieth century contradicts that. How does he reign in that criterion? And what supports that criterion? Simply his word? But who is he? Where is his reign? Where is his judging?

Actually, of course, he is no king at all. To call him a king is only to use picture language, to describe what he means in a metaphorical way. He is no king and never was. No, instead of being a king he was led to a cross, and the only kingship he knew was a cruel mocking before his death and a mocking title put up over his agony. And he, of course, is not the Son of Man of Jewish expectation, appearing with marvelous angels surrounding him and exercising an authority to which all are immediately obedient. Jesus is not that. No angels hover around his cross, for all that Christian iconography may have imagined them there. All the nations are not gathered before him. *All those people* are not immediately obedient to his word.

No, finally he is simply *there,* in the midst of the agony of many other people of the world, *there,* hidden away in the midst of all the suffering and dying and oppressed ones. And all that there is left of him, all that seems to remain, is just his prayer: "Father, forgive them," and the more agonizing prayer, "My God, why have you forsaken me." He is reduced finally to that. Not a king, not the Son of man, not the center of the angels, not the heart of the reigning and the ruling in the universe, he is reduced simply to his prayer, to waiting for God and his kingdom, waiting and crying out for God even in the midst of his death.

And in his death, of course, he is with the ones, identified with the ones whom he calls, in his story, his brothers. He is hungry with the hungry, thirsty with the thirsty, a stranger outside the camp with the strangers, naked with the naked, sick unto death with the sick, imprisoned and mocked with the prisoners.

He Is King in His Powerlessness

But *there,* confesses the faith, *there,* says the feast, *there* he rules. Christians have always understood the title over his cross as ironically true. He is king of the Jews and king of all that is. If he is reduced only to his prayer in the midst of the suffering of the world, then his prayer is, as the poet John Berryman has it, an "unconquerable beseeching." ("Ecce Homo," *Delusions, Etc.,* p. 44, Farrar, Straus and Giroux, 1972.) And faith says his prayer has an answer. God gives the kingdom and gives it already in the self-giving love of Jesus at his cross. As he is identified with those whom he calls his brothers, as he prays together with those whose need cries out for justice and for God, as he gives his love in that identification, he is *at the same time* the very gift of God, the very presence of the ruling, reigning God, giving forth his justice and establishing his kingdom. That is not apparent, but faith is the trust that it is so!

Where Does He Rule Today?

And where does he rule today, as we wait for what we hope to be the last day when that rule from the cross is manifested fully for *all those people,* for all the nations? Where does he rule today? Finally we have no other answer than to say he rules here in this Word. When the Word is in our midst, there he is ruling, dividing, judging, being with his brothers. For he is not dead, but is alive, and alive precisely here in this Word. In this Word spoken in our midst and in this Word heard in your hearts, there he rules. And all the angels of God hover around that Word, pointing to that Son of man whose story, whose cross-story, is told here. As people from all the nations are beginning to hear that story, as this Word is preached and spoken among all the peoples, already the nations themselves are thereby beginning to be gathered before him.

To Be Open to His Brothers and Sisters

To bear witness to his reign, to say that he rules in the *cross* and here in the *Word* which tells of the cross, is to be open to his brothers and sisters in their need. And that not because we misread the story to say that one must be open to other men since there is a "divine spark" in them (Jesus' solidarity with humanity is not in a mystical spark but in the actual cross!), nor as a way to lord it over the other, believing that somehow I and my strength can make it better for this poor, wretched one. To bear witness to Jesus' reign is to be open to his brothers and sisters, just because of the need of the others and because of my own need. When I see myself together with the brother and sister in their need, our mutual need forms a part of a common beseeching for the kingdom of God, a sign of our utter need for that kingdom, and a witness to the nature of Jesus' reign.

His Reign Is Not a Social Program

This "beseeching" is not a social program and it never has been. The Christian witness to the reign of Jesus Christ is not a way to organize *all those people* into some kind of coherent whole which will make for a better world.

Vladimer Soloviev, a Russian theologian about the turn of the century, said that when he encounters a beggar he knows that the social programs of both capitalist and socialist require that he ignore the beggar or urge the beggar to something else than begging. But in his desire to be a witness to the hope that is not in social programs but is in the kingdom of God, he knows that he must give to the beggar, not because that solves the beggar's problems nor the problems of the world, but because one is invited by the gospel to identify with the needs of the beggar and see those same needs in oneself. And so an act of hope joins in a beseeching for the kingdom.

When the Missionaries of Charity in India count it their task to gather in Christ's name the dying from the streets of Calcutta and Delhi and Bombay, bringing as many as they can into their home and allowing them therefore to die in the hands of love, they do not solve the problems of India's crowded and wretched cities. Nor do they really solve the problems of the dying. The dying still die. But they do a profoundly Christian thing. They join with them in their need, wrapping them in their arms of love, letting them die clean and cherished. And so they join together in a bodily beseeching for the kingdom.

When you and I suddenly realize that our rooms or our homes may be places of hospitality, that we may receive others there into a place of grace and peace in the midst of a world that is remarkably graceless and lacking in peace, when we see that that hospitality is at the heart of Christ's reign, we don't create the whole world into a remarkably hospitable place nor do we enter into a social program, but we join in the beseeching for the kingdom.

When the people in an average congregation suddenly understand that visiting the sick and the old is not just the responsibility of the pastor but of all of the congregation, they do it not as a social program nor as a way of building the membership roles but as a beseeching for the kingdom, an understanding of where the need is in our souls and in the souls of the brothers and sisters of Christ. And when the women of the Church in your home congregation make quilts for Lutheran World Relief, that quilting itself and all of its stitches can be a beseeching for the kingdom, a wrapping of the brothers and sisters of Christ in blankets which are also prayers.

These all are tiny signs, little blocks that are set up against death and disorganization, no social programs, seemingly hopeless things, foolish things. But they are a matter of being with the king where he reigns in his "unconquered beseeching."

Not Our Deeds But the Ground of Our Hope

But it must also be said that not to share this hopeless lot *may* mean that the one who refuses the needs of other people does not recognize the needs in himself and does not in fact wait for the kingdom of God, but only uses Christian language to mask his own attempt at ruling in his own kingdom, a kingdom carefully ordered for his own well-being. It *may* mean this because, on the other hand, our inability to help may also be part of our cry to God for *his* justice and *his* kingdom, while our hands are nailed down. But hear this: the text is not to be misread to mean that judgment in the kingdom of God depends upon what we do, that we must work hard to be accepted by the king. No, it depends much rather on the one who is the ground of our hope. If we hope for Jesus of Nazareth to reign, and believe that he already reigns in his utter extremity of need and death, if we wait for him, then we are free to wait with honesty about our own needs and inabilities and brokenness with openness toward the needy of his people whom he calls his brothers, his sisters.

The Hidden King Is Hidden Also in This Meal

So come and eat here at this table, for as he is hidden in the needs of the world, reigning there from the cross, he is hidden here in the signs of his littleness and death, hidden in this bread and cup. And yet here he truly reigns, truly gives life. From this meal he speaks to those who will hear and who in hearing are constantly surprised by the life which rises out of what seems to be only death and disorganization and hopelessness. He speaks here, from this meal, and says, "Come, ye blessed of my Father, receive the kingdom." Just so he speaks also from the midst of *all those people,* all those disorganized people, all those people in their needs, and says, "Come, ye blessed, and have that same kingdom." And so surely from the midst of his brothers and sisters and from this table he speaks already as if his voice came to us from the end, and says, "Come, ye blessed, into the only kingdom that truly is." Amen.

GORDON LATHROP
Pacific Lutheran University
Tacoma, Washington

HEALING AND WHOLENESS — ALL THANKS TO GOD!

Thanksgiving Day, U.S.A.
Luke 17:11-19

While they were on their way, they were made clean. One of them, finding himself cured, turned back, praising God aloud. He threw himself down at Jesus' feet and thanked him.

Things will be a lot better, experts are telling us, by the turn of the century, twenty-five years from now. Here's a sentence from a report on the crisis which has made this a most surprising and demanding year: "The prospects are bright from the year 2000 onward if some of the more exotic technological departures prove fruitful."

Surprised?

In a 1970 address on "The Hidden Enemies of Health" Dr. Paul B. Cornely surprised the American Public Health Association by beginning with this startling declaration: "The first and most important of the hidden enemies is the addiction to what all of us like to call the abundant life." Since then we have learned enough not to be surprised. We have experienced the inescapable truth that the misuse of technology and the dissipation of not inexhaustible resources in the pursuit of ever greater production and consumption can only spell disaster. There are those who tell us that the turn of the century will be upon us before we can count on brighter prospects. It will be the year 2000, they are saying, before we shall know again the kind of giddy affluence that once characterized our national life.

We are learning meanwhile that the abundant life characterized by Dr. Cornely as "hidden enemy number one" is not the abundant life promised by our Lord. We are learning to adjust to the demands being made on us by a society no longer able to support itself in the style to which it had become accustomed.

We had a great time *while it lasted.* Only here and there a voice was raised in warning, echoing the words of an infinitely wiser one who had a great deal to say about piling up treasures on earth and getting caught in the trap of depending on things.

Shall we say then that we have less to be thankful for today than we did a year ago, less than we had in 1965 or 1970? Shall we say, "Let's give thanks anyway, even if things are a lot worse than they used to be!"?

There are better ways. There is a helpful sentence in the Old Testament Lesson for Thanksgiving Day. Moses says to the people of God, "He humbled you and made you hungry; then he fed you on manna which neither you nor your fathers had known before. He let you know that man does not live by bread alone, but that man lives by everything that proceeds out of the mouth of God."

The Better Bread

God has ways of letting us know that he has greater and better gifts for us, that he has greater and better things in store for us, than the gadgets and goodies that we consider the necessities of life. We would do well, on a day and in a time like this, to think him for having the fatherly wisdom and love to humble us once in a while and to let us go hungry, so that we learn to recognize and appreciate the greater gifts that only he can provide, manna that neither we nor our fathers have known before, or, in the words of Jesus, the bread of life which comes down from heaven and gives life to the world.

The ten lepers of today's Gospel were granted healing and wholeness. They were cleansed of their leprosy. They had asked only for mercy. "Jesus, Master, have mercy on us!" Was it alms they were seeking, or just a kindly word? Did the ten really believe that he could cleanse them of their hideous disease, and that he would if he could? Who knows? We know only that they asked for mercy and received healing and wholeness. They were granted the gift of physical health. They were given release and relief from a then incurable disease. Nine of them went their way and one returned to give thanks. To that one Jesus said, that one who had thrown himself at his feet, "Rise and go your way; your faith has made you well."

Only one of the ten believed that he owed it to Jesus to offer thanks. Only one of the ten was sensitive to the source of the divine gift. Our Lord implies that only in that one was the gift complete. His faith recognized that the gift of healing he had received was from Jesus of Nazareth. He returned in a spirit of worshipful adoration, threw himself at the feet of Jesus, and gave thanks. In that moment another dimension was added to the gift of healing, the dimension of wholeness. Now the healing was complete. This is one of those times when I prefer the older translation, the one that has Jesus saying, "Your faith has made you whole."

New Every Morning

For it is healing and wholeness that I commend to your consideration as *your* reason to give thanks on Thanksgiving Day. For this is God's great gift to us in Jesus Christ, the healing and the wholeness that the angels of the holy Gospel shout from every housetop, the healing and the wholeness that knows no shortfall crisis, the forgiving grace that lets us fall asleep in peace each night, the mercy that is new every morning. It is manna for the humble and the hungry. It is the bread of God that gives life to the world.

Not long ago I heard someone say that health is generally defined as the absence of illness. The World Health Organization offers a greatly improved definition: "Health is happiness and well-being." A new dimension has been added. Health and happiness, healing and wholeness . . . these are more than mere words to the sensitive, to the thankful, to those who have faith.

They remind me of a great line in St. Matthew's story of the Wise Men as it comes out in Today's English Version: "How happy they were, what gladness they felt, when they saw the star!" There is mirth in those words, mirth and joy, for those who seek the Lord and find him, led by the star that is God's own special creation for each one of us. The Wise Men were few in number among those in whose skies the star appeared. The leper who gave thanks for his cleansing was one out of ten. But they were the happy ones. They were the ones who sought the Lord, who is always there for the finding. They were the ones whose faith bowed low in worship at the feet of Jesus. They knew the joy of thanksgiving for the gifts of God. "How happy they were! What gladness they felt!"

Sin and Forgiveness

We don't talk about sin very much these days, but we make much of forgiveness. We recognize that there is something that has come between us and God, something that has come between us and each other, that brings much grief and great sadness to us and to our world. Call it alienation, estrangement, a dislocation, a malfunction in personal relationships, call it anything you like, it's a problem to us. It places a burden of guilt on us. We hurt with it. We feel the pain of it. We run away from it. We try to drown it. We force ourselves to forget it. And we find that all this works only for a little while. We know it isn't really working at all. For it's there all the time, like that hideous and incurable leprosy of the miserable ten, for whom there was no hope and no relief and no cure.

Until, one day, they saw Jesus going by, and cried out to him in their loneliness and their misery, "Jesus! Master! Have mercy on us!"

If we have any sense at all, it means a lot more to us today than physical health. Is it really true, as the purveyors of patent medical elixirs of life try to tell us, that "if we have our health, we have practically everything?"

God's Many Ways

The healing and wholeness that becomes ours by the mercies of God in Jesus Christ offer infinitely more than that. There are passages in the Scriptures, in God's good word to us, that describe in more than a dozen ways what healing and wholeness mean when God comes into our life and deals with our problem through Jesus Christ. "We can trust him," St. John says in the first chapter of his first letter, "If we confess our sins to God, we can trust him, for he does what is right—he will forgive our sins and make us clean from all our wrongdoing."

He forgives, he makes us clean. Our sins are blotted out and swept away. He throws them behind his back. He crushes them underfoot. He throws them deep into the sea. He moves them to opposite poles. He forgets them, as only God can forget. He cancels the unfavorable record of our debts with its binding rules and does away with it completely by nailing it to the cross.

Reconciled

I didn't dream up those phrases. They come from the good word of God. In Christ he offers us healing and wholeness. We are no longer sick, no longer fractured, torn, divided. We are no longer alienated, strangers to God and to each other. We are reconciled. We are reconciled to God before the cross. We are reconciled to God through Jesus Christ. We are reconciled to God forever. In the words of today's epistle, "We are his offspring, his children. He is not far from each one of us, for in him we live and move and have our being."

If you know what I'm talking about, if you know what God is talking about in his word, if you know what Jesus has in mind for you, doesn't it make you want to rush into the arms of God, to throw yourself at the feet of Jesus and say, "Thank you, Lord!"?

When you think about it, as we've done today, it helps us to realize why God wants us to be reconciled with one another. It helps us to understand why Jesus says to us, "I have just one commandment for you. I want you to love one another."

Have a glad Thanksgiving. Have a happy day.

JOHN H. BAUMGAERTNER
President, English District—LCMS
Milwaukee, Wisconsin